ILO
Subregional Office for Central and Eastern Europe
Budapest

The Gender Dimensions of Social Security Reform in Central and Eastern Europe:

Case Studies of the Czech Republic, Hungary and Poland

EDITED BY
ELAINE FULTZ,
MARKUS RUCK AND
SILKE STEINHILBER

The Gender Dimensions of Social Security Reform in Central and Eastern Europe: Case Studies of the Czech Republic, Hungary and Poland
Budapest, International Labour Office, 2003

ISBN 92-2-113701-5

ILO publications can be obtained through major booksellers or ILO local offices in many countries, or direct from ILO Publications, International Labour Office, CH-1211 Geneva 22, Switzerland. Catalogues or lists of new publications are available free of charge from the above address, or by e-mail: pubvente@ilo.org
Visit our website: www.ilo.org/publns

Printed in Hungary

Bożena Balcerzak-Paradowska is a researcher at the Polish Institute of Labour and Social Studies. Her chief research interests are the demographic and socio-economic conditions of the family, with particular attention to single-parent families and families with many children. Her work focuses on the impact of a range of contemporary variables on the lifestyles and living standards of various types of families and population groups, as well as on female professional activity in the context of family and gender equality.

Agnieszka Chłoń-Domińczak is the director of the Department of Economic Analysis and Forecasting at the Polish Ministry of Economy, Labour and Social Policy. She previously worked in the Office of the Government Plenipotentiary for Social Security Reform, at the Gdansk Institute for Market Economics, and as a consultant to the Labour Ministry. She also worked briefly at the World Bank, where her research included a comparison of the implementation of Notional Defined Contribution systems in Poland, Latvia, Italy and Sweden.

Mária Frey is a labour economist working as a senior research associate at the Research Unit of the Hungarian National Labour Office. She has directed several research projects and published widely on such topics as labour market policies, flexibilization and reduction of working hours, male and female employment, and job creation outside the mainstream labour market. She received her Ph.D. in economics in 1989.

Irena E. Kotowska is head of the Demographic Unit at the Institute of Statistics and Demography, Warsaw School of Economics, and Vice President of the Social Sciences Department, Polish Academy of Science. Her main areas of research are work, family and gender, population policies, and demographic forecasting.

Magdalena Kotýnková is a senior researcher in the Department of Income Policy of the Czech Research Institute for Labour and Social Affairs. She received a master's degree in economic policy in 1971 from the University of Economics in Prague. She has long been engaged in the areas of income policy and income inequality. She has been a senior lecturer at the Department of Social Policy, University of Economics, Prague since 1999.

Věra Kuchařová is a senior researcher at the Department of Family Policy of the Czech Research Institute for Labour and Social Affairs. She received a master's degree in sociology from Charles University in 1979. Her areas of special interest are family policy, the gender aspects of social policy, and equal opportunities for men and women.

Erika Lukács, an economist, has worked as a civil servant and specialist in various fields of state administration, including the Hungarian Ministry of Health, Ministry of Welfare, and the Prime Minister's Office, as well as at a private insurance company. She has dealt with reform issues related to health care, the social protection system, family policy, family supports, pensions, and aging society. At present she is a deputy head of the Department of Pension Insurance and Aging Issues at the Hungarian Ministry of Health, Social and Family Affairs.

Anna Olejniczuk-Merta, an economist, is Deputy Rector for students' affairs at Leon Kozminski Academy of Enterpreneurship and Management in Warsaw. She specialises in issues relating to youth as consumers and in social services for youth, including education, health services, and the productive use of free time.

Ladislav Průša is Director of the Czech Research Institute for Labour and Social Affairs. He earned a master's degree in economics from the University of Economics in Prague in 1981. During 1992–2000, he worked with the Ministry of Labour and Social Affairs as head of the Department of Social Systems and subsequently as head of the Department of Social Services. He has been senior lecturer at the Department of Social Policy, University of Economics, Prague since 1992. His main research area is social services.

Silke Steinhilber is working towards her Ph.D. in Political and Social Science at the New School for Social Research in New York. Her research interest is in social and employment policy, social justice, and gender equality. Between 1997 and 1998, she participated in a one-year postgraduate training course at the German Development Institute. Between 1999 and 2001, she worked as Associate Expert on Women Workers' Rights and Gender Equality for ILO Budapest. She has since continued to collaborate with ILO Budapest on gender issues.

Irena Topińska is an associate professor at the University of Warsaw, Faculty of Economic Sciences. Her research interests include social policy, income distribution and the economics of poverty. She has consulted widely in Poland, Bosnia and Herzegovina, Belarus, Kyrgystan, Lithuania and Moldova for the Polish government, World Bank, ILO and private foundations.

Irena Wóycicka, an economist, is Head of the Social Security Department at the Gdansk Institute for Market Economics. Formerly she was Under-secretary of State in the Ministry of Labour and Social Policy and a member of the Supervisory Board of the Social Insurance Institution (ZUS). Her special fields of interest are social security financing and projections, the economic and social impact of aging, and social security program evaluation. She consults frequently with ILO.

This volume examines the gender dimensions of social security reform undertaken in the context of political and economic transformation in Central and Eastern Europe. It was completed as part of the International Labour Organization project, *Strengthening Social Security in Central and Eastern Europe through Research and Technical Cooperation*, supported by the French Government. The research component of this project examines the reconfiguration of social security schemes that has taken place since 1989, the process of social policy formation in the region's new multiparty democracies, and their early experience in implementing reform. Our objective is to offer countries still deliberating reforms pertinent information on recent experience and results of neighbors facing similar challenges and to empower governments' social partners as participants in social policy development.

This gender study is one component of the ILO's ongoing project to monitor regional efforts to restructure social security. We report elsewhere the results of other research, notably, the impact of old-age pension reform on retirement security; of disability pension reform on benefits, options for rehabilitation, and return to work; and of the role of social security, broadly defined, in addressing poverty and social exclusion emerging or persisting with the transformation. These studies also include analysis of the gender dimensions of the particular reforms they examine. They were published by ILO Budapest in 2002.

This study looks at social security reform in three EU accession countries – the Czech Republic, Hungary, and Poland – through the lens of gender equality. It examines two broad categories of benefits: family benefits (including maternity benefits, family allowances, and child care benefits) and pensions (retirement and survivors' protection). Both underwent major reform in the 1990s with important implications for women and men. However, as will be shown, the motivation to achieve gender equality was not often a force in shaping the reforms; and the gender dimension of major policy changes received relatively little attention, either during national reform deliberations or thereafter. Thus, it is the purpose of the study to reaffirm the importance of equal treatment in social security reform and to bring it into sharper view for public scrutiny.

Having adopted this focus, we must also recognize that social security is not the tool of choice for combating gender inequality in society. The sources of such inequality lie in labour markets, social and family domains, and cultural values, beyond the reach of social security systems. The *consequences* of unequal treatment can be remediated by social security schemes to some extent – for example, pension schemes might provide redistribution toward low-income workers, thus helping to compensate for the gender wage gap, and family benefits can assist parents in balancing work with child care responsibilities that fall disproportionately to women. Yet social security alone is a weak instrument for reshaping the entrenched beliefs and practices that sustain unequal treatment of women and men.

The study is organized to encourage cross-border comparisons of the impact of various reforms on women and men. To this end, the three country studies are laid out in a similar manner. After profiling the labour market and social context in which social security operates, each study looks first at family benefits and then at pensions, considering the reasons for reform, the specific measures adopted, and their impact on women and men. In examining the latter, the studies trace changes in government spending and benefits as a portion of household incomes over the 1990s. These efforts at quantification are impeded at critical points by a lack of relevant data, changing statistical measures, and inconsistencies in data collection from country to country. Nonetheless, several broad patterns stand out across the countries. These are highlighted in the comparative analysis provided in Chapter 1.

The quantitative effects of pension reforms turn out to be even more elusive, since these changes take longer to implement and simulations of their long-term impact have been undertaken in only one of the three countries (Poland). In this case, the comparative analysis in Chapter 1 relies heavily on the Polish simulations to illustrate the long-term effects of two major reform options – adoption of Notional Defined Contribution (NDC) schemes and pension privatization – on equality of treatment of women and men.

Two salient features of the Central European context are reflected in the design of the study. First, during the initial decade of transformation, changes in labour markets put social security schemes under great stress. High levels of unemployment, growth of the informal sector, and a loosening of job protections deeply affected social security benefits and financing, causing greater demand for some benefits (early retirement pensions) and less for others (extended maternity and family benefits). To highlight this influence, the initial section of each country study profiles labour market changes during the 1990s and their gender dimensions.

Second, Central Europeans hold diverse views as to the notion of gender equality, as to what it means for various areas of social and professional life, and even as to its desirability. This diversity is quite marked among women, some of whom defined or redefined their values in traditional terms during the transformation. While preserving its focus on gender equality as equal opportunity and equal treatment in all areas of life, the study also explores the various meanings it has for Central European women in relation to their family, social, and professional experience. These perspectives have been brought together from written questionnaires and a series of personal interviews in each of the three countries. The results form the final chapter of the study.

This volume includes the work of many authors. Silke Steinhilber, formerly the gender specialist at ILO Budapest, served as consultant to the project on gender issues. She organized and monitored the research, gave the comparative analysis of reforms its essential shape and content (Chapter 1), and herself researched the perceptions and attitudes of the women in the countries with respect to gender equality (Chapter 5). The analysis of reforms in the Czech Republic (Chapter 2) was undertaken by Věra Kuchařová, Magdalena Kotýnková, and Ladislav Průša under the auspices of the Research Institute of Labour and Social Affairs. Erika Lukács, formerly of the Office of the Prime Minister of Hungary, and Mária Frey of the Government's Labour Research Institute analyzed the Hungarian reforms (Chapter 3). In analyzing pensions, they received assistance from Krémerné Gerencsér Ildikó and Gabriella A. Papp of the Ministry of Social and Family Affairs, to whom they express their warm appreciation. The Polish study (Chapter 4) was the work of Irena Wóycicka (coordinator), Bożena Balcerzak-Paradowska, Agnieszka Chłoń-Domińczak, Irena Kotowska, Anna Olejniczuk-Merta, and Irena Topińska, carried out under the auspices of the Gdansk Institute for Market Economics. It includes financial projections made with the Institute's social budget model, developed in cooperation with the ILO and the Polish Ministry of Labour and Social Policy. Wouter Van Ginneken and Krzysztof Hagemejer of the ILO Social Protection Sector provided useful comments on several of the chapters in draft. Mercedes Birck provided administrative support and coordination among the researchers throughout the study. Eileen Brown supported the final editing and publication of the studies. We express appreciation to all for these efforts and thank the authors for their outstanding contributions.

ILO Budapest gratefully acknowledges the financial support of the Ministry of Social Affairs, Labour, and Solidarity of the Government of France for this analysis. We appreciate its support for strengthening social security in Central and Eastern Europe and particularly value its understanding of the significance of social security for social cohesion.

We at ILO Budapest hope that these studies, by casting light on the gender dimensions of social security reform, will help to bring consideration of gender equality to the forefront of policy development and action in Central Europe.

Petra Ulshoefer
Director

Elaine Fultz
Senior Specialist in Social Security

Markus Ruck
Expert in Social Security

Silke Steinhilber
Consultant on Gender Issues

July 2003

Chapter 1
The Gender Dimensions of Social Security Reform in the Czech Republic, Hungary, and Poland

Elaine Fultz and Silke Steinhilber

1. Introduction

The social security reforms that the new governments in the Czech Republic, Hungary, and Poland adopted in the 1990s affect women and men in quite different ways. The differential impact depends in large part on the particular benefits that were altered, and thus the domains of social and professional life touched by the reforms: work, unemployment, child bearing, parenthood, sickness, disability, or retirement. It is quite possible that different observers concerned with gender equality will assess these reforms differently, depending on their own views of what constitutes equal treatment, their priorities for addressing unequal conditions, and their notions of the shared rights and obligations of members of society. Without abandoning our own preferences, we have tried in what follows to provide an objective account of the gender dimensions of reform in the three countries.

The study analyzes two broad categories of benefits that address distinct areas of experience and need: on the one hand, a set of family benefits that supports parents with children (family allowances, child care benefits, and maternity benefits) and, on the other, one that replaces lost income as a result of old age or death (retirement and survivors' pensions). Although support in each case facilitates a retreat from the work force, the first may anticipate return while the second typically does not. More relevantly for this study, the first category includes a mix of benefits, some of which are shaped by biological differences (i.e., maternity benefits) and others that are provided without regard to these (family allowances and child care benefits), while both benefits in the second category address contingencies experienced by women and men.

Since the economic and social context shapes the need for benefits, the profiles of those who receive them, and their costs, this context is the starting point of analysis in each of the three countries.[1] The country studies show that women achieved a high level of work force participation under socialism, but the contexts in which they worked were characterized by significant gender inequality. This inequality persisted into the 1990s, with some indicators worsening or becoming more obvious, but on the whole falling within the range observed in Western Europe.[2] Unemployment rates were persistently higher for women than for men in two of the three countries, the Czech Republic and Poland, throughout the 1990s, a disparity that exists in all EU member states.[3] The gender pay gap was, and remains, in the range of 20–25 percent in all three countries, with the Czech Republic showing the greatest gap. These figures are comparable to those in the EU member states with the greatest pay inequality.[4] Gender segregation in employment is strong, with women being concentrated in services. Compared to the EU member states in 2000, however, the share of women in industrial employment is higher in all three countries.[5] Women are underrepresented in managerial jobs in all

---

[1] See section 1 of Chapters 2, 3, and 4.

[2] See EU DG Employment and Social Affairs, Unit Equality for Women and Men, Thematical statistical sheets (based on Eurostat, Key Employment Indicators), http://europa.eu.int/comm/employment_social/ equ_opp/statistics_en.html.

[3] In Hungary, women's lower unemployment rate is explained by a larger exodus of women from the work force in the early 1990s. See Lukács and Frey, section 1, this volume.

[4] These are Austria, the Netherlands, United Kingdom, and Ireland. See Eurostat 'Gender pay gap in unadjusted form – Average gross hourly earnings of females as a percentage of average gross hourly earnings of males' 2003, http://europa.eu.int/comm/eurostat/Public/datashop/print-catalogue/EN?catalogue=Eurostat&product=1-em030-EN.

[5] The highest share of women in industry is found in the Czech Republic, 27.3 percent. In Hungary, it is 24.8 percent, and in Poland 18.9 percent. In the EU, the average share of women in industrial employment is 14 percent. Source, see footnote 2.

three countries, although in Hungary and Poland they hold larger fractions of such positions than women in all EU member states with the exception of France.[6]

At the beginning of the 1990s, all three countries provided the benefits examined in this study on an unequal basis to women and men. Retirement age preferences existed for women, family benefits provided women with greater support for balancing their lives as workers and mothers, and, in two of the three countries, women had greater survivors' benefits (the Czech Republic and Hungary). While gender equality was part of the communist ideology, benefits were not aimed at achieving equal treatment of women and men. Rather, in an environment of substantial gender inequality, the benefits rewarded women for motherhood and eased their dual role of worker and principal family care giver.

In the period of rapid change following 1989, eliminating these gender differences was not among the highest priorities for reform. In these early years, gender equality was eclipsed by other concerns that were seen as more pressing, namely, the need for new benefits to protect workers and families against high inflation, job loss, and poverty.[7] The new governments' capacity to deliver such relief was an immediate test of their legitimacy, and they moved quickly, adopting measures to reconfigure existing social security schemes to meet these needs. Criteria for early retirement were liberalized for both women and men, pension benefits were improved in various ways, and new family benefits were established in an effort to compensate for inflation and the removal of subsidies on basic commodities.

As their economies gained a measure of stability in the mid- to late 1990s, all three governments set out to restructure social security more fundamentally. Even in this less extraordinary context, however, gender issues were not a major driving force in reform. This is attributable in part to the absence of a well-organized gender lobby in any country, to the divergent goals of the women's organizations that did exist, to the complexity of social security issues, and to the continuing existence of problems in labour markets that

---

[6]   See UN/ Economic Commission for Europe, 'Women and Men in Europe and North America,' New York and Geneva 2000.

[7]   See sections 1 and 2 of Chapters 2, 3, and 4.

captured greater attention.[8] The reforms of the later 1990s rather aimed at reshaping earlier emergency measures, containing scheme costs arising from them, and reflecting the new relationship between citizen and state. Family benefits were redirected toward the largest families and those in greatest need. Some family benefits were cut, either directly or by failure to provide regular cost-of-living adjustments. Pensions were made more individualized and earnings-related, although to a different extent and through different means within each country. In all three countries, retirement ages were increased.[9]

Although gender received little explicit attention, the new laws themselves raise major questions with respect to equal treatment. Among them, five stand out. Formulated below, these will be dealt with in the subsequent analysis.

- The channel through which family benefits for child care is made available is of importance in relation to women's attachment to the labour force. In national contexts where child care is still overwhelmingly provided by women, making such benefits available through the work place or contingent on employment creates incentives and rewards for labour force participation. Conversely, if child care benefits are restricted to those with low income or limited means, mothers who stay at home to care for young children may become isolated from the world of work and find their integration or subsequent reintegration into the labour market in later years more difficult.[10]

- Second, a basic issue arises as to what policies permit or promote more equal sharing of family caring responsibilities between women and men. In the course of the 1990s, all three countries made child care benefits available to men and women on an equal basis. As yet, equal treatment in this regard has had no discernible effect on the allocation

---

[8] Steinhilber identifies three distinctive sets of goals adhered to by women interviewed for this study: formal gender equality in social security, affirmative action to compensate for disadvantages in labour markets, and unequal treatment which recognizes women as partners in a family unit. Chapter 5, section 3, this volume.

[9] In Poland, early retirement was eliminated prospectively (2006). This will lead to an increase in the actual retirement age.

[10] In addition, some women will be ineligible due to income or resources that exceed the limit.

of child care responsibilities within the family, which continue to rest overwhelmingly with women. As populations age, elderly family members will pose increased requirements for care, while the need for family child care will be ongoing. It seems clear that women as a group cannot, as a matter of simple arithmetic, gain greater freedom to seek more diverse forms of income and fulfillment until men and women share the tasks of caring for family members more equally.

- Third, women have entered the new political era with privileges from the socialist years with respect to retirement. In some cases, the retirement age has been set by law to give all women the possibility to retire at an earlier age than men. In others, it is determined by the number of children a woman has raised. Clearly these privileges afford women and men unequal treatment in an area that does not relate to their biological differences. Is there a principled rationale for continuing them in the current era?

- Fourth, the 1990s witnessed a major regional trend in the direction of linking the magnitude of an individual's pension benefit more closely to his or her earnings and work history; in other words, in the direction of eliminating income redistribution toward low-income workers. This trend appears in both the public pension schemes and the new privatized ones. It is advantageous to women and men with higher incomes, and hurts all workers, women or men, with lower ones. Given that women earn significantly less than men during their professional lives and tend to work fewer years (both as a result of more time taken for bearing and raising children and more likely unemployment throughout much of Central and Eastern Europe), this trend affects them more negatively.

- Fifth, the partial privatization of pension schemes, such as took place in Hungary and Poland, raises a major question concerning the size of men's and women's pensions as a result of their different average life expectancies. This issue arises in the new systems of commercially managed individual savings accounts mandated by privatization laws. When the amounts accumulated in these accounts are converted to annuities at retirement, it will be necessary to consult one of two types of life expectancy tables: either one that treats women and men separately or a second that gives a single, joint life expectancy projection for both.

The use of the latter will result in the payment of an equal monthly benefit for a man and a woman who retire at the same age with the same history of contributions. However, since women on average live longer than men, they will, on average, accumulate higher total *lifetime* benefits than comparable men. On the other hand, the use of gender-specific tables will give a man and a woman retiring at the same age with the same histories of contributions the same total *lifetime* accumulations of retirement benefits but will give the woman a lower *monthly* benefit because her savings must, on average, be stretched to cover a longer lifetime.

What should we take as equal treatment for men and women with identical histories of earnings retiring at the same age? Identical total average accumulation over the entire period of retirement? Or identical average monthly benefits?

2. Family benefits: Overview of the Reforms

Family benefits are payments made in cash or in kind to support parents in bearing and raising children.[11] They include general allowances, paid to supplement wages according to the number of children in a family, as well as two benefits that are contingent on specific actions: giving birth (maternity benefits) and withdrawing temporarily from the work force to care for a young child (child care benefits).[12] Depending on program rules and the environments in which they operate, these benefits can have a different impact on men and women collectively across society. During the socialist period, all three countries developed an extensive array of family benefits. The

---

[11] In Hungary, family benefits are also paid through the tax system.

[12] ILO, *Introduction to Social Security*, Chapter 11, 'Family Benefit,' Geneva, Switzerland, 1984. The actual names of the benefits that fit the above definition of child care vary in the three countries. In the Czech Republic, it is the parental allowance; in Hungary, the child care fee, child care allowance and child raising allowance; and in Poland, the child care benefit and child raising allowance. See Table 1.

country studies examine the most relevant among these in shaping the life and professional choices of women and men.[13]

In contrast with pension reform, where major changes were adopted within short time periods in many CEE countries, the reform of family benefits has been more incremental and continuous. The sequence is simplest in the Czech Republic, where major reforms were implemented in 1995 and 1996.[14] In Hungary and Poland, by contrast, changes were made throughout the 1990s and continue today. Amidst this complexity, several broad trends stand out.

First, in the early 1990s, there was a decoupling of family benefits from employment status.[15] The new governments in all three countries used various family benefits, along with other forms of social security, to provide relief from the effects of inflation, job loss, and poverty.[16] This was accomplished by converting some employment-related benefits to universal ones while targeting others to families with low incomes or limited resources. Some new benefits were also created.

Later in the 1990s, fiscal pressures provided a major impetus for change. In Hungary and Poland, the governments adopted austerity programs that called for major cuts in overall social spending, including family benefits.[17] These were achieved through greater income testing of benefits, cuts in their level and duration, and omitting adjustments for inflation. The shift to income testing was most marked in Poland, where today eligibility for nearly all

---

[13] The Czech study examines four such benefits (the maternity benefit, child allowance, social allowance and parental allowance); the Hungarian study examines seven (the maternity benefit, family allowance, child protection benefits, tax credits, the child care fee, the child care allowance, and child raising benefit); and the Polish study, seven (the maternity benefit, child care benefit, the child raising allowance, the family allowance, the alimony fund, the guaranteed periodic benefit, and benefits for pregnant women and women raising children).

[14] Other less comprehensive reforms were enacted in 1990 and 1993 as well.

[15] Only maternity benefits were exempted from this process. Today they continue to be provided as employment-related insurance benefits in all three countries.

[16] Section 2 of Chapters 2, 3, and 4, this volume.

[17] Wóycicka et al., section 2 and 2(a), and Lukács and Frey, section 2, this volume.

benefits is based on the income or means of the family.[18] In Hungary, income testing (of the examined benefits) was adopted in the mid-1990s and then abolished later in the decade.[19] Income testing was less marked in the Czech Republic, where it was applied to some but not all benefits and in a manner that was not highly restrictive.[20]

A third pattern across the countries is provision of greater support for large families. In Hungary and Poland, these changes were part of broader efforts to redress stagnant or declining population growth. They were supported by certain religious groups and political parties favoring the restoration of traditional family roles or national values. In Hungary, a new child raising benefit was created for families with three or more children; and progressively larger tax credits were provided for the second, third, and subsequent children.[21] In Poland, larger families received a higher child raising allowance for their third and each subsequent child.[22] In the Czech Republic, although population growth was less ardently promoted, there too larger families received larger child allowances.[23]

Finally, all of the countries equalized benefits for men and women providing child care, thus eliminating provisions of preexisting law that had barred fathers from using these benefits or imposed stricter rules on them. In one country, Poland, equalization of one child care benefit was coupled with a cut in the rate of the benefit.[24] Given the gender wage gap, this was judged necessary to avoid an increase in spending outlays, since the benefit level was based on the worker's pay. See Table 1.

---

[18]   The child care benefit, a short-term payment for those who leave work to care for a sick child, remains employment related. Wóycicka et al., section 3, this volume.

[19]   Even when income testing was applied, it was rather loose, excluding only nine percent of families and seven percent of children from the family benefit. Lukács and Frey, Table 14, this volume.

[20]   94 percent of two-parent families with one economically active parent received the child allowance before it was income-tested (1996), and 93 percent received it afterward (1999). Kucharová et al., Table 2, this volume.

[21]   Lukács and Frey, Boxes 2 and 3, this volume.

[22]   Wóycicka et al, Box 1, this volume.

[23]   Kucharová et al., section 2, this volume.

[24]   This is the benefit for care of a sick child. Wóycicka et al, section 2(b), this volume.

Table 1
Equal treatment of men and women with respect to various national benefits
for child care, benefit and year equalized

Country	Benefit	Year equalized
Czech Republic	Parental allowance	1990
	Right to return to same job following allowance	2001
Hungary	Child care fee	1992
	Child care allowance	1992
	Child raising benefit	1998
Poland	Child care benefit	1995
	Child raising allowance	1996

Source: See section 2 of Kucharová et al., Lukács and Frey, and Wóycicka et al., this volume.

These varied changes in family benefits contrast with the limited change in maternity benefits. All three countries maintained these benefits as employment-related social insurance. Hungary, making a single change as part of a 1996 fiscal austerity plan, reduced the replacement rate of wages from 100 to 70 percent.[25] In 2000, the Polish government initiated a series of rapid changes in the duration of the benefit but ultimately restored its original duration of 16 weeks.[26] Throughout, Poland maintained an income replacement rate at 100 percent of the worker's current wage. Poland extended maternity benefits to fathers, allowing them to take two weeks of the total period available. The Czech Republic made a single small change, shifting the basis for computation of benefits from gross to net wages.[27] See Table 2.

---

[25] Lukács and Frey, Box 1, this volume.

[26] Poland first introduced an increase in the duration of benefits from 16 to 20 and then 26 weeks, followed by a cutback to 16 weeks. Wóycicka et al., section 2(a), this volume.

[27] In the Czech Republic, the percentage is calculated from the so-called Daily Assessment Base which is based on wages but entails a complex formula that can cause some variations from actual wage amounts.

	Table 2	
	Reform of maternity benefits	
	Pre-1989	**Reform and year**
Czech Republic	Social insurance benefit	Unchanged
	28 weeks' duration	Unchanged
	90% of previous net wage	1993, changed to 69% of previous gross wage
Hungary	Social insurance benefit	Unchanged
	28 weeks' duration	Unchanged
	100% of previous wage	1996, replacement rate reduced to 70%
Poland	Social insurance benefit	Unchanged
	16 weeks' duration	2000, increased to 20 weeks 2001, increased to 26 weeks 2002, reduced to 16 weeks for first child (2 available to father), 18 weeks for subsequent children
	100% of previous wage	Unchanged

Source: See section 2 of Kucharová et al., Lukács and Frey, and Wóycicka et al., this volume.

3. Impact of the Reforms

At the end of the 1990s we can discern four broad effects of the modifications previously outlined. First is a sharp decline in spending on family benefits as a portion of GDP in Hungary and Poland. While the definitions of benefits and years for which data are available differ, a trend is nevertheless clear: In Hungary, in 1990–2000, spending on the benefits under discussion fell in relation to GDP by nearly one-half, from 3.8 percent to 2.0 percent, and in Poland in 1990–98, from 1.7 percent of GDP to 1.1 percent.[28] See Table 3

---

[28] Lukács and Frey, Table 11 and Wóycicka et al., Figure 2, this volume.

and Figure 1. As a result, family benefits as a component of household income also fell sharply: in Poland (1993–99), for all households, from 3.8 percent to 1.4 percent and in Hungary (1993–99), for a family with two children, from 17.0 percent to 10.8 percent.[29]

Table 3
GDP per capita, family benefits – total and as a percentage of GDP, Hungary, 1990–2000 (1990 HUF)

Year	GDP per capita	Total expenditure in billions	Family benefits as a % of GDP
1990	201,573	78.5	3.8
1991	177,324	74.6	4.1
1992	171,221	69.7	3.9
1993	169,466	64.4	3.7
1994	176,020	58.8	3.3
1995	177,158	45.2	2.5
1996	176,630	36.6	2.0
1997	185,675	34.4	1.8
1998	192,641	38.8	2.0
1999	200,338	38.7	1.9
2000	201,915	39.6	2.0

Source: *CSO Statistical Yearbooks* and *Statistical Yearbooks of the National Health Insurance Fund Administration*, in Lukács and Frey, Table 11, this volume.

---

[29] Lukács and Frey, Table 17, and Wóycicka et al., Table 1, this volume. The figures for Poland represent only the family allowance, child care fee, and child raising allowance, as these are the only benefits for which household income statistics are available.

It is noteworthy that, in Poland and Hungary during most of the 1990s, the share of family benefits in household income declined significantly while the share of social security benefits overall remained relatively stable.[30] This suggests that as a category families were less well protected than other beneficiary groups, for example, old-age and disability pensioners.

Figure 1
Family benefits as percentage of GDP, Poland 1990–98

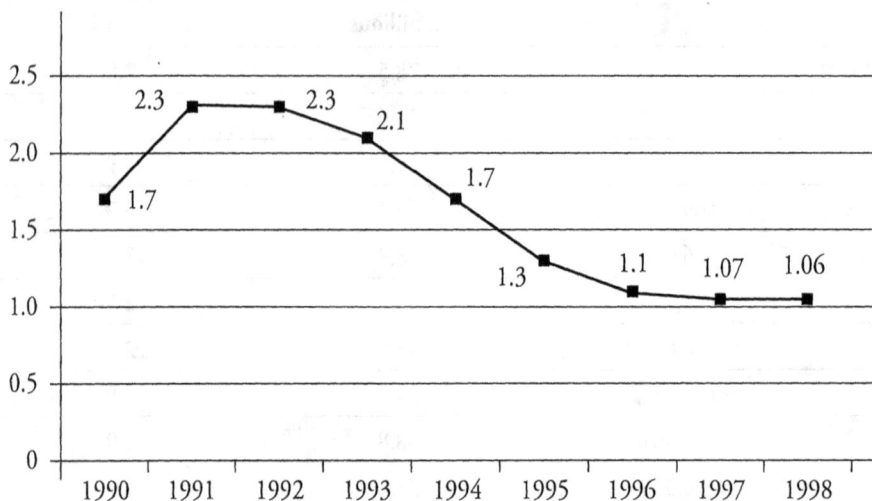

Source: Hagemejer, K.; Liwiński, J.; and Wóycicka, I., *Poland: Social Protection in Transition* (ILO: 2002) in Wóycicka et al., Table 3, this volume.

---

[30] In Poland, total social benefits ranged between 31 and 33 percent of household income during 1992–99, whereas in Hungary, social benefits dropped temporarily during the mid 1990s and were then restored. For a Hungarian family with one child, for example, social benefits were 21 percent of household income in 1993, 16 percent in 1997 and 20 percent in 1999, whereas the three family benefits dropped from 9.2 to 5.7 percent over this period. Wóycicka et al., Table 1, and Lukács and Frey, Table 17, this volume.

These losses contrast with the small gains posted in the Czech Republic. Here, in the postreform period (1996–2000) family benefits as a percentage of GDP increased modestly from 1.78 percent of GDP to 1.85. See Table 4. This increase resulted primarily from higher unemployment beginning in 1997 and a consequent increase in demand for the newly income-tested family benefits. In the Czech Republic, different levels of aggregation of family income data by household size complicate comparisons with the other two countries. What is clear, however, is that after the reforms, Czech benefits increased slightly as a fraction of family income in households of all sizes but somewhat more in larger ones.[31] This upward drift contrasts with the sharp decline in Hungary and Poland.

Table 4
Three family benefits, total spending and spending as a percentage of GDP, the Czech Republic, 1996–2000 (CZK, thousands)

Benefit	1996	1997	1998	1999	2000
Child allowance	12,194	12,495	11,493	12,474	12,748
Social allowance	6,244	6,224	6,273	6,251	6,199
Parent allowance	7,357	7,612	7,780	7,718	7,691
Total of three benefits	25,795	26,331	25,546	26,443	26,638
Gross domestic product (GDP)	1,447,700	1,432,800	1,401,300	1,390,600	1,433,800
GDP accounted for by the three benefits	1.78%	1.83%	1.82%	1.90%	1.85%

Source: Kucharová et al., Table A1.9, this volume.

In the second place, the reforms concentrated family benefits on families with low incomes. After Czech reforms (1995–96), the fraction of families receiving all three of the benefits examined in this study fell by one-half, while at the same time, those that remained eligible for all three received increases equal to three to ten percent of net family income.[32] This concentration

---

[31] Kucharová et al., Table 6, this volume.
[32] Ibid.

probably accounts in part for the fact that, in Poland at the end of the decade (1998), family benefits constituted 12 percent of income for families in the lowest income decile but just 0.15 percent for those in the top decile.[33] In Hungary, as previously mentioned, income testing was adopted and then discontinued.

The authors of all three studies express concern that the increased scope of income testing of child care benefits may reduce the incentives for women to engage in economic activity, especially women with low skills.[34] In Hungary and Poland, they raise similar concern about the relatively small gap between child care benefits and the minimum wage.[35] At the moment, however, we cannot quantify the strength of these incentives in the professional and life choices made by family caregivers.

Third, as previously described, all three countries gave equal access to child care benefits to women and men. Access alone, of course, cannot be expected to change entrenched modes of distributing child care between parents. While the data on use of these benefits is not complete, what does exist suggests that there has been no pent-up demand for access to child care benefits on the part of fathers. In the Czech Republic during 1995–98, fathers constituted less than one percent of child care beneficiaries, roughly the same as in Hungary.[36] In Poland, statistics on the use of child care benefits by men and women are not available. However, our authors were unable to find any evidence, even anecdotal, that men are using these benefits to stay home and care for their

---

[33] Wóycicka et al., Table 3, this volume.

[34] The statement actually refers to the 'child raising benefit' in Poland. There 'child care benefits' refer to short-term benefits for the care of a sick child, while the 'child raising benefit' is paid for caring for young children at home for extended periods. In Poland, means testing was applied to the child raising benefit but not the child care benefit. Wóycicka et al., footnote 13.

[35] In Poland, the guaranteed benefit is 88 percent of the net minimum wage, whereas in Hungary the combination of the child care allowance and child raising benefit equaled 84 percent of the minimum wage until 2001, when it was increased by 25 percent (from HUF 40,000 to HUF 50,000). Wóycicka et al., Section 2(f)(i), and Lukács and Frey, section 3; this volume.

[36] Kucharová et al., footnotes 26 and 27, and Lukács and Frey, Table 19, this volume.

children. Clearly, the main barriers to greater sharing of family responsibilities lie in inequalities in the labour market (the gender wage gap) and in cultural values.[37] Nevertheless, the equal treatment by these countries removes barriers to possible future shifts toward more equal sharing of responsibilities for child care between parents.

A final pattern worthy noting is anecdotal evidence reported in all three studies that women are increasingly reluctant to use employment-based rights to family benefits for fear of reprisals by employers in the form of job loss and unfavorable re-assignment.[38] There are, however, no estimates available on the scope of this phenomenon in any of the countries. From the perspective of gender equality in employment, these observations are a serious cause for concern.

To sum up, the reforms of family benefits have achieved mixed results. On the positive side, income-testing of some family benefits has succeeded in targeting scarce resources to those most in need. This has softened some of the financial shocks associated with the shift toward a market economy. Given that women have lower average earnings and higher rates of poverty, this targeting has no doubt benefited them accordingly. On the other hand, this change has shifted the nature of the support from wage replacement to poverty alleviation; and it has shifted the status of beneficiaries, mostly women, from holders of personal rights to petitioners of the state. At the same time, income testing provides a disincentive to economic activity. This threatens to capture some women in a trap of dependency on these benefits. While all three countries have extended equal treatment to men and women with respect to child care benefits, these reforms have not as yet been associated with any behavioral changes. Rather, the care of young children continues to be provided overwhelmingly by women, as before the reforms. In two of the three countries (Hungary and Poland), large cuts in family benefits leave working parents, mostly women, with considerably less support for efforts to balance family and professional responsibilities than they received before transition.

---

[37] Steinhilber, Chapter 5, section 2, this volume.

[38] Lukács and Frey, Section 3; Kucharová et al., pages 136 and 138, and Wóycicka et al., footnote 25, this volume.

---

4.   Pensions: Overview of the Reforms

In 1989, the national pension schemes of Czechoslovakia, Hungary, and Poland had several features in common. With no private supplemental arrangements in place, all served as the main providers of retirement income in their respective countries. All were financed on a pay-as-you-go basis through transfers from state-owned firms to a social insurance account within the state budget. There was little public accounting of the collection or allocation of these resources. Benefits were computed on the basis of a worker's final earnings, thus penalizing workers with steady earnings compared to those whose earnings rose as their careers advanced.[39] Retirement ages were relatively low: in Czechoslovakia, 60 for men and 53–57 for women; in Hungary, 60 for men and 55 for women; and in Poland, 59 for men and 55 for women.[40] Two countries, Czechoslovakia and Poland, provided pension privileges – i.e., higher benefit amounts and/or lower retirement ages for certain occupations, such as miners, pilots, and certain high-level members of the Communist Party. In the later socialist years, adjustments of pensions did not keep pace with increases in prices or nominal wages, to the economic detriment of older pensioners in comparison with those more recently retired.

In the early 1990s, rising unemployment caused a drop in contribution income in all three schemes. This was largest in Poland and Hungary, where the number of contributors declined by 15 and 25 percent respectively. In the Czech Republic, the number of contributors dropped by only eight percent.[41] The Hungarian and Polish governments liberalized early retirement in order

---

[39]   In Hungary, the best three out of five years before retirement were counted, with a rising replacement rate for those with longer careers. In Poland, the best two consecutive years out of the last ten were counted. In the Czech Republic, the benefit was based on the average wage earned in the five years immediately prior to retirement. Given the relatively compressed wage structures of these countries under socialism, the use of final earnings did not produce great differences in pensions.

[40]   For Poland, these are actual ages, based on early retirement options. The regular retirement age was 65 for men and 60 for women. Wóycicka et al., section 5, this volume.

[41]   Palacios, R., M. Rutkowski, and X. Yu, *Pension Reform in Transition Countries*, World Bank, Washington, D.C., June 1999.

to absorb excess unemployment, causing rapid increases in the number of pensioners – in the range of 20 percent in Hungary and 50 percent in Poland. In the Czech Republic, the increase was about 10 percent.[42]

In addition, all three governments took early action to improve pension benefits. Czechoslovakia and Poland took aim at the inequalities between old and new pensioners with a step-up in benefits. This adjustment was greatest in Poland, where it contributed to a sharp rise in pension spending.[43] In addition, all three governments regularized cost-of-living adjustments. Both Hungary and the Czech Republic established schemes of voluntary supplemental pension savings (1993–94). In the early period, Czechoslovakia moved decisively to eliminate pension privileges (1991).

As the decade progressed, the three countries enacted major pension reforms.[44] In general, these reforms aimed at containing scheme costs and at individualizing benefits. The Hungarian and Polish governments revised pension formulas so that benefit levels more closely reflected each individual's record of earnings, thus eliminating redistribution toward low-income workers. The Czech Republic, by contrast, adopted a new formula which continued to include redistributive terms. All three countries adopted laws that would increase the retirement age gradually. They also increased the number of years of earnings counted in computing pensions. This reduced the penalties for those with sustained flat wages and increased the rewards for contributions paid early in a career. In an effort to control costs, Hungary and Poland restricted the indexing of wages counted for pension purposes and reduced pension cost-of-living adjustments.[45] These same countries revised the

---

[42]   Palacios, Rutkowski and Yu, as previously cited.

[43]   During 1990–96, pension spending rose from 9.6 to 16.1 percent of GDP. Chlon, Agnieszka, 'The Polish Pension Reform of 1999,' Table 4, p.106, in Elaine Fultz, editor, *Pension Reform in Central and Eastern Europe, Volume 1, Restructuring with Privatization: Case Studies of Hungary and Poland*, Budapest: ILO–CEET, 2002.

[44]   Section 2, Lukács and Frey, Wóycicka et al., and Kucharová et al., this volume.

[45]   Hungary adopted the so-called Swiss method (benefit adjustments reflecting wage and price increases in equal proportions), while Poland moved to heavier reliance on price indexing (the ratio for adjustments was 85 percent reliance on prices and 15 percent, on wages).

pension credits for periods spent out of employment caring for young children, with the effect in both cases of reducing their value. The Czech Republic and Hungary made survivors' benefits for men and women equal.[46]

In a major policy shift in the late 1990s, Hungary and Poland introduced mandatory systems of commercially managed individual savings accounts.[47] These accounts replaced a portion of the countries' public, pay-as-you-go schemes and put part of workers' contributions (savings) with private investors. When these schemes are phased in, retiring workers will use their savings to buy an annuity, that is, a pension payable monthly until death. Proponents portrayed these reforms as needed to develop capital markets, boost economic growth, and increase the security of pensions through risk diversification. The Czech Republic debated this type of reform, but in view of the high transition costs has so far rejected it.

Unlike changes in maternity and family benefits that may be implemented quickly after enactment, pension reforms are usually implemented gradually over a period of years. The greatest time horizon belongs to the so-called radical reforms that replace one type of system with another, as is the case with pension privatization. This time lag makes assessing the reforms far more difficult in the short run. We can, however, make some educated guesses about long-run effects using existing data and macroeconomic simulations.

Using these approaches, the following three chapters identify the major gender dimensions of the reforms just described. A comparison of these analyses reveals several broad patterns across the countries. These relate to: 1) the retreat from income redistribution in pension benefit formulas; 2) changes in the retirement age; 3) crediting periods devoted to child care for pension purposes; and 4) the conversion of individual savings to annuities in the new private pension schemes.[48]

---

[46] No such action was needed in Poland since these were equal prior to 1989.

[47] These reforms are discussed in detail in another volume in this series. Elaine Fultz (ed.), *Pension Reform in Central and Eastern Europe: Volume 1, Restructuring with Privatization: Case Studies of Hungary and Poland,* Budapest: ILO CEET, 2002.

[48] Survivors' benefits are not included here. In two of the three countries (Czech Republic and Hungary) these were equalized for men and women during the 1990s, but these changes were of a secondary importance compared to those discussed here.

5. Impact of the Reforms

a) The retreat from redistribution. All three countries began the 1990s with pension policies that effected substantial redistribution of income from workers with higher earnings to those with lower ones. These schemes provided defined benefits computed on the basis of workers' wages in their final years of employment. The benefits were constrained by upper and lower limits that enhanced their redistributive character. In Hungary, a progressive scale within the pension formula provided further redistribution by weighting low wages more heavily. In the course of the 1990s, Hungary and Poland eliminated these redistributive elements entirely, while the Czech Republic revised its pension formula but retained elements of redistribution.

The governments achieved these changes in rather different ways. In 1998, the Hungarian government deleted the progressive term in the formula, thereby benefiting middle and upper income workers and disadvantaging those with low incomes.[49] This change is being phased in gradually and will become fully effective in 2013. The Polish government revised the formula twice in the 1990s. In 1992, it adopted a two-part formula that increased the weighting of individual workers' earnings, and at the same time provided some redistribution toward those with low incomes.[50] Seven years later, under the weight of large current deficits and unsustainable future ones resulting from the earlier adjustments, the government reformulated the public scheme to reduce both benefits and redistribution. This was accomplished by the introduction of a new Notional Defined Contribution (NDC) formula that makes an individual worker's pension directly proportional to total lifetime contributions.[51] In 1995, the Czech government adopted a new formula with

---

[49] Lukács and Frey, section 5, this volume.

[50] The latter was achieved through a constant term in the formula equal to 24 percent of the average wage.

[51] In the NDC scheme, benefits will be based on each worker's own contributions. The amount of the pension will be calculated by dividing the total lifetime contributions that s/he pays by the average statistical life expectancy of the worker's age cohort at the normal retirement age (gender neutral life tables will be used in this calculation). Thus,

two terms, both of which benefited low-income workers.[52] The first consists of a flat amount that is the same for all workers. The second uses the individual worker's earnings and gives greater weight to low wages.

At the same time that Hungary and Poland individualized their formulas (1998–99), they adopted new systems of private individual savings. This major policy shift redirected approximately 20 percent of contributions to individual accounts managed by commercial firms. By their nature, these accounts lack any redistribution toward low-income workers; and they offer no benefit promise at retirement. Instead, each worker will receive an annuity based on the investment performance of his or her own savings, minus administrative charges.[53] The method for converting savings to an annuity is of great potential importance for equal treatment and is discussed later.

The new formulas in the public schemes make no direct reference to sex and are therefore formally neutral with respect to equal treatment: A man and a woman retiring at the same age with identical earnings and contributions will receive the same monthly pension. The Hungarian and Polish reforms will of course leave workers with the lowest lifetime earnings with lower pensions. Since women figure prominently in this group, they will be disadvantaged in a way disproportionate to their numbers in the populations at large. The private component lacks any redistributive effect and will contribute further to their disadvantage.

The Polish study illustrates the likely future effect. Its simulation shows that the average pension paid to a woman who retires at age 60 under the old

---

benefits will decline automatically in response to increased life expectancy (unless the individual keeps working and delays retirement). Individual accounts will be established to record each worker's contributions. Past contributions will be adjusted at the rate of 75 percent of the real growth of wages which are subject to contributions. This reform applies to all those who were 49 or younger on the date the reform came into force. Others will continue to be covered by the preexisting defined benefit system. Wóycicka et al., Box 7 this volume.

[52] Kucharová et al., section 4, this volume.

[53] In Poland, if payments from both the public and private schemes fall below a certain level, the individual can receive a supplement from the state budget that brings his/her pension up to a specified minimum.

rules is about 82 percent of that paid to a man retiring at the same age.[54] After the new NDC and privatized schemes are fully phased in, the average woman retiring at 60 will receive just 74 percent of the average pension paid to a man with the same retirement age.[55] The declining female/male benefit ratio is largely the result of eliminating redistribution toward low-income workers and those with shorter work histories.

Not all women are losers under the Polish reform, of course; nor are women the only disadvantaged group: men with low earnings will be similarly affected. The greater impact on women results from their lower average earnings and shorter periods of contribution which the reformed pension system will no longer offset.

b) Retirement age. In all three countries, socialist retirement policies gave women an advantage. The possibility of retiring earlier than men was one of a number of advantages that encouraged and rewarded motherhood. In Czechoslovakia, women's preference ranged from three to seven years, depending on the number of children they had raised. In Hungary and Poland, women were afforded a five-year advantage (in Hungary, retirement at age 55 versus 60 for men; in Poland, 60 versus 65).[56]

In the current environment of pension financing difficulties, shrinking or stagnant fertility rates, and a projected drop in the ratio of active workers to retired persons, achieving equality with respect to retirement age by revising men's retirement age to agree with women's is not a plausible alternative. Practically, equality can be achieved only by eliminating women's preferences. In some sense, movement in the direction of equal treatment is a losing proposition for Central European women (we will argue below, however, that

---

[54]   Wóycicka et al., section 7, this volume.

[55]   Specifically, the typical retired woman retiring at age 60 will draw a pension equal to 22.4 percent of the average wage in the economy while her male counterpart will draw one equal to 30.4 percent. Should they both retire at age 65, the woman's pension would equal 29.2 percent of the average wage while the man's would equal 39.6 percent. In both cases the average woman's pension will be just 74 percent of the average man's. Wóycicka et al., section 7, this volume.

[56]   Section 4 of Kucharová et al., Lukács and Frey, and Wóycicka et al., this volume.

it should be seriously considered nonetheless). The difficulties associated with this change will probably fall most heavily on those women who, closest to retirement, planned to retire under the old rules but find themselves nearing retirement under the new ones. But it may also fall on the young and the aging as women, working to more advanced ages, are restricted from performing traditional roles as care-givers of aging parents and grandchildren. Reflecting these considerations, only Hungary has so far established equality of retirement ages. The Czech Republic has narrowed the gap between women and men, and Poland has chosen to maintain the preexisting five-year differential.[57] See Table 5.

Table 5 Retirement ages in the Czech Republic, Hungary, and Poland		
Country	Pre-1990	Current law
Czech Republic	60 for men, 53–57 for women	62 for men, 57–61 for women, being phased in by 1 January 2007
Hungary	60 for men, 55 for women	62 for both sexes, being phased in by 1 January 2009
Poland	65 for men, 60 for women, with early retirement options	65 for men, 60 for women, with early retirement eliminated beginning in 2007, with the exception of a narrow list of occupations, to be specified in future regulations

Source: Section 4 of Kucharová et al., Lukács and Frey, and Wóycicka et al., this volume.

However, it must be recognized that the value of the retirement age preferences that continue to exist in two countries is being eroded through the reforms described in the previous subsection. With the elimination of redistribution toward workers with low lifetime contributions, most women who exercise the option to retire early will receive substantially lower benefits

---

[57] Poland did, however, eliminate early retirement in the 1999 reform, effective in 2007. See Wóycicka et al., section 5, this volume.

than they would have before these reforms. This effect, too, is illustrated in the Polish simulations. See Table 6. Once the new mixed system is fully implemented, a woman retiring at age 60 with an average female's pension will receive an amount equal to only 57 percent of a man retiring at age 65 with an average male's pension. By delaying retirement until age 65, she would receive a pension equal to 74 percent of his. Given this large difference, the surest way to avoid further erosion of women's retirement protection is to bring the statutory retirement age for women into equality with men's. Without this equalization, the retreat from redistribution will leave women at substantially greater risk of poverty as the reforms are phased in. This risk provides strong justification for equal treatment.

Table 6
Average pension for a woman
(as a percentage of the average pension for a man) Poland, simulation for 2050

	With continuing earlier retirement for women (60, 65)	With equal retirement at age 65
Old system	75	81
New system	57	73

Source: Wóycicka et al., section 7, this volume.

c) Caring credits. During the socialist era, all three schemes provided credits toward a pension for years that workers (mostly mothers) spent out of employment caring for young children at home. While the rules for counting such periods varied across schemes, a year spent in such status was generally treated as equal to a year of employment, even though no contributions were paid.[58] This meant that periods of child care did not reduce the pension that a parent would receive. These credits were financed within the pension system by a cross subsidy from other contributors.

During the 1990s, Hungary and Poland revised the rules for crediting such periods, in each case diminishing their value. Hungary retained the old rules

---

[58] The treatment also varied depending on which child care benefit was received by the parent. See Lukács and Frey, section 5, this volume.

in the public component but applied the new rules in the new mandatory private component adopted in 1998. In this case, participants must contribute six percent of their child care benefit to a commercially managed individual savings account. As explained previously, their future pension benefits will be calculated as a simple return on this contribution – i.e., investment performance minus management fees.[59] As with all other contributions to the privatized component of the pension system, there is no employer matching contribution. Six percent of the child care benefit is a tiny amount, equal to less than US$ 4.00 per month. This policy is especially disadvantageous for middle- and upper-income workers, since the pension entitlements that they earn while working are substantially higher than those based on the child care benefit.

The Polish government took a different approach by providing a transfer from the state budget to finance pension credits for periods of child care (1999). This improves the transparency of pension financing and shifts the burden of financing pension credits for which no contributions are paid to the public at large. However, the subsidy is based on the minimum wage which makes the benefit much less generous than it was before this reform. As a result, most individuals who take leave from work to provide child care will receive lower pensions. As it is almost exclusively women who take leave and receive child care benefits, it is their earnings history, and consequently their pensions, that will be reduced. This reform also creates disincentives for men, who typically have higher earnings, to take child care leave.

d) Life expectancy and private pensions. Under the new mixed pension schemes in Hungary and Poland, part of each worker's monthly pension contribution is redirected to a commercially managed individual savings account. At retirement, the savings accumulated in this account will be converted to an annuity that will pay a monthly pension benefit until the worker's death. The annuity provider will set the level of this monthly benefit based on how long the worker is likely to live, that is, how many years the

---

[59] This private benefit will supplement the individual's public pension. The amount of the public pension will be reduced due to the diversion of a part of the contribution to the private tier.

savings must be stretched to cover. Since it is not possible to know this in advance, the provider will use a statistical estimate of the average life expectancy of all those in the worker's age group.

Two quite different methods for making this estimate are possible. The first will give a retired woman the same monthly benefit as it gives a man who retires at the same age with identical savings and investment earnings. This results from the use of a joint life expectancy table for both sexes. The second approach will give the woman in the range of 20 percent less, depending on the specifics of the situation. This results from the use of two distinct life expectancy tables, one for women that reflects the fact that, on average, they live longer than men. The simulations in the Polish study show that, using a joint table for both pension pillars, the average woman would receive a pension equal to 74 percent of that of the average pension for a man. Switching to gender-specific tables would reduce her benefit from 74 percent of his to 59 percent.[60]

What constitutes equal treatment in this situation? Should women and men with comparable histories of earnings accumulate equal benefits over the duration of their retirement? Or should they receive an equal monthly benefit?

From a public policy perspective, the latter approach is preferable for three reasons. First, the use of gender-specific averages would mask the substantial overlap that exists in the actual mortality of individual men and women. In fact, substantial numbers of men live longer than the average female life expectancy; substantial numbers of women die before they reach it; and substantial numbers of men and women live to be nearly the same age. Using group averages to set the pension benefits of individuals whose actual longevity does not match the averages would have a capricious effect, creating many unjustified winners and losers – i.e. men who outlive the female average but receive a higher pension nonetheless based on their own sex's shorter average longevity (winners), and women whose longevity falls short of the male average but who receive lower pensions anyway because other women live longer (losers).

---

[60] Wóycicka et al., Tables 13 and 14, this volume.

Second, though the new individual savings schemes of Hungary and Poland are privately managed, they are still part of the pension system and as such have public purposes. The most basic of these is to pool risks across the population so as to provide everyone a minimal level of protection against poverty arising from uncertain longevity. Paying lower benefits to those who live longer would defeat this objective, subjecting them to greater risk of poverty at every stage of their retired lives.

Third, women are by no means the only, or even most prominent, group in society with greater average longevity. If we apply group treatment to them, should we not also give smaller monthly benefits to nonsmokers who, on average, outlive smokers; to the more affluent members of society who, on average, outlive the less affluent; to members of racial and ethnic majorities who, on average, outlive members of minority groups; and to those free from genetic vulnerability to life threatening diseases such as cancer, hemophilia, or heart disease who, on average, outlive less lucky members of society?

For all three reasons, the preferred principle is that individuals with the same earnings history and the same *actual* retirement tenure should, in practice, receive the same monthly benefits.

This is precisely what the Hungarian law provides. It requires that annuity providers use the same joint life expectancy table in calculating monthly benefits for both women and men. In Poland, by contrast, the issue remains undecided; as yet there has been no legislation that stipulates how mandatory individual savings will be converted to pensions. In 1999, the Government presented a proposal to Parliament allowing the use of gender-specific calculations, and then in the face of heavy criticism there, withdrew it.[61] The successor government has not yet addressed the issue.

Beyond laws requiring equal treatment, there is need for regulatory structures that support compliance and enforcement of these laws. This need arises from the simple fact that the required use of joint life expectancy tables creates rational incentives for annuity providers to devise ways to attract men and discourage women. After all, the annuity for a woman will, on average, cost the provider more than an annuity for a man, for the simple reason that,

---

[61] Wóycicka et al., sections 5 and 7, this volume.

on average, women will collect their benefits for longer periods. For providers, averages matter. They might, for example, target men in advertising, dispatch agents to locations where men congregate, or offer gifts that men value. There are many other possibilities for subtle discrimination.[62]

Thus, both the method chosen for calculating the new annuities and the arrangements put in place for enforcing this method are of great importance for the future well-being of women.

To sum up, the first decade of transformation brought greater losses of pension protection for women compared to men in all three countries. These losses reflect two broad trends across Central Europe. First, the strong appeal of individualism in all areas of life shaped the politics of pension reform, leading to benefits in both the public and private schemes that more closely reflect contributions paid, that is, to a curtailment of redistribution. Second, tight fiscal limitations in all three countries constrained the options for achieving equal treatment in pension schemes, leading to reforms that imposed greater disadvantages on women in some regards.

The losses are most severe in Poland, where the particular combination of changes adopted – the elimination of redistribution in both the new public scheme and in the new commercially managed savings accounts in conjunction with continuing earlier retirement age for women – poses major disadvantages for women. They are least severe in the Czech Republic, where elements of redistribution so far retained in the pension system benefit women. In Hungary, the new equal treatment of women with respect to retirement age has helped to offset some of the economic losses that would otherwise be associated with reduced redistribution. The equal treatment implied in the adoption of gender-neutral life expectancy tables is an important step to avoid further disadvantages.

---

[62] This potential is greatest under a system such as that in Hungary where the law allows for multiple, competing annuity providers. Were there instead one single provider for the country, there would be no opportunity for that firm to discriminate in selecting its customers from among a larger pool of private scheme members. This option is among three arrangements being considered in Poland. Agnieszka Chlon, 'The Polish Pension Reform of 1999,' Framework 1, 'Options for providing annuities in Poland,' in Fultz (2002), p.135.

The four issues examined in this section call for attention and action by those with an interest in advancing women's interests. First, in those countries that have privatized their pension schemes, the use of gender-specific life expectancy tables (as opposed to unisex tables) would put women at considerable risk. In several CEE countries, it remains an open question whether this issue will be settled on the basis of social insurance principles or on the operating norms of private pension funds. Advocates of gender equality should weigh in. Second, there is great need for adherence to minimum standards that ensure that all those with low earnings will receive decent levels of protection in retirement. During the 1990s, the pendulum of public policy swung far in the other direction in many Central European countries; and corrections are needed. Useful benchmarks are provided by ILO Convention 102, Minimum Standards of Social Security, and the European Social Security Code. While this is not exclusively a gender issue, advocates of gender equality should lend their support. Third, the value of women's retirement age preferences is being eroded indirectly, as reduced redistribution in pension schemes makes payment levels increasingly inadequate for those who retire early. In this circumstance, equalizing the retirement age for women and men becomes a practical necessity. Finally, child care has been devalued for pension purposes in two of the three countries through credits that penalize parents, overwhelmingly women, who leave work to care for young children. Advocates of gender equality should join forces with all those who recognize the social value of child care to ensure that pension systems should not penalize such periods.[63]

---

[63] Germany, for example, takes several approaches to ensuring this. For every child born after 1 January 1992 a parent receives one pension credit point per year (calculated by dividing the insured wage for a calendar year by the average wage of all insured for the same year) during three years, regardless if s/he is employed or not (before the 2001 reform, credits were given for one year). If the parent is employed, the caring credits are added to the obligatory pension contributions from the wage. In addition, if a parent has a low income (e.g. because of part-time work) while the child is between three and ten years old, her/his pension contributions are boosted by 50 percent up to a maximum of the pension contributions from the average wage of all insured for the calendar year. Only one parent, typically the mother, can benefit from this rule. Parents without income from

Beyond these issues, the analysis raises a number of problems whose solution lies outside the social security system: i.e., the persistent gender wage gap in CEE countries, the higher unemployment rates that women experience in most of them, and the skewed division of responsibilities for child care between women and men that continues to exist across the region. As noted previously, social security alone is a weak instrument for reshaping the entrenched beliefs and practices that sustain unequal treatment of men and women in the larger environment. Rather, these problems require an integrated response that combines social security reforms with broader changes – i.e., changes in labour law, affirmative action, public education, and stronger legal protections against discrimination. Together these studies provide ample illustration of the need for broader action on gender issues that shape the impact of social security schemes.

---

employment who have two or more children below the age of 10 are credited an additional 0.33 pension credit points per year. The total entitlement must not exceed average contributions from all insured, and eligibility for the uprating of pension contributions between the 3rd and 10th birthday of the child is based on 25 years of contribution payments.

Chapter 2
The Gender Dimensions
of Social Security Reform
in Hungary

Erika Lukács and Mária Frey

1. Labour Market Transformation and Women's Employment and Life Choices

The gender impact of social security reforms should be analysed with reference to the labour market in which they occurred, since this larger context both creates pressures for reforms and influences their impact. The Hungarian labour market is therefore the starting point for this analysis. The 1990s were characterized by four main labour market trends:

- There was a huge loss of jobs between 1990 and 1997, but in contrast with some other CEE countries, the male and female work forces in Hungary absorbed these losses relatively equally.
- The official unemployment rate for women rose less than that for men, suggesting that more women than men who lost their jobs left the labour market permanently. In this sense, lower unemployment is not a positive situation for women, but rather masks deep discouragement.
- Despite the economic transformation, the labour market continues to be characterized by considerable occupational segregation by gender and by a persistent wage gap in favour of men.
- The decade was marked by changing attitudes toward employment among women. While the shift is not dramatic, a significant number of Hungarian women no longer see employment outside the home as a desirable objective.

Job Losses

During the transition shock of 1989–1992, Hungary lost around 1.1 million jobs, representing a fall of 21.4 percent in total employment. Employment continued to decline in 1993–1996, with a further drop of 5 percent, and stabilized only in 1997. Since then, employment has grown at around 1–2 percent a year.

Table 1						
Employment of the Hungarian population aged 15–64						
Year	Number of employed (in thousands)			Employment rates, %		
	Male	Female	Total	Male	Female	Total
1990[a]	2,745.1	2,338.9	5,084.0	82.9	67.3	74.9
1992[b]	2,185.6	1,838.3	4,023.9	64.6	52.3	58.3
1993	2,051.4	1,730.8	3,782.2	60.6	49.3	54.8
1994	2,033.0	1,679.3	3,712.3	60.3	47.8	53.9
1995	2,030.7	1,615.5	3,646.2	60.2	45.9	52.9
1996	2,021.4	1,601.1	3,622.5	60.1	45.5	52.6
1997	2,033.2	1,594.2	3,627.4	60.3	45.4	52.7
1998	2,029.7	1,649.3	3,679.0	60.6	47.3	53.9
1999	2,089.2	1,699.9	3,789.1	62.6	49.0	55.7
2000	2,108.8	1,716.9	3,825.7	63.3	49.7	56.4

a) Data refer to 1 January 1990 and are from the Census of the Central Statistical Office.

b) The Labour Force Survey was introduced in 1992. 1992–2000: Yearly average of the CSO LFS time series.

The employment rate of men, while consistently higher than that of women, declined slightly more than female employment; and it increased slightly more slowly in the period of 1997–2000. See Table 1.

Withdrawal from the Labour Market

After the demise of communism, unemployment rapidly climbed to its peak level of 11.9 percent in 1993. See Table 2. That peak reflected a 13.3 percent unemployment rate among men and a 10.3 percent rate among women. The female unemployment rate has consistently been lower than that of men in Hungary, in part because male-dominated industries, such as coal mining, metallurgy, and construction, were hardest hit during the economic restructuring. In addition, however, the lower unemployment rate for women masks a withdrawal of women from the labour market. While employed women have proved to be more successful than men in retaining their jobs, research shows that once a Hungarian woman becomes unemployed, it is much more difficult for her to be re-employed than for a man (Nagy, 2000, p.39).

Table 2						
Unemployment of the Hungarian population aged 15–64						
Year	Number of unemployed (in thousands)			Unemployment rate, %		
	Male	Female	Total	Male	Female	Total
1992	264.8	177.0	441.8	10.8	8.8	9.9
1993	313.4	198.5	511.9	13.3	10.3	11.9
1994	271.9	172.0	443.9	11.8	9.3	10.7
1995	260.4	153.9	414.3	11.4	8.7	10.2
1996	242.7	155.2	397.9	10.7	8.8	9.9
1997	212.6	133.2	345.8	9.5	7.7	8.7
1998	187.5	122.1	309.6	8.5	6.9	7.8
1999	170.6	113.9	284.5	7.5	6.3	7.0
2000	159.2	102.7	261.9	7.0	5.6	6.4

Source: CSO Labour Force Survey Time Series.

Some individuals withdrawing from the labour market were able to choose early retirement or a disability pension, the rules for which were relatively generous. As evidence of this, pensioners of working age actually outnumbered the registered unemployed by the year 2000. As can be seen in Table 3, the rate of increase was higher among women in both these categories.

	Registered unemployed			Pensioners of working age		
	Female	Male	Together	Female	Male	Together
1990	10.0	14.2	24.2	87.4	176.4	263.8
1994	256.0	376.1	632.1	161.8	275.9	437.7
1996	210.6	285.3	495.9	184.6	296.5	481.1
2000	184.4	220.1	404.5	246.6	322.0	568.6

Table 3
Number of registered unemployed and pensioners of working age in Hungary
(in thousands)

Source: Calculation based on data on labour force balances in January, 2000, CSO, Budapest, 2000.

Continuing Occupational Gender Segregation and Wage Gap

Gender segregation of occupations, already significant in Hungary, continued and even increased in some fields during the 1990s.

The transformation brought a reallocation of labour through downsizing, mergers, and liquidation of state-owned enterprises, while jobs were being created in the newly-established private enterprises. This reallocation also caused a shift of labour among the three broad economic sectors – agriculture, industry and services – with a clear migration of workers out of agriculture into the other two. As can be seen in Table 4, the shift to the services sector between 1992–2000 was modestly higher for women than for men; and there was also a modest decline in the number of women employed in industrial jobs.

Hungarian women and men not only tend to work in different sectors, but perform different jobs even when they are employed in the same one. The occupations in which women dominate are mostly focused on the provision of services, education, and treatment and care, whereas production is more typical in men's work. In Table 5, individual occupations have been grouped according to their degree of gender segregation.

Table 4
Female employment in Hungary by broad economic sectors, %

Sectors	Male		Female	
	1992	2000	1992	2000
Agriculture	14.3	9.0	7.7	3.6
Industry	40.4	40.8	28.7	25.1
Services	45.3	50.2	63.6	71.3
Total	100.0	100.0	100.0	100.0

Source: Time Series, Labour Force Survey, CSO.

Table 5
Occupational segregation in Hungary*, 1999

Occupations with	Percentage distribution of	
	individual occupations	female employed
90–100% women, 0–10% men	11	35.7
60–90% women, 10–40% men	19	34.2
40–60% women, 40–60% men	16	17.2
10–40% women, 60–90% men	27	11.7
0–10% women, 90–100% men	27	1.2
Total	100	100.0
In numbers	617	1,726,700

* Percentage distribution of individual occupations and employed women who work within totally segregated, heavily segregated and non-segregated occupations.

Source: Calculations based on CSO LFS data.

In 1999, 35.7 percent of women in employment were employed as clerks, social workers, nurses, cosmeticians, or in the textile and clothing industries. These occupations were almost exclusively female (at least 90 percent). A further 34.2 percent of women were in occupations that were predominantly female (60–90 percent). Only 17.2 percent of women in employment were working in jobs with a balanced male/female participation rate. These occupations included professional, professional support, and technical positions, as well as jobs in the printing industry and communal service. In fields such as mining, metallurgy, and construction, very few women can be found. Occupational segregation in 1999 followed practically the same pattern as had been identified in a similar survey conducted in 1994. The changes in the economy did not reduce gender segregation.

Women are underrepresented in senior and managerial positions, and their share of such positions declined between 1994 and 2000, as Table 6 shows.

Table 6
Distribution of employed women by and women's share in ISCO-88 Major Groups, Hungary

	Distribution, %		Women's share, %	
	1994	2000	1994	2000
Legislators, senior officials and managers	5.2	5.2	36.8	33.9
Professionals	12.8	15.2	56.7	58.2
Technicians and associate professionals	17.1	19.0	64.5	64.3
Clerks	17.1	14.0	91.2	92.3
Service workers and shop and market sales workers	17.3	18.9	56.7	55.4
Skilled agricultural and forestry workers	2.4	2.1	31.3	27.3
Craft and related workers	10.7	9.4	21.3	19.3
Plant and machine operators and assemblers	4.9	6.9	21.1	27.1
Elementary occupations	12.5	9.3	57.1	53.0
Total	100.0	100.0	45.9	44.9

Source: CSO Labour Force Survey.

On the other hand, almost all clerks are women, and they are also overrepresented in jobs requiring little or no training, as well as in the lower technical and professional categories. While women are well represented in the professional ranks, the 'glass ceiling' keeps them from reaching the level of senior officials and managers.

Women's inferior position in the labour market is accompanied by a noticeable gender wage gap (see Table 7). While the gap between male and female earnings was smaller in 2000 than in 1989 (82.8 percent compared to 88.9 percent of average earnings), the difference remains significant (nearly 20 percent); and it was slightly greater than that in 1999.

Table 7				
Gender wage gap in Hungary				
Year	Distribution of employed		Earnings as a percentage of average gross earnings	
	Male	Female	Male	Female
1989	53.8	46.2	114.9	82.8
1990	54.3	45.7	110.4	86.5
1995	55.7	44.3	110.6	88.6
1996	55.8	44.2	111.3	87.9
1997	56.0	44.0	111.9	87.4
1998	55.2	44.8	111.3	88.1
1999	55.2	44.8	110.0	88.9
2000	55.1	44.9	110.3	88.8

Source: CSO.

While average gender wage inequalities in comparable jobs have not changed much in the competitive sector, they have increased in the budgetary (public) sector to the detriment of women, as Table 8 indicates.

As unskilled workers were most affected by the drop in employment, the educational composition of the population of employed women has improved, with the proportion of those having higher education rising to 19.2 percent, and even surpassing that of employed men. See Table 9. As noted above, however, this improvement has not been accompanied by an increased share in managerial positions.

Table 8
Male and female earnings in comparable jobs in budgetary and non-budgetary sectors, Hungary 1997–2000

Sector	1997			1999			2000		
	Total	Male	Female	Total	Male	Female	Total	Male	Female
Budgetary	65.8	72	63.5	62.5	68.9	60.2	65.0	73.5	61.9
Competitive	100.0	104.9	92.2	100.0	105.0	92.1	100.0	105.1	92.2

Source: National Labour Centre Wage Survey.

The source of information is the representative annual survey of individual earnings with the reference month of May in each year. Data refer to earnings in comparable jobs.

Budgetary sector: state administration, public services (e.g. education, health) and armed forces. Competitive (non-budgetary) sector: private and public enterprises.

Table 9
Employed persons in Hungary* by highest educational attainment, %

	Male		Female	
	1992	2000	1992	2000
Less than/up to grade 8	25.9	16.0	32.8	19.1
Vocational and secondary schools	59.6	68.3	53.0	61.7
Higher education	14.8	15.7	14.2	19.2
Total	100.0	100.0	100.0	100.0

* Aged 15–74

Source: Time Series, Labour Force Survey, CSO.

Changing Attitudes toward Employment among Women

The decline in women's employment has been accompanied by measurable changes in values. Surveys show that, in the period just preceding the transition, employed women generally found their roles as workers appropriate and desirable. A 1988 Central Statistical Office survey carried out on a representative sample of working-age women in employment indicated that 81 percent of those questioned agreed with the idea that women should pursue paid activity. However, 71 percent of them said that the ideal solution for women would be part-time employment, while 10 percent preferred to work for pay at home (CSO, 1988). When the survey was repeated in 1995, it revealed a significant change in attitude. By that time, only some two-thirds of the working women who were interviewed answered that they were in favour of women's employment. Less than 20 percent of them thought that women should work full-time, 60 percent considered part-time employment to be desirable for women, and the remaining 20 percent said that it would be better for women to pursue their gainful employment at home. Thirty percent of the questioned women disapproved of female labour market participation (Frey, 1996).

In 1999, a new CSO survey was carried out on a sample which differed from the previous two. Only women aged 15–49 were surveyed, but this sample survey was drawn from the entire female population and not just those in employment (CSO, 2001). In this group, the proportion of women having a positive attitude to women's employment was also two-thirds (67 percent). However, the proportion of those who believed women should devote themselves only to child raising and housekeeping was more than a quarter higher than in the 1995 survey, or 27.6 percent. The rest (5.4 percent) did not have any opinion on women's employment.

Among women who with some connection to the labour market (the employed and unemployed), the acceptance of female employment is slightly above average (72.6 percent of the employed women and 70.3 percent of the unemployed approved female employment). Among women receiving the child care fee or child care allowance, the proportion believing that women should devote themselves to family and housekeeping is relatively high (33.3 percent of those receiving the child care fee and 39.1 percent of those receiving the child care allowance). 17.1 percent of the women who supported female employment found it desirable that women work full-time, while 77.5 percent preferred part-time employment.

2.   Family Benefits

Historically Hungary has had a rather generous social protection system, with child care benefits introduced gradually from the end of 1960s and subsequently becoming an integral part of the system. However, the changing economic and social conditions in the 1990s created a need for reform; and these benefits underwent significant changes.

In the communist era, the social protection system was linked almost entirely to employment, and open unemployment did not exist. The system therefore needed to be restructured to deal with a market economy in which unemployment was an overt problem. As a result of this restructuring, the following social protection sub-systems were established:

- a compulsory social insurance system, including health, pension, and unemployment insurance;
- family support schemes, which provided a mix of universal benefits, needs-related benefits, and earnings-related benefits;
- a social assistance system funded by the central budget and to some extent by the local governments; and
- social and child care facilities run by local governments.

Two of the social insurance elements, pensions and health care, were separated from the central state budget in 1990. Funded largely by contribution payments, these elements were to become an independent social insurance system.

In undertaking this restructuring, the governments faced financial, social, and political dilemmas. The economic crisis meant that there was increasing demand for social security benefits, but at the same time fewer resources to meet those demands. The first post-communist government (the Antall government) also faced the political dilemma of how to dampen high expectations and general enthusiasm for change without jeopardizing support for the new democratic system by introducing severe restrictions in existing benefits. The basic changes made over the decade occurred in several steps.

In 1989–90, some benefits that had previously been earnings-related (family allowance, several assistance supplements, maternity grant, and death grant[1])

---

[1] Parallel to this process, a fragmented social assistance system started to develop with responsibility split between the central and the local governments, which themselves changed in the 1990s. The benefits included an old age allowance, an income subsidy for the unemployed, regular social benefits, assistance to maintain a home, nursing allowance, temporary allowance, and death grant.

were removed from the social insurance system and funded by general revenues. As will be shown, this change made them more vulnerable to the financial pressures facing the state budget; and the eligibility criteria, availability, and level of these benefits were changed repeatedly during the 1990s.

During the centre-right Antall/Boross coalition governments (1990–94), entitlements remained unchanged, but price liberalisation and the sudden withdrawal of the price subsidies for basic goods resulted in high inflation, which devalued these benefits. The percentage of GDP allocated to family supports declined from 4 percent in 1990 to 2.67 percent in 1995. However, two new types of benefits, the *child raising benefit,* aimed at supporting larger families, and the *pregnancy benefit,* were introduced. The pregnancy benefit was equal to the family allowance from the third month of pregnancy and paid monthly. It was introduced under pressure from those who wanted the government to do something to decrease the number of abortions. Except for the introduction of these two benefits, there were no significant changes in social benefits during the Antall/Boross years.

The socialist (MSZP)/liberal (AFD) coalition government (1994–98), led by Gyula Horn, continued economic reforms and privatization. To address the budget deficit, the Horn government adopted a policy of fiscal austerity. Known as the 'Bokros-package'[2], this programme of comprehensive, radical measures was designed to stabilize the economy and bring the state budget into balance. It tightened eligibility for social benefits, income-tested some benefits, and decreased the real value of family benefits.

The Orbán government[3] (elected in 1998) reintroduced universal family benefits and created additional family-oriented preferences, such as tax credits.[4]

---

[2]   A set of restrictive measures initiated by the Minister of Finance, Lajos Bokros.

[3]   A coalition of the right-wing Fidesz-Hungarian Civic Party (MPP), the agrarian-right Independent Smallholders' Party Populist (FKGP) and the Hungarian Democratic Forum (MDF).

[4]   As will be shown, family benefits had been means-tested during 1996–98.

Changes in the Social Security Benefit Structures

While elements of the family support system were altered repeatedly, the variety of benefits was largely preserved, although the coverage for some of them has been reduced. The sequence of changes described above can be roughly categorized as follows:

- eligibility was expanded for some benefits, which became personal rights and were no longer linked to employment status;
- certain benefits were income-tested in mid-decade and later became universal again;
- the income replacement rate for benefits covered by social insurance declined; and
- new benefits were introduced.

The following table illustrates these changes.

Table 10
Main elements of family support system in Hungary by type of compensation, 1989–2000

	89	90	91	92	93	94	95	96	97	98	99	00
Family allowance												
Maternity benefit												
Child care allowance												
Child care fee												
Child raising benefit												
Birth grant												

▬ based on personal rights
▬ based on employed/insured status
▬ based on income test
▬ based on employed/insured status and income test

Based on Gábos András: *State of Families and Family Support in the 90s, Social Report 2000*, TÁRKI, 2000.

As can be seen from Table 10, the reforms were not uni-directional. The most dramatic changes occurred in mid-April 1996, when, in line with the Horn government's austerity plan, certain benefits became more targeted and less generous:

- the income-related child care fee was abolished;
- the maternity benefit was reduced from 100 percent to 70 percent of previous earnings;
- the family allowance, excluding those for families with three or more children, became income-tested;
- the child care allowance was raised and was income-tested according to the same rules as the family allowance; and
- the pregnancy benefit was replaced by a lump-sum birth grant which was 30–40 percent lower than the pregnancy benefit it replaced.

By the end of the decade, however, income testing had been abolished and the child care fee restored.

Because there was no statutory indexation of benefits, most of the family support benefits suffered considerable loss in value during the 1990s. Those benefits, the level of which is linked to the old age pension minimum (birth grant, child care allowance, or child raising benefit) or to earnings (maternity benefit, payments for caring for a sick child, and child care fee) were devalued less than the family allowance. However, budget restrictions affected the earnings-related benefits as well, and income replacement rates fell for the maternity benefit, payments for caring for a sick child, and the child care fee.

Coverage, Entitlement Structure

The structure of family support benefits which emerged from the reforms can be analysed according to three major functions: bearing children, caring for young children in the home, and raising a family.[5] The reformed benefits are described briefly in Boxes 1, 2, and 3.

---

[5] An attached table (Annex 1, Table A1.1) summarizes entitlements and other features of the family support system.

Box 1
Benefits related to child bearing:
The maternity benefit and birth grant in Hungary

The *maternity benefit* is an insurance-based benefit, available to women who had 180 insured days in the last two years before the birth of a child. It covers the 168-day-long maternity leave period (28 days before and 140 after the birth), and replaces 70 percent of the mother's last earnings. Until 1996, the replacement rate had been 100 percent.

Women are entitled to 24 weeks of maternity leave, but taking maternity leave is not mandatory. In addition to maternity leave, there are other provisions to protect a mother's health and safety. During pregnancy and until the child reaches one year of age, mothers may not be assigned night shift work or over-time. Maternity benefits and maternity leave are available only to mothers.

The *birth grant* is universal, but is contingent upon the mother having four medical visits during pregnancy. It is a lump-sum payment representing 150 percent of the minimum old age pension. Until 1992 there had been a flat-rate birth grant, and from 1993–1996 there was a pregnancy benefit, equivalent to the family allowance, payable from the third month of pregnancy. The current value of the birth grant, HUF 24,900, represents approximately 40 percent of the average net monthly earning, and is paid from the state budget. If the mother dies, the birth grant is paid to the father or to the person who takes care of the child.

Box 2
Child care benefits: Child care fee, child care allowance, and child raising benefit

First introduced in 1968, the *child care allowance* provides a flat-rate monthly amount which is equal to the minimum old age pension.[6] It is available to a parent who cares for a child up to the age of three years in his/her home. (In the case of a disabled child, the age limit is 10 years.)[7] A parent receiving the child care allowance can take a part-time job (up to four hours a day) as well as unlimited paid work at home if the child is at least 18 months old. Either the mother or the father can claim this benefit under the same conditions.

The *child care fee*, which was introduced in the mid-1980s, provides 70 percent of the former earnings for a parent who cares for a child under the age of two at home. Eligibility is based on a period of 180 insured days in the two years before the birth of the child. Either parent may claim this benefit. A parent is not allowed to be employed while receiving this fee.

The flat-rate *child raising benefit*, introduced in 1993, is for those who have three or more children in the family and covers for the period when the youngest child is between three and eight years of age. As with the child care allowance, this benefit is equal to the minimum old age pension, and the recipient parent can work no more than four hours a day outside the home. From 1993 until 1999, this benefit was income-tested. Until 1998, only mothers could claim this benefit, but now it can be claimed by either parent.

The child care fee and the child care allowance can be received sequentially, but not simultaneously. The general pattern for those who have accumulated the necessary insurance period is to claim maternity benefits for the first 140 days after the baby's birth, then the child care fee until the child reaches the age of two, and then the child care allowance when the child is between two and three years of age. If in this period a new baby is born, the beneficiary periods are extended, but the amount of the benefit is not increased.[8]

Those who have not accumulated the necessary period of insurance can claim the child care allowance from the child's birth until the child reaches the age of three.[9] In families of three or more children, a parent remaining at home to care for a child between the ages of three and eight can claim the child raising fee.

---

[6] It has been equal to the minimum old age pension only since 1996. Prior to that, there was a basic amount provided for each child cared for under three years of age (for the first child, HUF 700/month, the second, HUF 800/month, and the third and additional children, HUF 900/month) plus a flat-rate supplementary amount for each claimant. This supplement was raised year after year, so finally there was no significant difference in the amounts received if one cared for one or two children.

[7] Since May, 2001 it has been possible for a grandparent to claim the child care allowance in cases where the child is over one year old, if the parents agree to the arrangement, if the grandparent has no other earnings, and if the parent has no earnings activity. Therefore, a grandparent taking care of a child while the parent was a student could collect this benefit, but not a grandparent taking care of a child for a parent who was employed.

[8] Except in the case of the child care allowance, which is increased with the minimum pension.

[9] Between 1996 and 2000 the child care fee did not exist and the flat rate child care allowance was an income-tested social transfer. During this period there were two principal patterns: for those who had insurance, maternity benefits followed by child care allowance until the child was three; for those without insurance, child care allowance until the child reached the age of three.

Box 3
Family Benefits: family allowance, child protection benefits, and tax credits

The *family allowance* is payable until the child reaches the age of 16, or until age 20 if the child remains in school. In the case of seriously disabled children, no age limit is applied. This benefit was employment-related before 1990, universal between 1990 and 1995, income-tested (except in the cases of families with three or more children) between 1996 and 1999, and universal again after 1 January 1999. In 1998 this benefit was renamed the 'schooling benefit' for children of school age, and 'educational support' until the child reaches school age. The amount of the family allowance benefit increases until the third child, and is higher for single-parent families than for two-parent families.[10]

The *regular child protection benefit* was paid from 1998 to 2000 to families whose per capita income did not exceed the minimum old age pension. Its amount was 20 percent of the minimum old age pension per child. The benefit was distributed by local governments and financed, up to 80 percent, by the central budget. Since 2001, this benefit has been renamed the *supplementary family allowance*. The benefit is slightly higher, but the qualifying conditions remain unchanged.[11]

The *irregular child protection benefit* is available to families with temporary cash flow problems or facing emergencies. The amount is determined and paid by local governments.

Tax credits, which had existed on a small scale until 1995, were re-established and expanded in 1999. In the first year, for the first and the second child the benefit was HUF 1,700 per month, and for the third or additional child, HUF 2,300 per month. In 2000, these amounts were HUF 2,200 and HUF 3,000 per month per child in the respective categories. In 2001, these allowances increased again and the amount for the second child was increased (HUF 3,000, HUF 4,000, or HUF 10,000/month per child for the first, second, third or additional child).[12]

---

[10] For details on family allowance payments by type of family and number of children, see Table A2.3 in Annex 2.

[11] HUF 4,000/month per child instead of HUF 3,660/month per child.

[12] The revenues loss from these tax credits was HUF 33 billion in 1999, HUF 40 billion in 1999–2000, and for 2001 it is estimated that it will reach HUF 80 billion. It is estimated that nearly 1.1 million families have made use of tax credits. The total number of families in Hungary is just over two million. Some of the families which cannot use the tax credit because their income is too low may receive the supplementary family allowance in (a flat rate of HUF 4,000 and HUF 4,200 HUF/month per child in 2001 and 2002).

Changes in Expenditures

How did these frequent and multi-directional changes affect program expenditures? As shown in Table 11, the real value of aggregate family benefits declined significantly over the decade, however it is measured – in total expenditures, in benefits per capita, or as a percentage of GDP. While all three of these measures began to increase in the late 1990s, the gains compensated for only a small portion of the previous losses. As a portion of GDP, real spending on family benefits was only about half as great in 2000 as it had been in 1990.

Table 11

GDP per capita, family benefits per capita, and total expenditures on family benefits in Hungary 1990–2000 (in HUF adjusted to 1990 values)

Year	GDP per capita	Family benefits per capita	Total expenditure in billion	% of GDP
1990	201,573	7,569	78.5	3.8
1991	177,324	7,215	74.6	4.1
1992	171,221	6,702	69.7	3.9
1993	169,466	6,255	64.4	3.7
1994	176,020	5,728	58.8	3.3
1995	177,158	4,413	45.2	2.5
1996	176,630	3,585	36.6	2.0
1997	185,675	3,391	34.4	1.8
1998	192,641	3,840	38.8	2.0
1999	200,338	3,846	38.7	1.9
2000	201,915	3,941	39.6	2.0

Source: CSO Statistical Yearbooks, Statistical Yearbooks National Health Insurance Fund Administration.

While the real value of expenditures declined overall, some benefits were eroded more than others, as shown in Table 12. In general, those benefits which were based on earnings or on the minimum old age pension fared better than the family allowance, whose real value declined by the end of the decade to just 39.5 percent of its 1990 value (see row 1 versus rows 4 and 10).

Table 12

Selected average monthly family benefits per capita in Hungary;
in nominal value, in real value, and as % of average net earnings 1990–1999

	1990	1994	1995	1997	1999
Change in real value of family allowance to families with two children (1990=100)	100.0	65.0	50.7	44.8	39.5
Family allowance to families with two children as % of net average earnings	41.0	28.2	25.1	22.0	18.8
Amount of child care allowance in nominal value (HUF)	3,350	7,600	8,500	11,500	15,350
Change in real value of child care allowance (1990=100)	100.0	86.5	78.9	69.6	68.7
Amount of child care allowance as % of net average earnings	33.1	33.0	31.8	30.1	30.7
Amount of child care fee in nominal value (HUF)	5,198	11,495	13,613	19,165	—
Change in real value of child care fee (1990=100)	100.0	84.3	84.1	77.0	—
Amount of child care fee as % of net average earnings	51.4	49.9	52.6	51.8	—
Amount of child raising benefit in nominal value (HUF)	—	6,800	8,500	11,500	15,350
Change in real value of child raising benefit (1993=100)	—	92.5	97.3	83.1	82.0
Amount of child raising benefit as % of net average earnings	—	29.5	32.8	30.1	30.7

FA = Family allowance; CCA = Child care allowance; CCF = Child care fee; CRB = Child raising benefit.

Source: CSO Statistical Yearbooks, Statistical Yearbooks National Health Insurance Fund Administration.

Gábos, A., *Position of and Support to Families in the 90s*, TARKI, Social Report 2000.

To disaggregate this trend in another way, Table 13 presents spending over time for each of the separate family benefits. Among these varying patterns, it is possible to discern the effect of restrictions enacted under the Horn government's austerity program (see highlighting). With the elimination of the child care fee, more parents claimed the (less generous) child care allowance. Income testing reduced the expenditures on family allowances, and the reduction in the replacement rate for the maternity benefit caused a significant drop in expenditures on it.

Table 13
Expenditures on various family benefits in Hungary,
1990–1999 (HUF, billions)

Year	Family allowance (schooling benefit)	Child care allowance	Child raising benefit	Maternity grant	Pregnancy allowance	Birth grant	Maternity benefit	Child care fee	Pay for caring for sick child	Child protection benefit
1990	64.3	3.8	—	0.7	—	—	4.1	9.7	1.1	
1991	82.2	5.8	—	0.7	—	—	5.2	12.0	—	
1992	92.0	7.1	—	1.1	—	—	6.4	14.7	1.2	
1993	103.2	8.3	—	0.2	2.1	—	7.2	17.3	1.4	
1994	107.7	10.3	3.2	—	2.2	—	8.3	18.8	1.5	
1995	100.7	11.3	5.4	—	2.1	—	8.9	20.4	1.4	
1996	95.5	14.2	6.6	—	1.1	0.3	8.3	22.3	1.3	
1997	105.9	27.1	8.6	—	—	1.7	6.0	12.7	1.4	
1998	121.0	39.0	11.0	—	—	1.9	6.9	1.2	1.7	24.8
1999	132.6	44.8	11.1	—	—	2.1	7.8	—	2.0	28.2
2000 budget	133.8	28.0	12.9	—	—	2.7	7.1	36.3	2.1	35.8

Source: *Statistical Yearbook 1999*, National Health Insurance Fund Administration.

Changes in Number of Beneficiaries

There were also substantial shifts in the number of recipients of various family benefits, as can be seen in Table 14. Most dramatically, between 1990 and 2000, the number of children receiving a family allowance declined by nearly 350,000. This change was due primarily to the lower birth rate, but the drop between 1996–98 also reflects the income testing of the allowance in those years. The effect was not great because the income threshold for exclusion was relatively high (around the 7th decile of family per capita income). As a consequence, the proportion of those excluded from the system was relatively low – nine percent of families and seven percent of children.[13]

Data of Table 14 on beneficiaries of the child care allowance, child care fee, and maternity benefit reflect the worsening employment situation of women. It is noteworthy that the number of those receiving the child care allowance rose despite a steady decline in the birth rate over the decade (in 2000 there were 30,000–35,000 fewer births than a decade before). Compared to 1990, the proportion of parents of children aged zero to two that received the child care allowance or child care fee rose from 70 percent to 85.7 percent, reflecting an increasing tendency for parents (in practice, mothers) to care for young children in the home. Because of the loss of jobs, fewer women were eligible for the insurance-based child care fee and instead collected the child care allowance, and in those years when the child care fee was abolished (1997–98) more women yet switched to the child care allowance. Over the past decade, the number of women giving birth who had previously been employed declined markedly. While in 1990 three-fourths of those giving birth were formerly in employment, their share in 1999 was only about 50 percent, another indication of the loss of jobs for women.

---

[13] In addition, the percentage of children below 18 years of age whose families were entitled to receive family allowance increased from 91.1 percent to 95.6 percent over the decade because of the increasing rate of secondary school attendance. This increase is netted into the overall decline.

Table 14
Number of beneficiaries of the family support system in Hungary
(per year in thousands)

Type of benefits	1990	1991	1992	1993	1994	1995	1996	1997	1998	1999	2000
Family allowance (number of children)	2,498.3	2,532.0	2,508.5	2,443.8	2,432.4	2,354.0	2,186.3	2,113.8	2,041.1	2,154.5	2,152.6
Regular child protection benefits (number of children)	101.0	152.3	201.1	250.0	288.3	384.6	405.6	656.2	742.7	804.1	786.3
Maternity benefit (number of women)	47.1	46.4	43.6	40.7	38.8	37.6	32.0	24.3	22.7	21.7	22.5
Birth grant/pregnancy benefit (number of women)	119.2	116.8	114.7	48.2	50.5	50.1	39.9	82.6	92.1	88.7	91
Child care allowance (average monthly number)	94.7	108.9	113.0	115.4	116.4	117.9	124.4	182.2	234.0	245.0	192.8
Child care fee (average monthly number)	155.0	150.9	148.0	143.1	135.9	128.5	118.4	56.8	9.9	—	53.8
Child raising benefits (average monthly number)	—	—	—	—	24.1	n.d.	44.6.	48.1	52.0	55.4	52.6

n.d. = No data available.

Source: CSO Yearbooks.

Availability and Cost of Child Care

An important consideration for women considering employment outside the home is child care. Some observers have hypothesized that the transition to a market economy in Hungary and other CEE countries would make quality child care much more expensive, thereby indirectly limiting women's employment options. While data with which to verify this claim are very limited, it does not tend to support it. The situation and factors at play appear to be more varied and complex.

In terms of availability, the situation differs between nurseries and kindergartens. The past two decades witnessed a continuous decline in the availability of the former, especially outside the larger cities. Between 1980 and 1999, both the number of nurseries and the available slots dropped dramatically, by approximately 60 percent, with most of the losses occurring between 1990 and 1995. See Table 15. This resulted from the interplay of several factors, including the decreasing birth rate, the consequent need for nurseries to close and consolidate in order to achieve greater economies of scale, and the popularity of the earnings-related child care fee. Introduced in the mid-1980s, this fee prohibits recipients from accepting outside employment. Its use increased significantly in the years following its introduction, accentuating the trend of nursery closures.[14]

Table 15
Nurseries – institutions, slots, enrolment, and utilization rates in Hungary

Year	Number of institutions	Number of slots	Number of children actually enrolled	Slots per hundred children aged 0–2 years	% utilization of slots
1980	1305	64,502	69,768	13.6	81.6
1990	1003	50,250	40,825	13.7	61.8
1995	628	31,020	37,696	9.0	70.4
1999	549	26,071	31,983	8.8	77.6

Source: *Social Statistical Yearbook*, 2000, National Statistical Office.

---

[14] The average number of beneficiaries doubling between 1985 and 1990, from 67,000 to 155,000 recipients.

The supply of kindergartens, by contrast, has been reduced only minimally. More than 86 percent of children of the target age attend kindergartens, a rate higher than 10 years ago. Between 1990 and 1999, only 17 kindergartens and 15,000 places were lost, while live births decreased by 30,000 over the same period.[15] Kindergartens are available throughout the country, including in villages.

In terms of the affordability of fees charged by these institutions, it is important to note that today most child care facilities are owned and run by local governments, financed from general revenues, and provide a substantial subsidy for families. This means that families, except those using private nurseries and kindergartens, do not pay the total costs of child care. The fees paid by parents cover only about one-fifth of the costs, while the remainder is paid by local governments (e.g. in the kindergartens the subsidy was about HUF 16,700 per month per child in 1998,[16] and parents paid a HUF 4,000 monthly fee). The amount of the fee is legally regulated, calculated on the basis of the costs of food and raw materials, and set by the local government. Fees therefore can differ from one locality to another, with the highest fees reported for Budapest. These fees increase by at least the inflation rate for basic foods. Child care costs can be substantial for those whose earnings are low and have two or more children, representing 40–50 percent of the minimum or low wages. However, for three or more children there is 50 percent standard discount in fees, and low-income families can obtain additional relief through local governments.

Religious groups, employers, foundations or private individuals operate fewer than five percent of kindergartens, caring for three percent (11,726 out of 374,874) of all children. Their fees can differ substantially from those charged by the state-run facilities.

While data on child care costs over time are not available, these indicators do not suggest that these costs are a significant barrier to the employment of women. Rather, it appears that the main causal factors reducing women's employment are those discussed earlier – the combination of a real loss of jobs, the availability of benefits for the care of young children at home, and a certain attitudinal shift with respect to out-of-home work among women.

---

[15] *Educational Yearbook, 1999*, Ministry of Education.

[16] *Statisztikai Tájékoztató, Oktatási Évkönyv, 1998*, Budapest, 1999.

Impact of the Changes at the Household Level:
Changes in Benefits as a Percentage of Family Income

Income inequality increased considerably in Hungary in the 1990s, and families with children lost some ground. At the beginning of the decade, the incomes of the upper deciles exceeded those of the lower by a factor of four, but this had increased to a factor of 7.5 by 1997. In 1987, 42 percent and in 1996, 45 percent of children were found in the lowest three income deciles.[17] Table 16 shows that, over the decade, the per capita net income of families with children declined as a percentage of the net income of active households with no children. The degree of decline varied directly with the number of children.[18]

As Table 17 illustrates, the proportion of family income represented by social benefits first declined and later stabilized for all types of families over the decade. The total share of social benefits in family income fell from 1993 to 1997 due to the government's austerity plan and the cutback in benefits. By 1999 the proportion of social income in the net income had bounced back considerably for most families.[19] Given that the cuts in the family allowance that were made earlier in the decade were not restored, we must attribute this rebound to increases in other types of social income, most probably pension income.[20]

---

[17] Living standard (1988–1997), Central Statistical Office, 1998.

[18] At the same time, the portion of family benefit payments directed toward the lower three income deciles increased quite dramatically, from 44.2 percent in 1987 to 60.2 percent a decade later. This larger increase was, however, the result of means testing of the family benefit.

[19] A question arises as to why there was no rebound for families with two children. This is not entirely clear. The best explanation that we find for this phenomenon is that a larger portion of families with one child or multiple chidren tend to be eligible for social assistance. The former is the case because single parents are overrepresented among one-child households.

[20] The real value of pensions increased by 6.4 percent in 1998 and 3.8 percent in 1999.

Table 16				
Per capita net income of Hungarian households with children as a percentage of income of active households without children, 1991–2000 (selected years).[21]				
Denomination	1991	1997	1999	2000, first half year
		Household budget survey		
	Yearly processing		Quarterly processing	
Active households without children	100	100	100	100
All households with 1 child	83	72	73	73
with 2 children	73	62	67	65
with 3+ children	58	46	49	47

Source: CSO, *Household Statistics 2000*. First half year.
Household Budget Survey, Annual Report, 1993, 1997, 1999. CSO.

---

[21] A child is a dependent member under 20 years of age, living in the household. The basis of comparison is always data of active households without children. For 1991 data of active households with children, for 1997–2000 data of all households with children constitute the object of comparison.

Table 17
Share of social income in total household income
by number of dependent children, Hungary

Denomination	Household with			
	One child	Two children	Three or more children	Average of all families with children
1993				
Family allowance as % of net available income	7.0	14.5	24.2	8.7
Child care fee as % of net available income	1.1	1.5	2.5	1.2
Child care allowance/aid as % of net available income	1.1	1.0	2.7	0.9
Social income total/Net available income	21.0	25.1	38.0	23.8
1997				
Family allowance as % of net available income	3.9	9.4	18.3	5.0
Child care fee as % of net available income	0.5	0.4	0.7	0.3
Child care allowance/aid as % of net available income	2.1	2.1	7.5	1.7
Social income total/Net available income	16.3	20.1	35.0	19.5
1999				
Family allowance as % of net available income	3.6	8.2	16.4	7.3
Child care fee as % of net available income	—	—	—	—
Child care allowance/aid as % of net available income	2.1	2.6	8.8	3.3
Social income total/Net available income	20.4	21.0	38.8	23.2

Source: *Household Budget Survey, Annual Report, 1993, 1997, 1999.* CSO.

'Average' box represents both active and inactive families; other boxes reflect only active households.

Impact on Gender Division of Household and Child Care Work

Women in Hungary continue to bear the double burden of employment and household/child care work. The time-balance survey (see Table 18) shows that while employed men devoted a total of 493 minutes to earning activities, household, and child care activities on an average day in 1986 and 471 minutes in 1999, employed women devoted a total of 538 minutes to these activities in 1986 and 511 minutes in 1999.

Strong differences between men and woman are observeable in the balance between paid and unpaid work. Data in the time-balance survey show that the women in all categories devoted more time to housework and child care than did men.

Although the time spent by both genders on child raising has risen in recent years, an 'average woman' still spends two and a half times longer than an 'average man'; while employed women spend less time on child rearing than they had previously (a decline of 16 percent), they still spend more time than men. Table 18 outlines the different gender patterns.

Overall, the time spent in earning-productive activity decreased over the 12-year period; however, the time spent in earning-productive activity by employed women increased, meaning that those women who did have paid work were working longer hours. Although the gender differences in time devoted to housework declined in this period, woman still spent 2.6 times longer on housework than did men. Child care activities also remained mostly in the charge of women. The earning-productive activity of women who were on child care leave decreased substantially (by 88 minutes/day, to one quarter of the previous level) and nearly equal to the additional time they reported spending on child care activities (+76 minutes/day).[22] This reflects the strengthening of traditional patterns fostered by a declining labour market and the lack of support for combining employment and child raising.

---

[22] Those receiving the child care allowance and child raising fee are limited to no more than four hours' paid outside work per day.

Table 18
Time spent on earning-productive and housework/child care activities
by 18–74 year-old Hungarian population by employment status
(based on an average day in autumn, in minutes per day)

	Male			Female		
	1986	1999	Difference (1999–86)	1986	1999	Difference (1999–86)
Earning-productive activity						
Employed	419	395	–24	315	330	15
Pensioner	226	143	–83	124	87	–37
On child care leave	—	—	—	119	31	–88
Housewives	—	—	—	163	89	–74
Student	125	28	-97	90	22	–68
Unemployed	—	156	—	—	85	—
Average	*357*	*282*	*–75*	*228*	*188*	*–40*
Housework						
Employed	59	58	–1	190	153	–37
Pensioner	87	105	18	243	234	–9
On child care leave	—	—	—	256	256	0
Housewives	—	—	—	274	286	12
Student	42	27	–15	76	49	–27
Unemployed	—	114	—	—	262	—
Average	*62*	*71*	*9*	*206*	*186*	*–20*
Child care activities						
Employed	15	18	3	33	28	–5
Pensioner	2	5	3	2	8	6
On child care leave	—	—	—	185	261	76
Housewives	—	—	—	20	58	38
Student	—	—	—	—	—	—
Unemployed	—	27	—	—	58	—
Average	*11*	*14*	*3*	*31*	*35*	*4*

Source: 1986–87 and 1999–2000 survey of lifestyle-time-utilisation of population, CSO, Budapest 2000.

Another indication of the unequal distribution of child care activities is the negligible percentage of men claiming child care benefits. Although the child care fee and child care allowance may be claimed by either parent, a look at Table 19 shows that for most years of the decade fewer than one percent of the beneficiaries were men. In the middle of the decade, at the height of the economic crisis, this figure climbed to two percent, indicating the difficulties men were having in the labour market. As job prospects increased, the number and percentage of men claiming child care benefits sank to new lows.

Table 19
Number and percentage of male beneficiaries of child care fee/allowance,
Hungary 1990–2000

Year	Number of male beneficiaries (thousands)	% of men in the total number of beneficiaries
1990	1.2	0.5
1991	1.3	0.5
1992	1.8	0.7
1993	1.7	0.7
1994	2.2	0.9
1995	5.2	2.1
1996	4.6	2.0
1997	2.0	0.8
1998	1.0	0.4
1999	1.0	0.4
2000	1.0	0.4

Source: CSO Labour Force Survey.

Wider Economic and Social Impact of the Reform of Family Benefits

Social security reforms introduced to deal with the consequences of the transition to a market economy have had a mixed impact on women's employment and life prospects. While certain measures improved their immediate economic situation, others limited their opportunities. In this context, transitional and long-term effects have to be distinguished.

In the short term, the widely used child care benefits temporarily relieved unfavourable labour market effects.[23] However, by encouraging the withdrawal of mothers (in rare cases, fathers) from the labour market and, through the new child raising benefit, which made it possible for mothers to receive benefits for 14 or more years while giving full time care to children, these benefits also make it more difficult for mothers to return to the labour market. After such a long absence, their skills are obsolete, and there are no guarantees of a job on return.[24]

Although there are no hard statistics on this phenomenon, social workers and employment advisors report that some employers offer only short-term contracts to women of child-bearing age, thereby avoiding the obligation to grant them maternity and child care leave. There are also reports of women feeling pressured to forgo using the full period of maternity leave and leave for caring for a sick child because they fear losing their job.

The low level of wages combined with the wide availability of family benefits may have dissuaded some groups of women from entering or re-entering the labour market. The negligible difference between minimum wages and amount of the flat-rate child care allowance or child raising benefit (in 1998 – HUF 3,557/month; in 2000, HUF 3,275/month) provided little incentive for seeking a job. Moreover, low-income families are entitled to child protection benefits. These benefits offer a moderate income, so it could have been a reasonable decision, especially for poorly educated younger women in larger

---

[23] The child rearing benefit is an exception since it is for large families, and only three percent of employed women receive it.

[24] To illustrate this, assume that a family has three children. Depending on the timing of their births, the mother can claim at least five, but theoretically a maximum of nine, years of child care fee or child care allowance. After that, she can claim the child raising benefit between her youngest child's third and eighth year, providing five more years of benefits. If she then has another child, she can claim yet another child care allowance followed by another five years of the child raising benefit. Since the child rearing benefit has only existed since 1993, there are no actual statistics demonstrating such a pattern. We describe this as a theoretical possibility.

families, whose labour market position is weak, to accept benefits instead of taking a job. Table 20 compares earnings, the minimum wage, and family benefits for selected years.

	Child care allowance, child raising benefit	Child care fee	Family allowance (average /family)	Regular child protection benefit*	Average net earning	Minimum wage**
			Table 20			
	Selected child care benefits, earnings, and the minimum wage in selected years, Hungary (HUF)					
1990	3,350	5,198	3,539	—	10,108	—
1995	8,500	13,613	5,841	—	25,891	10,797
1998	13,700	28,027	8,375	2,777	45,162	17,257
2000	16,600	—	8,463	3,250	53,890	19,875

*   It was renamed supplementary family allowance in 2001.

**   Net amount.

Benefits and wages are per month.

Since 2001 there has been a considerable increase in the minimum wage (HUF 40,000 in 2001, and HUF 50,000 in 2002), which has made a significant difference between the minimum wage level and flat-rate child care benefits.

Another trend of concern is increasing numbers of women who give birth to a child before they establish themselves in the labour market. In 1990, the rate of those dependent and without a job when giving birth was 12.3 percent; in 1991, 14.4 percent; in 1995, 18.4 percent (including unemployed women giving birth, 26.9 percent) and in 2000 28.8 percent (combined with unemployed women, this rate increased to 34.8 percent).[25]   Many of these women have no entitlement to maternity benefits or the child care fee, and thus receive the flat-rate child care allowance.

---

[25]   *Demographic Yearbooks, 1990, 1991, 1995, 2000.* CSO, 1991,1992, 1996, 2001.

Given women's vastly greater responsibility for child care, the most feasible option for those who wish to stay attached to the labour market seems to be to postpone or give up plans to have children. Those groups of women who choose to begin a family before obtaining any work experience find it difficult to enter the labour market later on. As a result, young women more and more frequently postpone or even give up marriage and children in order to pursue a career. As changing conditions offer women a more distinct choice between a family and a career, there is a widening gap between these two roles.

Changes in Fertility Rates

As early as 1960, the birth rate in Hungary had slipped below the population maintenance level. The net reproduction rate has been falling ever since, except for a slight increase between 1999 and 2000. Over the past decade, the median age for childbirth rose into the 25–29 cohorts. It is interesting to note that from the early to mid-1990s, the rate of decrease was less than that in the surrounding post-communist countries, and the birth rate rose between 1990 and 1991 before resuming its fall. When the elimination of the child care fee was followed by a sharp drop in the birth rate, some attributed this to the negative effects of the reform, while others cited other factors such as high inflation, declining living conditions, and lack of economic prospects. However, surveys show that the majority of Hungarians consider establishing a family and having a baby to be of intrinsic value that cannot be reduced to economic factors.[26]

The decline in the fertility rate masks another dynamic at work: changing family composition. Between 1990 and 1996, the number and percentage of families with two children declined, while the number and percentage of families with three or more children rose. The most common type of family was one with a single child, and the number and proportion of families with one child grew from 1990 to 1996.[27]

---

[26] S. Molnár Edit: *A gyermekvállalás konfliktusai, Szerepváltozások, Jelentés a férfiak és nők helyzetéről 1999.* TÁRKI-SzCsM.

[27] In 1990 32.9 percent of families had one child, 26.3 percent had two children, and 6.5 percent had three or more children. In 1996 the figures were 33.7 percent, 26 percent and 7.2 percent. *Statistical Yearbook of Hungary, 2000.*

Table 21
Indicators of live births and fertility, Hungary 1953–1998

Year	Live birth rate	Total fertility rate	Net reproduction rate
1960	14.7	2.02	0.917
1970	14.7	1.96	0.912
1980	13.9	1.92	0.909
1990	12.1	1.84	0.889
1991	12.3	1.86	0.885
1992	11.8	1.77	0.839
1993	11.4	1.69	0.804
1994	11.3	1.64	0.784
1995	11.0	1.57	0.750
1996	10.3	1.46	0.693
1997	9.9	1.38	0.655
1998	9.6	1.33	0.638
1999	9.4	1.29	0.615
2000	9.7	1.33	0.635

Source: *Demographic Yearbook*, CSO 2001.

Women and Poverty

Certain groups of Hungarian women face disproportionate risks of poverty. Single women with children have a risk about 2.5 times greater than the national average. In 1998, nearly one-third of these single-parent families were in poverty.[28] The number and percentage of families headed by single mothers grew slightly during the decade, from 361,000 familes in 1990 to 379,000 families in 1996 (from 12.5 percent of all families to 13.1 percent).[29]

---

[28] Central Statistical Office, 1997: *Data on Single Parent Families*, Budapest, KSH, p.80.

[29] In the same time period, families headed by single fathers declined from 3.1 percent to 2.4 percent. *Statistical Yearbook of Hungary, 2000.*

Roma women are at particular risk of poverty. Because of the lack of job opportunities and the high number of children, the majority of Roma are poor. While half of Roma women had work in the 1980s, their employment rate dropped sharply to 16.3 percent by 1993. In the early 1990s, most of the young Roma women lost their jobs (the employment rate in the 15–24 age group was 8.2–13.9 percent).[30]

A disproportionate share of children can be found in the lowest decile of per capita income in Hungary: This share grew during the decade, indicating that child support benefits were not sufficient to make up for the loss of income of a working parent. The difference in poverty rates between children and the elderly indicates the relatively better position of pensions compared to family benefits.

Table 22
Percentage of certain age groups in Hungary
in the lowest decile of per capita income

Age group	1987	1992	1997
0–2	20.7	19.6	27.8
3–6	17.0	19.2	22.7
7–14	15.1	15.6	18.8
15–19	7.2	13.9	15.9
20–24	6.0	11.9	10.1
25–29	12.9	12.3	12.3
30–34	11.5	9.3	12.2
35–39	9.7	9.7	6.9
40–44	6.4	7.2	8.9
45–49	4.7	8.0	7.4
50–54	5.4	5.5	3.2
55–59	6.0	5.5	5.1
60–69	9.8	5.8	0.9
70–	11.7	4.1	1.4

Source: Household Income Surveys, CSO, (Spéder, 2001, p.50.)

---

[30] Béla, Janky: 'Situation of Gypsy women; Changes in Roles – Report on the Situation of Women and Men,' TÁRKI-SzCsM.

3. Pension Benefits[31]

The rather generous Hungarian pension system of the late 1980s required adjustment in the face of inflation, unemployment, and the economic crisis of the early 1990s. Under the former system, one needed to accumulate only ten years of insurance to qualify for pension benefits; and benefit amounts were based on wages in the final years before retirement (best three out of five). However, because of inflation and the lack of regular indexation of benefits, benefits for those who had been retired longest became devalued; and because of the short qualifying period and generous provisions for early retirement, there was a weak relationship between contributions and benefits, and a high dependency ratio. At 60 for men and 55 for women, retirement ages were comparable with those in many CEE countries.

Over the 1970s and 80s, the combination of rising wages and the natural maturation of the pension system (i.e., retirement by successive cohorts with benefits based on increasing numbers of years of contributions) raised aggregate pension expenditures. These increased from 3.5 percent of GDP in 1970 to 8.8 percent in 1990.[32] The economic transition brought additional stresses through a combination of reduced employment and increased early retirement (including an increase in disability pensioners). The ratio of pensioners to active contributors (i.e., the system dependency ratio) increased sharply, from 51.4 percent in 1989 to 83.9 percent in 1996.[33] Table 23 shows the proportion of early retired and new disabled pensioners in the past decade.

---

[31] The authors wish to acknowledge that the chapter on Pension Benefit is based on a study written by Gabriella A. Papp, Head of Pension Department and Krémerné Gerencsér Ildikó, Deputy Head of Pension Department from the Ministry of Social and Family Affairs.

[32] Augusztinovics, Maria *et al.*, 'The Hungarian Pension System Before and After the 1998 Reform,' in Fultz, Elaine, editor, *Pension Reform in Central and Eastern Europe, Volume 1: Restructuring with Privatization, Case Studies of Hungary and Poland* (Budapest: ILO CEET, 2002), p.29.

[33] Augusztinovics et al., 2002, p.30.

Table 23
New pensioners (without survivors' benefit),
Hungary 1990–1999

	Total*	Disabled pension*	Early retirement pension*	Disabled pension, % of total	Early retirement pension, % of total
1991	193.2	66.3	43.6	34.3	22.6
1992	181.4	64.4	46.1	35.5	25.4
1993	165.9	62.7	43.0	37.8	25.9
1994	152.3	62.4	41.0	41.0	26.9
1995	142.7	61.0	34.0	42.7	23.8
1996	149.8	62.0	44.0	41.4	29.4
1997	139.7	55.4	42.4	39.6	30.4
1998	99.5	49.3	16.6	49.5	16.7
1999	89.8	48.0	3.3	53.5	3.7

*   Number of persons, in thousands

Source: *Statistical Yearbook of National Pension Fund, 1999.* Budapest.

In order to make the pension system sustainable in the face of these problems, some adjustments were introduced in the early 1990s:

- From 1990, the minimum service period required for pension eligibility was raised from ten to 20 years.
- In 1992, the statutory indexation of pensions according to the rate of increase of net earnings was introduced. Since real wages were falling sharply, this meant that benefit adjustments were lower than inflation. Also introduced was a new formula for the calculation of the pension base that would increase gradually to include lifetime earnings. In addition, a ceiling was placed on employees' wages that are subject to contributions.

- Between 1992 and 1995, social benefits (such as child allowances and some social support schemes) were gradually separated from the pension insurance fund.
- In 1993 private supplemental saving schemes were introduced. [34]

The Horn government introduced a set of pension amendments as a part of its comprehensive reform of the public sector. Among other changes, these amendments raised and equalized the retirement ages for men and women, gradually phasing in an increase for both sexes to age 62, and tightened eligibility requirements for early retirement. In addition, the physicians who made disability assessments were instructed to use more rigorous standards.

While these measures restored the immediate viability of the pension scheme, there was wide agreement that it needed more comprehensive reform in order to improve fairness and create stronger incentives for earners to pay contributions. In addition, there was a need to strengthen financing in anticipation of the aging of the population, expected to affect the system from 2020 onward. Competing blueprints for reform emerged, one formulated by the Pension Insurance Fund's self-governing body and a second by the Finance Ministry, with support from the World Bank. After a long period of stalemate, the basic outline of the Finance Ministry proposal was adopted in 1997 and became the basis for the reform of 1998. It provided for partial privatization of the pension system, restructuring it as a so-called multi-tiered system. The new pension structure is as follows:

- a compulsory pay-as-you-go tier, which would ensure a moderate income replacement rate, together with a cap on the wages subject to contributions (twice the average wage);
- a second compulsory tier consisting of commercially-managed individual savings accounts. This tier would provide each worker with an annuity based on his or her own savings;

---

[34] Due to the considerable tax credits offered, these voluntary schemes – especially the pension schemes – became widespread quickly: in 1996 they had nearly a half million members (469,000 persons), and in 2000 more then one million members (1.044 million at mid-year). Although the legislation favoured mutual funds, the most successful schemes were run by banks and insurance companies. *Report on the Development of Second Quarter of 2000*, Hungarian Financial Supervisory Authority, 2001.

- a third voluntary tier consisting of individual savings, including the new supplementary schemes operating as mutual funds and/or run by private insurers or banks (this had of course already been authorized in 1993); and
- a means-tested basic old age annuity financed from general revenues for those unable to obtain adequate protection against poverty from their own earnings (zero tier).

For new entrants into the labour market, participation in the privatized second tier was obligatory, while the remainder of the work force was given a one-time choice of whether to join a private pension fund or not. During a limited period (September 1997–August 1999), the current work force could choose between remaining in the public system or joining the mixed system (tiers one and two), and until December 2000 they were allowed to switch back from the mixed system into the public scheme.[35]

The 1998 reform also revised public pension benefits, with one of the main changes being the gradual elimination of digression (redistribution) in the formula. However, most of the public scheme changes concerning the pension formula were delayed and will not become effective until 2009–13. To the contrary, the rules governing the annual pension increase were to begin to change immediately: the switch from indexation according to wage increases to the so-called Swiss index (half by wages, half by prices) was to be completed in a three year transitory period.

Changes of the Pension System with a Gender Impact

Benefit Formulae

With the enactment of the structural pension reform in 1998, there are three benefit formulae: the first is the current formula, while the second and third

---

[35] This date was subsequently extended and then eliminated, allowing all members of the mixed system to return to the public system. However, less than one percent have opted to do so.

ones enter into force after 2013 for beneficiaries of the reformed pay-as-you-go and mixed systems.[36]

- **Current formula (effective until 2013):** The pension formula has two main components: (1) countable individual earnings, and (2) a multiplier based on the number of contributory years.

  (1) *Countable individual earnings* – Countable earnings consist of those amounts earned since 1988 and, since the ceiling on wages subject to the employee *contribution* was enacted in 1992, only of earnings which fall below it.[37] To compute a benefit, these earnings are first indexed (partially) to reflect average wage increases in subsequent years of the worker's career, then totalled and finally divided by months of work to arrive at a monthly average. Next, the average earnings are subjected to a degressive (redistributive) scale. Under this scale, a higher fraction of low earnings are counted for pension purposes than of higher earnings.[38] Clearly the degressive scale favours those with lower incomes. Because of the gender wage gap, the scale is generally more favourable for women than for men.

  (2) *The multiplier* – A percentage figure representing the length of service is constructed based on a weighted scale. This multiplier represents the accrual rate for a pension: it determines what portion of average monthly countable earnings are returned to the worker in the form of a pension for each year of work. This scale also favours those workers with fewer years of service: the first ten years of the service period are assigned the value 33 percent; from

---

[36] A proposal has recently been put forward to convert the mandatory public pillar into a notionally-defined contribution system, but details have not yet been worked out.

[37] Previously the reference wage had been either the average wage over ten consecutive years from the past 20 years or the wages of the best 20 earnings years.

[38] For example, at the level of twice the average net wage, only 40 percent of earnings are counted for pension purposes. Above this, earnings of HUF 125,000–141,000/month are assessed at 20 percent; and earnings above HUF 141,000 are counted at only 10 percent. These amounts are for 2000.

ten to 25 contributory years, the multiplier falls to two percentage points per annum; and in the service period 25–36 years, it falls to one percentage point per annum. Above 36 years of service, the pension accrues by 1.5 percentage points per annum, as indicated in Table 24. Given women's greater tendency to have periods out of the work force for child rearing, this weighted multiplier is also of particular benefit to them.

Table 24
Calculation of Hungarian pension until 2013

Service time (year)	Percentage of average monthly net earnings
10	33
20	53
25	63
36	74
And an additional 1.5% for each additional year	

- **Pension formulae after 2013**: The new formulae are simpler than the current one and lack its digressive (redistributive) features. The pension benefit level in the new system will depend on the number of years of service and the average individual monthly earnings up to the ceiling on wages which are subject to the employee contribution.

  For those in the public pension scheme alone, the pension accrual rate will be 1.65 percent of average earnings for each year of service. For those in the mixed system, this rate will be 1.22 percent. The rate is lower for the latter group because a portion of their contributions is being diverted to a private pension fund in the second tier, where it is invested to provide a supplemental annuity.[39]

---

[39] Depending on investment yields, years of service, administrative charges, and other factors, this annuity may be higher or lower than the portion of the public pension benefit the individual must forego (1.65 versus 1.22 percent of earnings above) in order to join the mixed system.

Service period (years)	Pension as percentage of average monthly earnings, public scheme	Pension as percentage of average monthly earnings under public scheme for those in the mixed scheme
20	33	24.4
25	41.25	30.5
30	49.5	36.6
35	57.75	42.7
40	66	48.8

Table 25
Hungarian pension as a percentage of countable earnings after 2013

Comparing the formulae, it is clear that the new formulae favour longer service periods and higher incomes and are therefore more favourable to men on average.

Pension Age

Under the 1997 pension reform, men born in 1939 reached the new pension age of 62 in 2001, while women born in 1947 will be the first cohort to whom the new pension age of 62 will apply.

In addition to the introduction of a uniform retirement age, the new program makes the conditions of early retirement more stringent. Previously, one could become eligible for early retirement a maximum of five years before the standard pension age. Under the new legislation, this has been reduced to three years, and the length of required service for early retirement has increased as well.

Because Hungarian women's average life expectancy at the age of 60 is five years longer than that of men, they can expect to be retired and drawing a pension for a longer period. In this sense, they are advantaged by a uniform retirement age relative to men. However, earlier retirement under the previous law was also an advantage for women when combined with the current benefit formula which favours those with lower earnings and shorter work careers. With the 1998 pension reform, however, these features of the benefit formula will be eliminated. In their absence, a lower retirement age for women would have meant considerably lower benefits.

Survivors' Benefits

The 1997 reform brought significant changes in survivors' benefits which may affect women's position negatively in the long run. Prior to the reform, survivors had been subject to a rule that they could receive only one pension benefit, either a pension earned in their own right or a survivor's pension. In cases of dual eligibility, they would receive the highest. The reform changed this rule, allowing a maximum of *two* benefits for each person instead of one. Thus, a widow or widower could receive a benefit in that capacity in addition to a pension based on his or her own earnings.

At the same time, however, the level of the survivor's pension was decreased, from 50 to 20 percent of the deceased spouse's pension.[40] (Up to 2009, a transitional rule exists for those widows and widowers who do not have a pension in their own right. Such individuals will still get 50 percent of the pension as a survivor benefit.)

Because of the decreasing participation of women in the labour market in the past decade, it is predicted that many will have lower pensions or no pension at all of their own. In this respect, the eventual reduction in the survivor's pension could increase the dependency and vulnerability of women in their old age.[41]

Annuity Rates in the Mandatory Second Tier

As described earlier, the second tier in the multi-pillar system provides individual savings accounts. At retirement, an individual must use these savings to purchase an annuity. Thus, a question arises concerning how annuities will be calculated: will the average life expectancy of each age cohort be calculated for its male and female members combined, or will the calculation be made separately?

---

[40] Augusztinovics et al., 2002, p.39.

[41] This is also a problem for men, as the male participation rate decreased to an even larger extent than the female rate, and women's share in employment increased. On the other hand, the survivor's pension is indeed more important for women than for men.

The law requires the former; that is, that gender-neutral life expectancy tables be used in the mandatory, fully-funded individual savings schemes. This decision can be seen as positive in preventing discrimination against women.[42] However, no benefits are payable from the new private pension schemes; and private pension and insurance companies in Hungary generally do not use the gender-neutral calculation required by government. Thus, there are still important unanswered questions about how the annuities will eventually be calculated.[43]

Caring Credits (Child Raising, Care for Elderly)

The public pension scheme currently provides credits toward a pension for periods of taking care of children and the elderly. In the new fully-funded private tier, such credits are significantly restricted. This is, of course, a major disadvantage for women.

In the public scheme, a year of caring is given the same service credit as a year of employment. However, if child care benefit is the sole source of income, then at retirement the benefit is not countable as income, nor is the credited year counted as part of the earning period. Thus, in this case that year is ignored when average previous earnings are calculated; it affects only the *multiplier* which determines the ratio of pension to average previous earnings. On the other hand, those persons who are working while receiving caring benefits (recipients of the child care allowance and child raising benefit are allowed to take a four hours/day part time job as well as unlimited home paid work) can choose the most advantageous method of calculating the pension: the child care benefit may be added to actual earnings if this is more advantageous for the individual.

Periods for receiving the child care allowance are limited to a maximum of three years per child. In the case of overlapping child care periods, this term might be shorter; and for a child who suffers from severe illness/disability this period may be up to ten years. The periods of payment of child raising benefit for larger families are covered as well, and they may add five years or more to the service period.

---

[42] However, some also hold that this provision is discriminatory against men.

[43] No benefits will be payable until 2009.

Similarly, periods when one is receiving the insurance-related maternity benefit, child care fee, or the benefit for caring for a sick child are counted for their full value in calculating the basis for a pension. These benefits are earnings-related, and their amounts are proportional with earnings.

Periods when one is receiving the nursing fee, a payment for taking care of the elderly, are also credited as service for pension purposes; but the earnings are counted at the amount of the benefit, not that of former wages.[44] This is in conformity with the fact that the government budget pays pension insurance contribution according to the amount of the benefit.

The fully-funded system does not offer the same advantageous recognition of caring credits. For those who chose the mixed system, or new entrants who were mandated to join, these credits described above are available only at a rate of 75 percent of the public scheme. In the fully-funded scheme, an individual on child care leave is credited only for his or her actual contributions, which amount to six percent of the benefit he/she is receiving; and there is no employer or government contribution in the fully-funded second tier. Thus, someone receiving the child care allowance or child raising benefit would have contributed only HUF 996/month in 2000, or less than US$ 4.00. In the second tier, benefits are computed as a straight return on contributions, plus investment returns and minus administrative charges; so low contributions for caring periods will be directly reflected in lower pension benefits.

---

[44] There were some modifications in the 1990s in the rules regarding the payment of contributions to ensure correct coverage of caring credits. The employers' pension contributions levied upon the caring benefits are paid into the Pension Insurance Fund by different payers depending on the type of benefit. For social transfers, such as the child care allowance, payment is made from the central budget; for child raising benefits and nursing fee, by the local government; and for insurance-related benefits, by the employers' fund. An individual's eight percent contribution is deducted from the amount of the benefits. In the case of beneficiaries who have entered into the mixed system, two percent of this sum is transferred to the Pension Insurance Fund, while the remaining six percent is credited to the fully-funded individual savings account.

Impact of Other Periods Out of Full Legal Employment (e.g. Unemployment, Part Time, Atypical Work)

There are no particular gender impacts.[45]

Simultaneous Eligibility for Different Benefits

The latest changes of the widow/widowers' pension in 1998 provided for simultaneous entitlements in the public pension scheme, which are payable alongside a pension in one's own right without any limitation. This will produce mixed results for women, as described earlier, due to the reduction in the amount of the widow/widowers' benefit that was made simultaneous with this change.

Simultaneous benefits are expected to become common later on in the multi-tiered system, where the amounts of the voluntary or mandatory private schemes will be added to pensions from the public system. There are no special gender impacts.

---

[45] Here the whole period covered by unemployment benefits and unemployment aid prior to retirement is recognized as a service period for pension calculation purposes. The Labour Market Fund pays the employers' contribution to the Pension Insurance Fund, and the personal contribution is deducted from the benefit. In the public scheme, the same rules apply to unemployment as to caring benefits; that is, they are based on previous individual earnings. Conversely, in the private pension scheme, the same consequences arise as with the child care benefits: only the individual's contribution amounting to 6 percent of the unemployment benefit will be added to the fully-funded pension account. Therefore, recipients of these benefits who are in the mixed scheme suffer considerable losses in their eventual annuity.

With less than full time employment, a certain income is required (the income threshold is 30 percent of the minimum wage irrespective of the length of working time) before one is obliged to make insurance contributions. In 1997, the rules on the calculation of the service period were modified, and part-time employment was distinguished from other types of employment. If the earned income is less than the minimum wage, a proportional service period is calculated (e.g. work at half of the minimum wage for two years will be counted as one year of service period). In the case of casual workers and home work contracts, where working time cannot be determined, the service period is counted proportionally if the income is below the minimum wage.

Compliance, Differences in Payment Contributions

There is no differentiation in payment of contributions related to gender. In the pay-as-you-go system, the employer contributes an amount equal to 18 percent of the wage, and the employee pays 8 percent. If an employee is in the mixed system, s/he contributes 2 percent of this 8 percent to the first (public) pension tier and 6 percent to the second, fully-funded private tier. The employer makes no contribution to the second pillar.

Conclusions: Pension Options, Employment Choices, and Gender Relations

Changes in the pension system between 1990 and 1997 entailed negative as well as positive effects on women. Previously, the disadvantages that derived from women's shorter service periods and traditionally lower earnings were compensated for by some special pension rules, such as the degressive (re-distributive) scale for earnings assessment and the weighted accrual rate, which were not aimed specifically at women, but which nonetheless proved favourable for them. In addition, the pension system provided an earlier statutory retirement age for women.

These benefits were greatly reduced by the pension reform. The multi-tiered system that was introduced in 1997 and will become effective in 2013 has many features that place women at a disadvantage. Although not explicitly intended to harm women, the new system, when compared with the old one, is less advantageous for those with lower incomes and shorter service periods. Therefore, women in general are expected to fare worse than men as they suffer from a wage gap and have longer periods without paid labour. Although the consequences are negative for women in both the public and the mixed schemes, the disadvantages are greater in the latter, where the annuities will be directly related to the total sum of contributions. In the public system and the first pillar of the mixed system, those receiving child care allowance and unemployment benefits have their earnings credited at the level of their former wages, but their contributions to the fully-funded scheme are limited to six percent of their actual benefit (rather than their previous wage). Those who spend years out of the labour market caring for children and family members will have a significantly smaller accumulation in the second pillar than those who had uninterrupted employment.

One aspect of the mixed scheme that is beneficial to women is the decision to use gender-neutral life expectancy rates even in the private tier instead of sex-differentiated ones in calculating annuities.

The old pension system had some provisions that mitigated income inequalities, unfavourable labour market trends, and the unequal distribution of child care activities. Under the multi-tiered system, benefits will correspond more directly to contributions, there will be greater differentiation in benefits, and the gender wage gap and unequal sharing of child care activities will put many women in an unfavourable position. The reduction in the widow's benefit and the elimination of the guaranteed minimum pension also have negative consequences that have a greater impact on women than on men.

Annex 1

Table A1.1
Family benefit system 2000

	Entitlements	Duration	Value	Paid by	Changes since 1989
Maternity benefit	180 insured days in last two years before child birth	168 days (28+140) at least 28 days before childbirth	70% of last earnings	Social security	Until 1996 100% of former earnings; then reduced to 60–70%; since 1998 unified in 70% of former earnings
Benefit for caring for sick child	180 (270) insured days in last two years	Until the child reaches one year of age; children between 1–3 years of age for 84 calendar days per child; children between 3–6 years of age for 42 calendar days per child (84 for single parents); children between 6–12 years of age for 14 calendar days per child (28 for single parents).	60–70% of last earnings depending on insured period	Social security	Until 1996 the amount was 75% of last earnings

Table A1.1 (*continued*)
Family benefit system 2000

	Entitlements	Duration	Value	Paid by	Changes since 1989
Birth grant	Universal, but is offered to mothers who had 4 medical visits during pregnancy	One-time birth allowance	150% of the minimum pension amount (HUF 24,990, % of net minimum wages) 41.4% of average net earnings	General revenues	Until 1992 flat-rate maternity grant. In 1992 pregnancy benefit introduced, its amount equivalent to family allowance. From the 3rd month of pregnancy, in 1995 maternity subsidy introduced.
Child care fee	For those parents who care for a child at home under age 2; 180 insured days in last two years before child birth	After maternity benefit until the 2nd birthday of the child	Earnings related: 70% of former earnings	General revenues	Until 1996 paid by social insurance; in the case of 180 or 270 insured days the income replacement differed (65%, 75%).
Child care allowance	For those parents who care for a child at home under age 3 (under age 10 for a disabled child)	Until the 3rd birthday of the child	Flat rate monthly income the same as the minimum pension (HUF 16,600) 27.5% of average net earnings	General revenues	

Table A1.1 (*continued*)
Family benefit system 2000

	Entitlements	Duration	Value	Paid by	Changes since1989
Child raising benefit	Universal for parents, with 3 or more children	5 years, between years 3–8 of the youngest child	Flat rate monthly income, the same as the minimum pension (HUF 16,600) 27.5% of average net earnings	General revenues	• Introduced in 1993, income-tested (3 times minimum pension level), available only to mothers. • In 1996 income-tested by term of limit of FA. • In 1998 income-test abolished; available to either parent.

Table A1.1 (*continued*)
Family benefit system 2000

Entitlements	Duration	Value	Paid by	Changes since1989
Family allowance	Universal	Education support until the child reaches school age (6). Schooling benefit: during primary education (6-16 years of age) and during secondary and vocational education up to 20 years of age; no age limit in cases of serious infirmity	• Monthly HUF 3,800/4,500/5,900 in the case of 1/2/3 children in family per child; • For single parent monthly HUF 4,700/5,400/ 6,300 per child in respective groups; • For seriously ill/ disabled child HUF 7,500; • For foster child HUF 5,400; HUF 3,800/7,500 spread on 6.3–12.4% of net earnings per child.	General revenues	• Universal 1990–1995. • Since 1995 income-tested for families with one or two children. • Became universal again after 1999.

Table A1.1 (*continued*)
Family benefit system 2000

	Entitlements	Duration	Value	Paid by	Changes since1989
Supple-mentary family allowance	Income-tested and assets-tested if the per capita income in the family does not exceed the minimum old-age pension (HUF 16,600) and assets are less than 25 times or 75 times the minimum old age pension	Until the child is independent	Fixed sum per child, regularly 20% of the minimum pension; but in 2000 and 2001 the amount is HUF 4,000 and 4,200, as declared in state budget 6.6% of average net earnings per child	General revenue costs shared between state budget and local authorities	• Until 1997, regular educational assistance on a discretional basis. • In 1997 renamed for regular child protection benefit, and based on personal right. • Since 2000 renamed supplementary family allowance.

The table shows the present range of family support benefits. The figures reflect 2000 benefit levels. Average net earnings HUF 60,303/month (*Statistical Yearbook of Hungary 2000*).

Annex 2

Table A2.1

Composition of unemployment among working-age population*

Main categories of working-age population (in thousands)	1 January 1990	1 January 1994	1 January 1996	1 January 1997	1 January 1998	1 January 1999	1 January 2000
Employed*	4,599.2	3,708.7	3,632.6	3,643.6	3,672.8	3,754.0	3,833.0
Unemployed	1,357.6	2,362.9	2,448.1	2,501.2	2,464.1	2,362.9	2,374.5
Out of which:							
– Unemployed	24.2	632.1	495.9	477.5	464.0	404.1	404.5
– Receiving child care allowance/ child care fee	244.7	254.6	230.6	247.1	239.0	244.0	243.3
– Receiving child raising benefit	—	24.1	44.6	48.1	52.0	55.9	53.8
– Students	531.6	577.7	605.3	631.2	675.9	687.1	699.7
– Pensioners	263.8	370.5	404.4	409.0	512.1	535.4	568.6
– Other inactive	293.3	503.9	667.3	688.3	521.1	436.4	404.6
Unemployment rate (%)	22.8	38.9	40.3	40.7	40.1	38.6	38.3

Table A2.1 (continued)

Composition of unemployment among working-age population*

Main categories of working-age population (in thousands)	1 January 1990	1 January 1994	1 January 1996	1 January 1997	1 January 1998	1 January 1999	1 January 2000
			WOMEN				
Employed*	2, 074.1	1,678.5	1,582.5	1,589.6	1,600.9	1,656.2	1,690.9
Unemployed	775.5	1,233.8	1,333.6	1,387.7	1,369.8	1,300.9	1,318.4
Out of which:							
– Unemployed	10.0	256.0	210.6	202.1	202.6	181.3	184.4
– Receiving child care allowance/ child care fee	243.5	252.4	226.0	245.1	238.0	243.0	242.3
– Receiving child-raising benefit	—	24,1	44,6	48,1	52.0	55.9	53.8
– Students	255,1	287,8	301,1	317,4	338.6	346.2	350.0
– Pensioners	87,4	151,2	160,7	149,4	207.5	228.6	246.6
– Other inactive	179,5	262,3	390,6	425,6	331.1	245.9	241.3
Unemployment rate (%)	27.2	42.4	45.7	46.6	46.1	44.0	43.8

Table A2.1 (*continued*)
Composition of unemployment among working-age population*

Main categories of working-age population (in thousands)	1 January 1990	1 January 1994	1 January 1996	1 January 1997	1 January 1998	1 January 1999	1 January 2000
			MEN				
Employed*	2,525.1	2,030.2	2,050.1	2,054.0	2,071.9	2,097.8	2,142.1
Unemployed	582.1	1,129.1	1,114.5	1,113.5	1,094.3	1,062.0	1,056.1
Out of which:							
– Unemployed	14.2	376.1	285.3	275.4	261.4	222.8	220.1
– receiving child care allowance/ child care fee	1.2	2.2	4.6	2.0	1.0	1.0	1.0
– Students	276.5	289.9	304.2	313.8	337.3	340.9	349.7
– Pensioners	176.4	219.3	243.7	259.6	304.6	306.8	322.0
– Other inactive	113.8	241.6	276.7	262.7	190.0	190.5	163.3
Unemployment rate (%)	18.7	35.7	35.2	35.1	34.6	33.6	33.0

* The upper limit of working age for women was increased from 54 to 55 on 1 January 1997, and to 56 from the beginning of 1999. Out of the male population, until 1999, the age group of 15–59 was considered to be of working age. This was increased to 60 in the year 2000.

The employed do not include those on child care leave who, in accordance with the CSO classification based on international standards, are regarded as part of the economically inactive population.

Source: Calculations based on the data of labour force balances on 1 January 2000, CSO, Budapest, 2000.

Table A2.2
Real terms and % of GDP of the main family benefit provisions 1990–1999

Year	Total expenditure* in billion HUF		
	Actual price	At price of 1990	As % of GDP
1990	78.5	78.5	3.8
1991	100.8	74.6	4.1
1992	114.9	69.2	3.9
1993	131.0	64.4	3.7
1994	142.0	58.8	3.3
1995	139.9	45.2	2.5
1996	139.9	36.6	2.0
1997	156.0	34.4	1.8
1998	201.1	38.8	2.0
1999	220.5	38.7	1.9
2000 budget	249.6	39.6	2.0

* Family allowances, child care fee, child care allowance, child support grant, birth grant, regular and irregular child protection benefit are included.

Source: *Statistical Yearbook 1999*, National Health Insurance Fund Administration.

Table A2.3
Amount of family allowance as prescribed by law (in HUF)

Date of change of the rule, income category	For one child		For two children, per child		For three or more children, per child		For sick children and physically or mentally disabled children
	Married couples	Single parents	Married couples	Single parents	Married couples	Single parents	
January 1990	1,770	2,070	2,070	2,200	2,200	2,200	1,770
August 1990	1,870	2,170	2,170	2,300	2,300	2,300	1,870
December 1990	1,970	2,270	2,270	2,400	2,400	2,400	1,970
January 1991	2,170	2,570	2,570	2,900	2,900	3,000	2,170
January 1992	2,370	2,820	2,820	3,250	3,250	3,400	2,370
September 1992	2,800	3,100	3,100	3,800	3,800	3,800	2,800
February 1993	2,150	3,250	3,250	3,750	3,750	3,950	2,150
April 1996							
HUF –18,000	2,150	3,250	3,250	3,750	3,750	3,950	5,100
HUF 18,301–18,750	2,000	2,300	2,300	2,700	3,750	3,950	5,100
HUF 18,751–19,500	1,100	1,300	1,300	1,500	3,750	3,950	5,100
May 1997							
HUF –21,200	3,400	4,000	4,200	4,800	5,200	5,600	6,600
HUF 21,201–23,000	1,700	2,000	2,100	2,400	5,200	5,600	6,600
May 1998							
HUF –24,000	3,800	4,500	4,700	5,400	5,900	5,300	7,500
HUF 24,001–26,000	1,900	2,250	2,350	2,700	5,900	6,300	7,500
January 1999	3,800	4,500	4,700	5,400	5,900	6,300	7,500

Source: Yearbook of Welfare Statistics 1999, CSO 2000.

Table A2.4
Number of male beneficiaries of child care fee/allowance 1990–2000

Year	Number of male beneficiaries (thousands)	% of the total
1990	1.2	0.5
1991	1.3	0.5
1992	1.8	0.7
1993	1.7	0.7
1994	2.2	0.9
1995	5.2	2.1
1996	4.6	2.0
1997	2.0	0.8
1998	1.0	0.4
1999	1.0	0.4
2000	1.0	0.4

Source: CSO Labour Force Survey.

Table A2.5
Female employment rates(%),
according to age and number of children, 1996

Female	26–29	36–39	46–49
Without children	82	82	71
With one child	52	80	71
With 2 children	35	78	62
Three or more children	11	41	40

Source: MONEE Project, p.2.

Table A2.6

Proportion of poor persons in the adult (16+) population and among employees by gender, 1992–1998

	1992	1994	1996	1998
Adults				
• Male	9.2	10.7	11.4	9.1
• Female	11.4	10.4	10.9	10.0
Employees				
• Male	4.0	5.6	5.6	3.5
• Female	2.5	3.2	3.2	4.5

Source: Hegedűs Rita, Spéder Zsolt: 'Relative poverty and earning disadvantages.' In: Pongrácz Tiborné, Tóth István György (edit.): *Changes of Roles (Szerepváltozások)* TÁRKI-SZCSM, Budapest, 1999. pp.116–124., p.118.

Table A2.7

Poverty rates by gender and female/male earnings ratio, 1992–1998

	1992	1994	1996	1998
% of employed persons earning less than 50% of average earnings				
• Male	5.0	8.3	7.5	10.6
• Female	16.0	18.2	17.6	13.4
Rate of average of earnings				
• Female/Male	73.7	77.7	84.0	79.2
Average monthly earnings*	16,836	24,931	31,024	40,775

*   In March of responded years.

Source: Hegedűs, Rita, Spéder, Zsolt: 'Relative poverty and earning disadvantages.' In: Pongrácz Tiborné, Tóth, István, György (edit.): *Changes of Role (Szerepváltozások)* TÁRKI-SZCSM, Budapest, 1999. pp.116–124., p.118.

Table A2.8 Number of beneficiaries of pensions and pension-type provisions and average provisions, 1990–1999				
Year	Expenditures on pensions and other pension-type provisions (billions)	Average number of beneficiaries of pensions and other pension-type provisions (thousands)	Average sum of provision per person (HUF/ month)	Average net earnings of full employees (HUF/ month)	Average sum per person as % of average net earnings (replacement rate, %)
1990	202,118	2,520.2	6,683	10,108	66.1
1995	582,205	3,026.6	16,030	25,891	61.9
1999	1,117,236	3,141.0	29,639	50,076	59.2

Source: National Statistical Yearbooks, Central Administration of National Pension Insurance.

Table A2.9
Number of pensioners by own right and average amount of pension

Title	Number of beneficiaries (thousand)	Average amount of pension (HUF/month)	Pension as % of employee net earnings
Male			
1990	987	6,708	66.3
1995	1,033	16,566	64.0
2000 (January, before increase)	1,063	33,828	67.5*
Female			
1990	1,104	5,598	55.4
1995	1,285	13,059	50.4
2000 (January, before increase)	1,412	26,855	53.6*

* Percentage of employee net earnings in 1999.

Source: National Statistical Yearbooks, Central Administration of National Pension Insurance.

Table A2.10
Number of new entrants into old-age pension system
and amount of pension by year

Title	Number of new entrants	Average period of considered work history (year)	Average amount of pension (HUF/month)	Pension as % of employee net earnings
Male				
1994*	15,697	35.6	15,023	65.3
1995	13,223	37.5	18,445	71.2
1999	14,267	39.5	38,952	77.8
Female				
1994*	25,768	31.2	11,613	50.5
1995	23,379	31.7	13,955	53.9
1999	23,030	34.5	30,653	61.2

* There are no data by gender available for earlier years.

Source: National Statistical Yearbooks, Central Administration of National Pension Insurance.

Table A2.11
The number of survivors' pensions, average benefits

Title	1999		2000	
	Number of beneficiaries (thousands)	Average pension amount, and as % of employee net earnings	Number of beneficiaries (thousands)	Average pension amount and as % of employee net earnings
Male				
• Widow's/parent's pensions (main benefit)	—	—	6	16,385 (29.4%)
• Widow's/parent's pensions (supplementary provision)	—	—	69	6,440 (11.5%)
Female				
• Widow's/parent's pensions (main benefit)	241	4,906 (48.5%)	210	22,974 (41.1%)
• Widow's/parent's pensions (supplementary provision)	232	...	497	7,851 (14.1%)

Source: National Statistical Yearbooks, Central Administration of National Pension Insurance.

Table A2.12
Changes in real value of pensions

Calendar year	Index of real earnings 1990=100	Consumer price index	Individual pension index	Changes in real value of individual pension (%)	Changes in real value of net earnings (%)	Changes in real value of individual pension position related to net earnings (%)
1991	125.5	135.0	125.6	–7.0	–7.0	0.1
1992	121.3	123.0	120.0	–2.4	–1.4	–1.1
1993	117.7	122.5	118.0	–3.7	–3.9	0.3
1994	127.3	118.8	124.8	5.1	7.2	–2.0
1991–1994	228.1	241.7	222.0	–8.2	–5.6	–2.7
1995	112.6	128.2	115.4	–10.0	–12.2	2.5
1996	117.4	123.6	112.6	–8.9	–5.0	–4.1
1997	124.1	118.3	119.5	1.0	4.9	–3.7
1998	118.4	114.3	121.6	6.4	3.6	2.7
1995–1998	194.2	214.3	188.8	–11.9	–9.4	–2.8
1999	112.7	110.0	114.2*	3.8	2.5	1.3
2000	111.4	109.8	110.8	0.9	1.5	–0.5
1990–2000	556.1	625.6	530.3	–15.2	–11.1	–4.6

Source: Central Administration of National Pension Insurance.

Annex 3

Table A3.1
Costs of child care in comparison with family benefits, 1990–98 (in HUF)

Year	1990			1995			1998		
Income groups*	Min. wage	Average net earnings	Average net earnings of white collar workers	Min. net wage	Average net earnings	Average net earnings of white collar workers	Min. net wage	Average net earnings	Average net earnings of white collar workers
1. Monthly net earnings	4,518	10,108	12,707	10,797	25,891	32,603	17,257	45,162	58,536
2. Family and child care benefits									
Child care allowance, child raising benefit		3,303			8,236			13,725	
Family allowance for 1 child		1,970			2,750			3,800	
Family allowance for 2 children		4,540			6,500			9,400	
2.1. Benefits total									
For 1 child		5,273			10,986			17,525	
For 2 children		7,843			14,736			23,125	
3. Child care costs**									
Kindergarten fee for 1 child		616			1,823			3,326	
Kindergarten fee for 2 children***		1,232			3,646			6,652	

Table A3.1 (*continued*)
Costs of child care in comparison with family benefits, 1990–98 (in HUF)

Year	1990			1995			1998		
Income groups*	Min. wage	Average net earnings	Average net earnings of white collar workers	Min. net wage	Average net earnings	Average net earnings of white collar workers	Min. net wage	Average net earnings	Average net earnings of white collar workers
4. Amount by which benefits exceed child care costs									
For 1 child (See 2. and 3.)		4,657			9,163			14,199	
For 2 children (See 2. and 3.)		6,611			11,090			16,473	

* Monthly net earnings of full-time employed, CSO.

** Figures represent kindergarten costs in Budapest, but the costs of infant nurseries are comparable. Sarolta Jeney from the Budapest municipality provided the data.

*** Families with three or more children receive a 50% reduction in fees at kindergartens and nurseries.

Magdalena Kotýnková, Věra Kuchařová, and Ladislav Průša

1. Labour Market Transformation and Women's Employment and Life Choices

The social security afforded women in the Czech Republic is heavily influenced by the conditions they face on the labour market, including the availability of jobs, wage levels, and the extent to which employers accommodate workers' family-related needs and responsibilities. These contextual factors cause the social security system, though largely gender neutral in its legal provisions, to have differential impacts on women and men. Given this interrelationship, the necessary starting point for analysing social security is Czech women's labour market participation.

Czech women have a long tradition of engagement outside the home, and this pattern has been only slightly affected by the transformation. In the former Czechoslovakia, the share of women in the economically active population was 36.5 percent in the wake of World War II (1948). Over the next two decades it rose by a quarter to around 44 percent, a ratio maintained with only small variations until the transformation began in 1989. In 2000, women's 44.3 percent share of the active labour force was not markedly different from a decade earlier.

These figures do not tell the full story, however, since the economically active population includes both workers and those who are officially un-employed. During the early 1990s, unemployment rose among both men and women; but it increased more rapidly and rose to higher levels among women.

Between 1990 and 1993, it climbed from 0.8 percent to 5.4 percent for women, whereas for men the increase was from 0.7 percent to 3.4 percent. Over the remainder of the decade, there was an approximate doubling of both rates: female unemployment increased from 5.4 percent in 1993 to 10.4 percent in 2000, while male unemployment increased from 3.4 percent to 7.9 percent in this same period (see Annex 1, Table A1.5). While not reflected in official unemployment figures, the tight job market also led some women to make different choices at the beginning or end of their careers. This is shown in:

- decreased employment of younger women who are remaining longer in formal education or are on maternity/parental leave; and[1]
- a decrease in the number of employed female pensioners and in the number of employed women of post-productive age.[2]

In addition, working women face difficulties on the labour market which result from legacies of the communist period and subsequent the restructuring of the Czech economy. Under the communist regime, women had a high employment rate but low representation in the ranks of management and in better-paid jobs. There was also a marked feminization of some employment sectors or occupations, including education, social services, and the textile industry. At the same time, however, the state assisted women in harmonizing family and work, with the provision of housing, nurseries, and other services

---

[1] While the number of full-time university students grew in 1991–2000 by 66 percent, the number of women students increased by 73 percent. Similar data for non-university higher education (introduced in 1996) show increases of 110 percent (total) and 119 percent (women) (*Statistical Yearbook of the Czech Republic*, CSO 2000). In 1995 the period of eligibility for parental benefits was extended to the fourth birthday of the child. Previously it covered the period until the child reached the age of three (for further details see section 2).

[2] The percentage of employed pensioners among all women pensioners was 4.4 percent in 1993, 5.3 percent in 1996 and 4.5 percent in 1999. The real number of employed women aged 60+ (both pensioners and those with deferred retirement) decreased during period 1993–1999 by 13 percent; the share of employed women among all women aged 60+ fell in the same period from 5.7 percent to 4.9 percent (data from the standard Labour Force Survey of the Czech Statistical Office). These figures reflect the lack of employment opportunities for older women.

(Cermakova, 1997, p.391). Economic transformation has changed these conditions unevenly and brought different results for women depending on their professions and educational status. Today women's ability to find work is more dependent on age, family situation, education, and place of residence.[3] Reflecting this, the position of some women is significantly worsened by a combination of limited or obsolete skills, motherhood, old age, or regional economic difficulties. In regions with high unemployment rates, some employers offer women lower pay than men and/or inferior working conditions (Kucharova, Zamykalova, 2000). On the positive side, the restructuring has resulted in increased employment in services – here women's share of employment rose from 61 percent to 68 percent.[4] However, as the higher unemployment rate shows, this gain has not offset the loss of employment in other sectors.[5]

In addition, longstanding wage disparities between men and women continue to exist. Women today receive, on average, just 73 percent of men's earnings, but this indicator conceals a high degree of variation. Wage disparity decreased at the beginning of the 1990s, but then the trend reversed itself, in part because women were unable to access a proportionate share of the new management positions. One factor which plays a major role in creating wage disparity is change in enterprise ownership: in state-run firms women earn over 80 percent of what men earn, whereas in foreign firms they earn less than 60 percent (*Human Development Report*, 1999, pp.71–73). See Annex 1, Table A1.7.

---

[3] The level of economic activity of women increases along with the level of education. In the first quarter of 2001 it was 22.5 percent for those with basic education, 59.3 percent for women with vocational education, 70.1 percent for women with completed secondary professional education, and 77.8 percent for women with university education. An inverse relationship between unemployment and education can be seen, with 20.9 percent of women with basic education unemployed, 11.9 percent of those with vocational education, 7.2 percent of those with completed secondary professional education, and 2.9 percent of women with university education.

[4] At the same time the share of women working in agriculture decreased from 6.6 percent to 3.4 percent.

[5] See Cermakova 1997, p.392.

Today government employment policy recognizes women as among the more vulnerable groups of workers (*National Employment Plan, 1999*, and *National Plan of Action in Employment Policy, 2000*, produced by the Ministry of Labour and Social Affairs). Measures recently introduced to address this situation include better monitoring of employers' practices concerning equal treatment, support for retraining for return to work after maternity leave or parental leave, and assistance for school leavers and graduates.[6] To improve the situation over the longer term, the National Employment Plan attempts to reduce the differences in boys' and girls' preferences in education.[7]

The level of women's education, which had been relatively high (with emphasis at the upper secondary level) during the communist era, improved during the 1990s. This supports an apparent shift of the female labour force towards professions requiring higher qualifications. See Annex 1, Table A1.6.[8]

---

[6] See also *Operational Programme for Human Resources Development in the Czech Republic*, www.mpsv.cz.

[7] Differences between girls' and boys' education can be distinguished by types of schools and fields: Fifty-nine percent of those studying at grammar schools are girls, as are 58 percent of those involved in secondary school technical studies (chiefly in the fields of medicine, in which 97 percent are women, teaching with 94 percent and economic administration with approximately 80 percent). In apprenticeship facilities just 39 percent of students are women. In higher professional schools 69 percent of all students are women. Women enrolled at universities are concentrated in literature and languages (where 81 percent of the students are women), in teaching (74 percent), medicine (66 percent), and in the social sciences (in total, 61 percent of social sciences students are women). Only 24 percent of the students in technical fields are women, and just 7 percent of those studying machine engineering and electrical mechanics are women. The proportion of women among university graduates rose from 52 percent to 62 percent in the years 1996–1999. Women more frequently finish their studies with a bachelor's degree, men with a master's (data from the Institute of Information in Education, Prague).

[8] According to the 9-point ISCO-88 employment classification, for example, in 1993–2000 the share of women in the three highest categories increased by 4.1 percentage points, and the share of men by 6.8 points. While the share of women remains higher here (40 percent compared to 35 percent for men), 8 percent of employed men are employed in the highest category , while only 3.6 percent of employed women are in this group, and growth rate for men in this category is faster (by 2.2 percentage points for men compared to 1.1 for women).

However, women remain seriously underrepresented in management positions. Fifty-eight percent of women graduates do not hold a managerial position, compared to just 39 percent of men.

While entrepreneurship has opened up as an employment avenue for both women and men, it continues to attract fewer women. The share of self-employed women among all employed women recently reached – and seems to have stabilised at – 7.4 percent for those self-employed without employees and 2.1 percent for entrepreneurs with employees. Comparable figures for men are 13.2 percent and 5.4 percent.

The choices and trade-offs facing Czech women changed during the 1990s. While family budgets are often dependent on two incomes, women also report social and cultural reasons for maintaining their high rate of activity. For younger and more highly qualified women, these are increasingly important.[9] As will be shown, government is playing a decreasing role in reconciling work and family with various support services. Yet despite the combination of diminished support and more demanding working conditions under the free market system, women have maintained their level of economic activity. They have reacted to the changing social and economic conditions by delaying or forgoing motherhood and by devoting larger amounts of time to work at the expense of the family. The life choices of individuals vary, and the differentiation of women's values and behavioural patterns is increasing. On the one hand, those with higher education face increasing professional demands; on the other hand, women with poor qualifications are confronted with narrowing options on the job market. All women are confronted with the lack of effective support, especially from employers, for combining work and family (Souvislosti, 2000; *Women in Transition*, 1999).

---

[9]   This has been confirmed repeatedly in sociological research during the 1990s, for examples see: Kucharova, Zamykalova 1998; Kucharova, Nedomova, Zamykalova 1999; Cermakova 1997.

2. Family Benefits

Reasons for Reform

The social security system in place up to 1989 was conceived in the second half of the 1950s under the communist socio-economic system. This system was not able to handle the problems brought about by the shift from a planned national economy to a market economy. This was in part because there was duplication and inefficiency in the former system, which provided more than 60 benefits.[10] The larger reason, however, was that the system was not conceived of with large-scale unemployment as a possibility.

During the early 1990s, the central concern of the Czechoslovak government was economic transformation. The government introduced changes to the social security system principally to moderate the impact of new economic policies which created hardship for the population, thus making the transformation more politically acceptable. These changes represented an adaptation of the preexisting social security system rather than a fundamentally new policy direction. As the 1990s progressed, more substantive social reforms were initiated under the new Czech government. However, gender inequalities were still not at the forefront of policy makers' attention. These issues only began to be addressed later in the decade, particularly as part of the preparation for entry into the EU.[11]

There were two main reasons why gender issues were not the main focus of the social security reforms of the 1990s. Firstly, a system for protecting mothers had already been developed and was in place. Secondly, women's rights had been part of official government policy under the previous regime, and there clung to the concept of gender equality some of the hypocrisy of the

---

[10] There was also gender discrimination, in that fathers were not eligible for certain parental benefits.

[11] For instance, a Department of Equal Opportunities (at the Ministry of Labour and Social Affairs) was not established until 1998.

past when women had been 'honoured' in the official ideology. In practice, however, gender inequalities had existed under the communist regime, and some of them were intensified or became more apparent during the period of transformation as a result of changes in the labour market and a weakening of the role of the state in helping families with children.

Overview of Reforms

The government drew up a scenario for economic and social reform in 1991 and, at the same time, experts from the Ministry for Labour and Social Affairs started planning a new system of social security. The first task was to create a social safety net to protect the population from the negative consequences of economic transformation. This safety net included new measures to protect families with children, especially those with low incomes. In 1991 a household subsistence minimum was established as the minimum income benchmark in society.[12] It serves as the criterion for claims to income-tested benefits as well as the base for calculating these benefits. See Annex 2. At the same time, in response to rising prices, the government formulated rules for cost of living increases in benefits.

The Ministry reorganized social security into three parts: social insurance, social assistance, and state social support. Maternity benefits were (and are) provided as social insurance, while social protection of families with children was transferred to the state social support subsystem.[13] These benefits include support for birth of a child, as well as for parents caring for children. All state social support benefits were (and are) financed from general revenues as part of the state budget. They are paid out through district authorities, the lowest level of state administration.

In 1995, the Czech Parliament introduced the state social support scheme with a new act (Act no. 117/1995 Coll.) which sets out nine benefits, some

---

[12] Act no. 463/1991 Coll.

[13] Some state social support benefits were provided before as either social insurance or social assistance.

of which were income-tested.[14] The broad objective of the act was to simplify preexisting forms of social support and to target these benefits to the neediest families. This reform was launched in two stages. In the first (starting on 1 October 1995), those provisions dealing with non-income-tested benefits came into force. [15] In the second stage (starting on 1 January 1996), those provisions concerning benefits that are dependent on the income of all persons of the household were implemented.[16]

Gender-related Changes

Maternity benefits – Only minor changes have been made in maternity benefits. The most significant was a revision in the benefit formula. Up to 1 January 1993, the formula provided benefits equalling 90 percent of a worker's *net* income[17]. After that date, it was decreased to 69 percent of a worker's *gross* income.[18] The change had one basic objective, which was the adaptation of the sickness insurance system (of which maternity benefits are a part) to market conditions, especially growing numbers of the self-employed and new tax system.

---

[14] The test for claims to benefits takes into account a family's income. The state social support system sees the family as the cohabitation of parents and dependent children in a shared household. A dependent child means a child who has not yet reached the end of compulsory education as well as a child up to a maximum age of 26 in case of full-time higher education or disability. Only a citizen with permanent residence in the Czech Republic or a legal resident, and the co-assessed members of his/her household, can claim state social support benefits.

[15] Parental allowance, maintenance allowance, birth grant, funeral grant.

[16] Child allowance, social allowance, housing allowance and transport allowance.

[17] The base for calculation was a worker's average net income of the previous three months.

[18] The base for calculation is a worker's average gross income of the previous three months; the average proportion of income tax is approximately 20 percent of gross income and the average proportion of net income equals approximately 80 percent of gross income.

Eligibility requirements have not altered since 1956: 270 days of participation in sickness insurance in the last two years before delivery.[19] Nor was the duration of maternity benefits altered in the 1990s: they continue to be available for 28 weeks, or 37 weeks in the case of a multiple birth or a single mother, as they have been since 1987.

It is important to note that all employed women giving birth are entitled to maternity *leave* whether or not they fulfil the requirements for a cash benefit. The basic entitlement is the same as for maternity benefits: 28 weeks of leave, or 37 weeks in the case of single mothers, as well as of multiple births. Maternity leave usually starts six weeks before the expected birth of the child. While the law does not oblige a woman to take maternity leave, if she takes time off from work for the birth of a child, the leave must last at least 14 weeks, six of which must follow the child's birth.

Family allowances and child care benefits – Here changes were made in two phases, first in the early 1990s and a second group of reforms in mid-decade. The early changes were:
- In 1990, the *state compensatory allowance* was created in response to the liberalization of consumer goods prices, chiefly foodstuffs. Between 1990 and 1995, it was paid out to all children.
- Also in 1990, the *parental allowance* replaced the maternity allowance. The latter was provided exclusively to mothers caring for children up to three years of age; since then, it has been available to either parent.[20]

---

[19] A maternity benefit is provided to the father only exceptionally in those cases when he acts as a substitute for the mother in the period during which the woman is entitled to maternity benefits, but she is unable to take care for a child for some valid reason, such as death or disability due to serious disease. However, since 1990, fathers have been entitled to parental benefit following the birth of a child.

[20] Act no. 382/1990 Coll., on parental allowance. But a more fundamental legislative change with potential to change the gender division of roles was the introduction of parental leave in 2000 (the amendment took effect 1 January 2001). Between 1990 and 2000 a man could take care of a child up to three years of age, but the Labour Code did not specifically guarantee his right to return to his job as it did for a woman, although fathers had a right to parental allowance identical to that for mothers.

- Late in 1993, the *child allowance* was targeted toward children as beneficiaries instead of parents.[21] Before the change, this allowance had been dependent on parents' participation in sickness or pension insurance. Its amount depended only on the size of the family. Afterward, the benefit was made available to children in all families, but both the number of children and their ages determined its amount in a particular family.

The second set of changes aimed to concentrate benefits narrowly on those most in need and, at the same time, to improve the adequacy of protection for this group. The former was achieved primarily through income testing. With one exception, the changes made in this second round became effective on 1 January 1996 (the parental allowance became effective on 1 October 1995).

- The *state compensatory allowance* was replaced by *the social allowance.* This is an income-tested benefit whose aim is to compensate for a temporary fall in the income of families with children. Its amount depends on the size of the family's income in the preceding calendar quarter. The subsistence minimum is used as the criterion for awarding the benefit as well as for calculating its amount (see Annex 2).
- The *child allowance* was income-tested. Today this is the basic benefit for families with children, which helps cover the costs associated with feeding and raising a child. It is awarded depending on the family's net income in the preceding calendar year. The size of the benefit continues to depend on a child's age, as before the change. The subsistence minimum is used as the criterion for awarding the benefit as well as for calculating its amount (see Annex 2).
- The *parental allowance* continues to be non-income-tested, but it is paid out under very strict conditions requiring full-time care for a child under the age of four. It imposes restrictions on the carer's earnings, and allows the carer to put the child in child care for no more than three (later raised to five) days a month. The base for calculating the size of the benefit is also the subsistence minimum.

---

[21] Since children were the beneficiaries, the amounts were stated for different childrens' ages instead of the number of children in a family.

Impact of the Changes: Public Spending

Maternity Benefits

(a) **Changes in beneficiary caseloads:** The numbers of maternity bene-ficiaries are not recorded in any central register, in part because benefits are distributed through employers as well as through the District Social Insurance Administration offices. However, a rough approximation may be obtained by examining maternity leave statistics (see Table 1). Entitlements for maternity leave and maternity allowances are not identical but also probably not markedly different. The numbers in both groups dropped in the 1990s following the decrease in fertility, but there is a discrepancy between the decrease in live births and num-bers of women on maternity leave – by 30 percent in the former and by 54 percent in the latter. One reason is that only employees may take maternity leave (subject to the Labour Code) while all mothers of newborn children are entitled to maternity benefits if they participate in sickness insurance and meet the defined conditions (subject to Social Insurance Act).

(b) **Changes in program expenditure:** During 1990–2000, program expen-ditures increased by 104 percent. Since entitlement conditions did not change significantly (see the previous section), most mothers continued to collect the allowance, and fertility rates dropped, this increase appears to be due largely to increases in nominal wages during the period.

(c) **Changes in average expenditure per beneficiary:** The lack of statistical data on mothers as beneficiaries does not allow for an assessment of these changes. For an approximate picture of trends see Table 1.

Table 1
Data illustrating the changes in expenditures and beneficiary caseloads, Czech Republic

	1990	1991	1992	1993	1994	1995	1996	1997	1998	1999	2000
Expenditures per year*	1,349	1,397	1,441	1,623	1,732	1,722	1,811	1,963	2,028	2,151	2,759
Live births	130,564	129,354	121,705	121,025	106,579	96,097	90,446	90,657	90,535	89,471	90,910
Women on maternity leave**	70,000	59,000	53,290	47,573	41,848	40,245	37,766	38,202	36,282	33,863	31,875
Average women's gross wages (base for maternity benefits calculation)											
Women aged 25–29							9,090	10,234	10,807	11,738	12,716
Total							9,449	10,730	11,036	11,793	12,640

* Millions CZK.

** 31 December in the given year.

Sources: Ministry of Labour and Social Affairs; *Populacni vyvoj Ceske republiky (Development of the Czech Population)*, issued 1996–2001, Prague, Charles University; *Zeny a muzi v cislech (Women and Men in Figures)*, 2000, Prague, Czech Statistical Office; Statistical Yearbooks of the Czech Republic, Czech Statistical Office; *Fakta o socialni situaci v Ceske republice (Facts on the Social Conditions in the Czech Republic)*, 1997, Czech Statistical Office.

Family Allowances and Child Care Benefits

(a) **Changes in beneficiary caseloads** – In principle, income testing was intended to target benefits on lower-income families and improve the protection available to them. In practice, the targeting effect has been relatively modest. As can be seen in Table 2, a high percentage of Czech families with children continued to collect the *child allowance* after the reform. Families (one- or two-parent) with an economically inactive parent are more likely to receive this benefit.

Table 2
Proportion of total families in the Czech Republic
with children which collected the child allowance in 1996 and 1999,
by type of family and economic activity of parents*

Year	Two-parent family		Single-parent family	
	Both EA	One EA	Parent EA	Parent EI
1996	84.15%	94.31%	89.61%	96.03%
1999	75.66%	93.18%	89.29%	NA**

EA = Economically active.
EI = Economically inactive.
* See note on sources for data in tables, Annex 4.
** Not available.

While the child allowance is paid out to the great majority of Czech families, only about a quarter collect the *social allowance*, whose chief aim, as described above, is to help families cope with a drop in income. As can be seen in Table 3, this benefit is particularly prevalent among single parents who are economically inactive; but the portion of two-parent families covered has increased since the reform. This is probably a reflection of increased unemployment in the late 1990s.

After the introduction of income testing, the overall number of families collecting social benefits fell. Whereas the child allowance and state compensatory allowance had previously been universal, after the 1996 reform 12.7 percent of families received neither benefit, 63.8 percent of families received only the child allowance, and only 23.5

percent of families received the child allowance plus the social allowance. The distribution of benefits among different types of families is shown in Table 4.

Table 3
Proportion of total families in the Czech Republic with children which collected social allowance in 1996 and 1999, by type of family and economic activity of parents* (%)

Year	Two-parent Family		Single-parent Family	
	Both EA	One EA	Parent EA	Parent EI
1996	16.76	34.47	37.94	77.84
1999	21.68	46.59	37.50	NA**

EA = Economically active.
EI = Economically inactive.
*   See note on sources for data in tables, Annex 4.
** Not available.

Table 4
Proportion of families in the Czech Republic collecting social benefits (child allowance and social allowance) in 1996 by type of family and economic activity of parents* (%)

	Two-parent family		Single-parent family	
	Both EA	One EA	Parent EA	Parent EI
Proportion of families collecting neither child allowance nor social allowance	15.85	5.69	10.39	3.97
Proportion of families collecting only child allowance	67.39	59.84	51.67	18.19
Proportion of families collecting child allowance and social allowance	16.76	34.47	37.94	77.84
Total	100.00	100.00	100.00	100.00

EA = Economically active.
EI = Economically inactive.
*   See note on sources for data in tables, Annex 4.

As shown in Table 5, the distribution of the child allowance corresponds closely with the overall distribution in family structure (see lines one and two), whereas families with one parent or one economically inactive parent receive a larger share of the social allowance (see lines one and two versus line three).

Table 5
Structure of families collecting social benefits
(child allowance and social allowance) in 1996
by type of family and economic activity of parents* (%)

	Two-parent family		Single-parent family		
	Both EA	One EA	Parent EA	Parent EI	Total
Structure of all families	66.93	21.04	10.78	1.25	100.00
Structure of families collecting child allowance	64.72	22.80	11.10	1.38	100.00
Structure of families collecting child allowance and social allowance	47.64	30.83	17.38	4.15	100.00

EA = Economically active.
EI = Economically inactive.
* See note on sources for data in tables, Annex 4.

(b) **Changes in aggregate program expenditure** – While the benefits under consideration are only three among nine State Social Support benefits, they are the highest expenditures in this category by far, comprising 85 percent of total State Social Support spending. See Annex 1, Table A1.9. Since 1996, there has been a modest growth tendency in expenditure on these benefits resulting from indexation and rising caseloads, the latter of which is mainly as a consequence of rising unemployment since 1997. Specifically, the share of State Social Support benefits as a proportion of GDP has increased by 0.26 percentage points, from 1.96 percent in 1996 to 2.22 percent in 2000.

(c)   **Changes in average expenditure per beneficiary** – The nominal value of the parental allowance, child allowance, and social allowance rose considerably over the last decade. Between 1992 and 2000, the parental allowance doubled, the average child allowance increased by 150 percent, and the average social allowance increased four times. See Annex 1, Table A1.11. This was largely due to cost of living adjustments in all three benefits and, for the social allowance, to the reform policy of concentrating this form of assistance on those most in need. While indexing occurred regularly throughout the 1990s, the method changed. From 1991 to 1995, these benefits were indexed in line with price increases. Since 1996, indexation has been in accordance with the Act on State Social Support, which calls for benefit adjustments at the same time as increases in the subsistence minimum which is used in their calculation. When compared to wage changes over the 1990s, these adjustments boosted nominal benefits by slightly more than the minimum wage but less than the average wage, which rose faster over the period. See Annex 1, Table A1.11.[22]

Impacts of the Changes: The Household Level

The statistics presented so far show the effects of the reforms from the perspective of government spending. This section will examine their effect of household budgets, seeking to show how great or small their impact was on the net income available to families. It will also examine available evidence of the impact of reforms on the division of household and care work within families and, finally, inquire into how they affect families' ability to meet rising child care costs.

(a)   **Changes in benefits as a percentage of family income**
      Maternity benefits – There are no statistics available which distinguish maternity benefits as part of overall family incomes.

---

[22]   However, the rate of increase was much less after 1996 when the subsistence minimum was used for benefit adjustments. See Annex 1, Table A1.11.

Family allowances and child care benefits – The overall impact of the reforms just described was to reduce the numbers of families that receive the State Social Support family benefits while increasing the amount of these benefits for the neediest families. The portion of families that collect all three benefits dropped by half after the reforms, from 20.1 percent in 1992 to 9.98 percent in 1996. At the same time, those families that continued to be eligible for all three benefits received increases equal to 3 to 10 percentage points of net family income. See Table 6. With income testing, there also emerged a group of families (about 12 percent) which receives neither child allowance nor the social allowance.

Table 6
Percentage of families' net income accounted for by child allowance, social allowance and parental allowance in 1992 and 1996 by type of family, for all families that received all three benefits, Czech Republic* (%)

No. of children	Two-parent family		Single-parent family	
	1992	1996	1992	1996
1	19.18	24.23	53.24	62.72
2	24.22	26.67	57.94	63.61
3	30.54	33.75	58.06	69.62
4	31.70	40.67	95.13	56.65***
5	42.86	53.54	NA**	96.08

*   See note on sources for data in tables, Annex 4.
**   Not available.
***   The apparent contraction between 1992 and 1996 for this group may be due to the small number of single-parent families with four children in the two samples – only five in 1992 and eight in 1996.

The components of this change are as follows:
1. *Child allowance* – The child allowance has generally declined in importance in family budgets over the period examined. This is true for most single- and two-parent families, for most families with active and inactive parents, and for most families with larger and smaller numbers of children. See Table 7.

Table 7

Percentage of families' net income accounted for by child allowance in 1992, 1996 and 1999 by type of family, economic activity of parents and number of children* (%)

No. of children	Two-parent Family						Single-parent Family					
	Both parents EA			One parent EA			Parent EA			Parent EI		
	1992	1996	1999	1992	1996	1999	1992	1996	1999	1992	1996	1999
1	2.03	2.54	2.06	2.55	2.87	2.26	3.82	5.45	3.86	6.82	9.28	NA
2	6.09	4.86	4.35	7.16	5.57	4.15	10.83	9.44	6.44	17.38	13.69	NA
3	11.64	7.99	8.04	12.56	9.18	6.40	18.97	13.25	6.51	22.44	19.08	NA
4	15.98	10.93	7.00	14.62	11.86	9.71	21.39	21.90	NA	42.23	17.99	NA
5	20.29	11.19	NA	19.94	17.14	11.83	33.26	29.10	NA	NA	21.19	NA

* See note on sources for data in tables, Annex 4.

EA = Economically active.

EI = Economically inactive.

NA = Not available.

2. *Social allowance* – Since 1996 the social allowance has been collected by only a quarter of Czech families, but this allowance represents a more significant proportion of many families' net income than before. The largest effects can be observed in single parent families with several children. See Table 8.

3. *Parental allowance* – The parental allowance is not income-tested but is paid out to parents who provide full-time care for a child up to four years of age. Its percentage share of a family's net income tends to fall with the number of children, as other social benefits increase. It has more or less maintained its value to families during the 1990s, but with some variations. See Table 9.

(b)   **Impacts on the gender division of household work and care for children**
The social security reforms so far enacted have not appreciably changed the gender division of labour in the Czech Republic. No significant changes in women's employment rate occurred after the introduction of the new family benefits under the State Social Support scheme. A decrease in fertility in the 1990s can be ascribed to a range of social, cultural and economic factors; and it seems that changes in state support for young parents, even when defined very broadly, play only a marginal role.[23] In families with higher incomes, State Social Support allowances provide only a modest supplement to total income; and they do not create a serious counterweight to the tendency of women to return to employment after their youngest child reaches the age of three or, at most, six.[24]

---

[23]   In addition to changes in the system of family benefits, there have also been changes in some other family support systems which existed in communist times. The Ministry of Education no longer organizes child care facilities; the abolition of state ownership of houses has meant the end of a state housing policy which supported young families; and low-interest state loans for young families have been abolished. Discussion about influence of different factors is found in: Vecernik, Mateju 1998, Kucharova, Tucek 1999, Fialova 2000.

[24]   For instance, for families with incomes equal to 1.8-three times the subsistence minimum, child allowances (1 April 2000–30 September 2001) amounted to CZK 224–324 per child. The subsistence minimum in a two-parent family with two children aged five and eight was CZK 10,320, the income ceilings for entitlement to child allowance were CZK 18,576–30,960, and the child allowances for these two children would have been CZK 474.

Table 8

Percentage of families' net income accounted for by social allowance in 1992, 1996 and 1999 by type of family, economic activity of parents and number of children, Czech Republic* (%)

No. of children	Two-parent family						Single-parent family					
	Both parents EA			One parent EA			Parent EA			Parent EI		
	1992	1996	1999	1992	1996	1999	1992	1996	1999	1992	1996	1999
1	2.46	4.29	3.85	4.32	4.71	4.54	4.65	7.90	14.93	11.36	13.24	NA**
2	4.19	4.89	4.68	6.28	6.40	4.67	7.45	10.95	14.20	13.91	17.58	NA**
3	6.43	10.71	5.42	8.10	9.94	6.54	10.25	20.92	20.61	14.96	24.22	NA**
4	8.19	11.21	9.76	8.39	11.98	11.39	12.76	22.26	NA**	22.27	28.95	NA**
5	9.38	12.86	12.57	11.96	16.01	NA**	18.35	NA**	NA**	NA**	38.18	NA**

* See note on sources for data in tables, Annex 4.

EA = Economically active, EI = Economically inactive.

** NA = Not available.

Table 9
Percentage of families' net income accounted for by parental allowance in 1992, 1996 and 1999 by type of family and number of children, Czech Republic* (%)

Number of Children	Two-parent family			Single-parent family		
	1992	1996	1999	1992	1996	1999
1	12.31	13.78	9.84	35.06	39.75	NA
2	10.81	12.51	10.46	26.65	28.88	NA
3	9.88	12.47	9.92	20.66	24.48	NA
4	8.68	12.38	7.77	20.63	17.91	NA
5	10.97	13.81	NA	NA	15.64	NA

* See note on sources for data in tables, Annex 4.
NA = Not available.

The high degree of economic activity among Czech women means that most of them must divide their time and energy between their job and family. While male partners generally participate in domestic work to a greater extent when women are employed, they typically devote only half the time spent by women; and this difference is even greater in households with small children where a woman is on maternity or parental leave (Cermakova, 1997; Souvislosti, 2000).

Sociological surveys (Kucharova, Zamykalova 1999, Souvislosti 2000, Tucek, Friedlanderova, 2000) point to a discrepancy between women's opinions on the division of labour in the family and their actual behaviour. In contrast to their voiced support of gender equality, they continue to pattern their behaviour on an acceptance of a gender division of tasks and responsibilities in the family.[25] This situation has shown little change over the last decade.

---

[25] In the survey *Family* 2001, in 83 percent of married couples, women always or usually do the everyday housework (e.g. cooking, cleaning). In Tucek (2001, pp.110–111) women's and men's daily time budgets on weekdays do not differ much in the hours spent in employment (men 36 percent, women 33 percent of the day), but more in the hours spent on housework (men seven percent, women 15 percent).

In some social subgroups, particularly among the well-educated, urban young people, changes in the division of men's and women's roles in the family have been noted. However, this is less a result of social security benefits than of the reported preferences for modern cultural patterns, which include a more individualistic life style (Vecernik, Mateju, 1998).

Although the introduction of parental allowance in 1990 represented a fundamental change in the legislative conditions for the gender division of roles, few fathers utilize the chance to care full-time for their child.[26] During 1995–98, parental allowances were provided to almost half a million women but fewer than four thousand men, or less than one percent of the female beneficiary population.[27] This failure on the part of fathers to make use of parental allowance is attributable not only to traditional views of the roles of men and women in Czech society, but also to the negative financial consequences for the family. Because of the gender wage gap, the income of the family tends to decrease less during the period of care for a small child if it is the woman who stays home. The value of parent allowance in 2000 equalled 29 percent of the average wage of women aged 25–29 years working full-time, but only 20 percent of the average wage of men under the same circumstances. Another factor working against the equal sharing of child care was the unequal availability of parental leave. Up until 1 January 2001, a man wishing to take leave to care for his child did not have the same entitlement to return to his job as a woman did.

---

[26] The approximate number of men caring for children and the family can be illustrated by the following data that, however, include men and women regardless of the type of family and form of family cohabitation (i.e. including one-parent families with fathers as the head of the household). During 1993–98, the percentage of men caring for a family or household within the group of economically inactive persons (aged 15 years or more) decreased from 0.7 percent to 0.4 percent. At the same time this share decreased among women from 17.5 percent to 16.1 percent, largely as a result of the decline in the birth rate.

[27] Souvislosti, 2000, p.52.

(c)   **Changes in the affordability of child care**

One important feature of the transformation from a gender perspective has been the reduction of state subsidies for child care. Questions arise as to how child care costs have changed since the beginning of the transformation, how these costs compare with the child care benefits now provided to families, and whether the gap between costs and benefits has become so significant that it impedes some women from accepting work or improving their skills. Though there are no reliable statistics with which to address these questions definitively, available information does not support the notion that child care options have decreased significantly, nor does it suggest that they have become unaffordable on a broad scale. As shown in Annex 5, family benefits exceeded the child care costs in all years and in all cases examined, except for mothers earning 150 percent of the average wage and living in a household with an income level three times the subsistence minimum in 1996 and 2000. Thus, for the majority of Czech women, it does not appear that women's out-of-pocket (net of subsidies) costs for child care, needed to enable them to accept employment or improve their skills, have risen over the decade to the extent of making work or education significantly more difficult to pursue.[28] These findings are in line with sociological surveys (e.g. *Family* 2001), as well as with data presented earlier showing only an insignificant decrease in economic activity among Czech women.

Wider Economic and Social Impacts of the Reforms

Maternity benefits – The Czech maternity leave and benefits scheme were for many years among the most generous and family-supportive in the world. At the same time, they were structured for a centrally controlled economy and with relatively level incomes. With the transformation, reforms were necessary to adapt the system to the higher diversity of the market economy, as well as

---

[28] The findings from the same model for the less frequent family type with two children at a kindergarten are similar to what we present here for a family with one child.

the increased diversity of the social and professional structure of the female population. The adopted adaptation of the benefit formula was aimed at ensuring equal conditions for mothers with different economic (employment) status.

Family allowances and child care benefits – The objectives of the reforms were to provide greater assistance to needy families and to simplify the complex system of benefits in place during the communist period. These goals have been largely achieved. In an era characterised by increasing social inequality, the reformed system of State Social Support for families with children tends to average out differences in household income, helping to prevent larger families and lower income families from becoming socially excluded. In addition, the restructuring of the previous system of multiple, and often duplicative, allowances into just three allowances has improved transparency and public understanding of the system.

Against this generally positive assessment, some shortcomings of the reform should also be noted. First, the use of some family benefits has been inhibited by inconsistencies between social security laws and other statutes. The lack of alignment between parental leave and parental allowance benefits is one such problem. At present, an employer is obliged to grant parental leave to the mother or father of a child up to the age of three years. In the fourth year, the mother or father still has the right to parental allowance; however, the employer is no longer obliged to accept that employee – the parent – back into employment. Because of the fear of unemployment and the need to increase the family income as soon as possible by a second income, about 80 percent of women return to work before or immediately after the end of parental leave (*Family Life Patterns*, 1996).

Second, a high degree of redistribution through state social support has led to fears about the benefits' disincentive effect on economic activity. Such worries are particularly felt among the middle classes, who often bear a tax burden disproportionate to what the system offers them in the way of social allowances (Vecernik 1998). One expert has estimated that the number of families that abuse allowances is as high as 50 percent (Mares, 2000, p.145), but this estimate is subject to high uncertainty. Moreover, social workers' experience suggests that the disincentive effect applies mostly to those persons at higher risk of unemployment.

Concerning the opposite problem – low take-up rates by people who are reluctant to apply for income-tested benefits – a qualified estimate has indicated that this could result in non-receipt of benefits for 10 percent of families with the right to child benefits and nearly 40 percent of families with the right to social allowance (Mares, 2001, p.85).

Finally, the family allowances under the new State Social Support system have had little or no effect on the falling birth rate in the Czech Republic. Since this was not a major objective of the reform, it does not come as a major surprise. Rather it seems that the decline in the total fertility rate which occurred during the 1990s – from 1.89 percent to 1.13 percent – has been driven by changing social attitudes. State social support allowances cannot be a solution to this problem, nor are they perceived by the public as such.

Conclusion

Because the Czech government did not take gender issues explicitly into account when framing social security reform, women's needs are addressed only indirectly in those cases where they are part of another disadvantaged social group such as low-income families, the unemployed, or single-parent families. Still, in this indirect way, the reform has had a positive gender impact. Because the reformed system takes into account factors which are associated with increased poverty among women in the transforming Czech economy – i.e. status as single head of household, lower wages, and higher rates of economic inactivity due to responsibilities for child care – it is targeted to help combat poverty among women in general and, in particular, female-headed households.

At the same time, the government's lack of explicit focus on women's needs in drawing up the reform has resulted in replication and intensification of some gender inequalities (Souvislosti, 2000, p.45). While social security itself is not the root cause of these continuing inequalities, we can identify certain relations between the reform and their perpetuation:

- The family has become the basic subject of social policy. Conditions of entitlement to benefits take into account the situation of the whole family (or household), not that of individual members. In this approach, a woman is predominantly perceived first as a mother and second as an individual, and some women's individual rights are restricted to conform to their roles as mothers (e.g. restrictions on placing a child in day care for even short periods during parental leave prevents women from working or upgrading their skills).

- Employers' obligations toward pregnant women and the mothers of young children worsen women's access to employment. This obligations relate not so much to the payment of benefits, which are financed through social insurance, but to the provision of leave from work. Although it is hidden and thus difficult to prove, professionals in labour offices and in trade unions report that employers prefer women employees without family responsibilities; and some of them offer women only temporary employment contracts.

- The fixed and relatively low amount of the parental allowance provides a strong economic incentive for parents to assign child care to that parent whose earnings are lower, usually the mother.[29]

- Full-time caring for a disabled child or an elderly family member is supported by higher allowances or longer period of entitlement, which is undoubtedly helpful for women. However, this longer period out of employment may make a woman's return to work more difficult or may have a negative impact on her eventual pension.

- By supporting larger families the system creates conditions for a social trap for women in these families, particularly for those with fewer educational and job qualifications. Women with low qualifications and many children risk being trapped in their role as mothers and recipients of social security benefits, unable to enter, or re-enter, the labour market.

---

[29] The amount is low for better-educated women with higher earned incomes.

3. Pension Benefits

While the Czech government adopted significant pension reforms in the early and mid-1990s, the restructuring of the national pension system remains under debate. This section traces the developments, first describing the features of the former, communist-era pension system; then, the changes introduced since 1990; and finally the reforms that continue to be considered today. Current disagreements centre on a) whether to partially privatize the pension scheme as has been done in some other CEE countries (e.g. Hungary and Poland) by establishing a second tier consisting of mandatory, commercially managed individual savings accounts; and b) how to improve and expand voluntary options for supplemental pension savings.

Reasons for Reform

The system of pension security in place at the end of the 1980s was heavily shaped during the communist period. Under this system, preferential treatment was given to certain types of workers, mostly from male-dominated occupations. In addition to such unhealthful or high-risk occupations as mining, the privileged categories included pilots and some artists. There were also so-called personal pensions for 'meritorious' professionals in fields such as science, culture, health care, and defense. Many recipients of such pensions were high-level officials in the communist party ('Instructions about Social Security,' 1989, Prague, Ministry of Health Care and Social Affairs, pp. 19–20, 41–43, and 52).

Since inflation was not officially recognized in the communist period, pensions were defined in fixed sums and there was no benefit indexing. As a consequence, there were differences between pensions awarded at various times, and 'old pensions' were significantly lower than those more recently granted.

The financing of pensions was from general revenues in the state budget, rather than from an earmarked contribution. There was, however, a benefit formula according to which pensions were calculated in relation to the earnings from which taxes were collected.

The retirement age was 60 for men, and for women ranged from 53 to 57, depending on the number of children reared.[30] While widows were provided survivors' benefits based on their deceased husband's pension, widowers had no such rights.

Because Czechoslovakia did not experience the same level of economic turmoil as some other CEE countries in the early 1990s, the government did not find it necessary to use the pension system to absorb high unemployment. Thus, the system did not fall into deficit in the early years of the transformation. There were, however, strong public sentiments in favour of pension restructuring. These related mainly to equity issues – i.e. to the perceived unfairness of pension privileges, opaque pension financing, and the absence of inflation adjustments in benefits.

Overview of Reform

During 1990–92, the new Czechoslovak government moved quickly to eliminate pension privileges and to adjust the pensions of the oldest pensioners to reflect past inflation, thus bringing their benefits up to par with the benefits of those who had retired more recently.

In 1993, social insurance contributions as a payment separate from taxes were introduced, and the new Social Security Administration was charged with collections. Contributions were set as a percentage of a worker's gross income, with approximately one quarter coming out of his or her pay and the employer contributing the remaining three quarters.[31]

In 1994, the government provided authority for voluntary supplemental pension savings in private pension funds. The new private funds were organized on the so-called civic principle, so that any Czech citizen could par-

---

[30] Retirement age for women without children was 57 years, 56 years for women with one child, 55 years for two children, 54 years for three or four children, and 53 years for five or more children.

[31] The insurance contribution was set at 6.5 percent of the gross wage to be paid by the employee, and 19.5 percent to be paid by employers. The self-employed paid pension insurance contributions equal 26 percent of the tax base.

ticipate in any fund. To encourage such supplemental retirement savings, the law provided a government matching payment up to a ceiling. Today almost half of the economically active population participates in a voluntary private fund.[32]

The 1995 Pension Insurance Act, which went into effect in 1996, made major changes in public pension eligibility and benefits.[33] It provided for a gradual, scaled increase in the retirement ages of both men and women.[34] It also aligned the widow's and widower's pension entitlements, established new rules for early retirement (a compromise necessary to gain support for increasing the official retirement age), and introduced a new two-part benefit formula for pensions. Under this formula, all workers receive a flat-rate benefit (an identical sum for all pensioners) supplemented by a sum derived from a wage-related formula.[35] The 1995 reform also enlarged the period of work taken into account in computing benefits and allowed certain groups of non-wage earners, including housewives, to participate in pension insurance on a voluntary basis.

Contributions to pension insurance formed part of the general state budget through 1995. Because the pension system was in surplus during most of the early 1990s, the amounts collected in excess of those needed to pay benefits were spent on other government purposes. The Czech public objected strongly to this practice, leading to the establishment of a separate pension account within the state budget in 1996.

---

[32] Calculation of the authors from data of the Ministry of Labour and Social Affairs and the Czech Statistical Office.

[33] Act No. 155/1995 Coll.

[34] The pension age is being gradually increased over the decade 1996–2006, so that it will be 62 years for men and 61 years for women without children in 2007. The pension age still decreases for women on the basis of the number of children, as it did up to 1995. The increase in the pension age is calculated so that, for each year (1996–2006), two months are added for men and four months for women to the pension age that was valid in 1995. This means that, in 2001, the pension age for men was 61 years, and the pension age for women without children was 59 years and, for women with two children, 57 years.

[35] See section 5, benefit formula.

In 1996, the contribution rate was decreased by two percentage points. Combined with the economic recession in 1997, this change caused the pension system to fall into deficit and has required supplements from the state budget in each subsequent year. The ruling Social Democratic party has attempted to increase the contribution rate but, as a minority government, it has been unable to gain parliamentary support for its proposals.

In 1997, an amendment reduced the value of so-called substitute periods, that is, periods out of the labour force which are credited as years of work for pension eligibility purposes. Substitute periods are provided to those caring for children up to four years old (or if the child is severely disabled, up to 18 years) or for an incapacitated relative, as well as for periods of secondary or university education or military service. Until 1997, individuals received credit for the full duration of such periods. Since then, with the exception of army service, care for a child, and care for dependent relatives, the substitute periods are counted only for 80 percent.

Though the government continued to propose reforms of the pension system in the late 1990s, a legislative stalemate has prevented their enactment. Parliament has declined to approve legislation establishing an independent agency with a tripartite governing board to administer social security, as well as declining to authorize the establishment of supplemental occupational pensions by employers. Part of the parliamentary opposition is a protest vote by those who want to move forward with privatising the public pension scheme, as occurred in Hungary and Poland. So far, the government has rejected privatisation as a reform strategy, instead seeking to maintain and strengthen the existing public pension system. Thus, the current Czech pension system is based on two pillars: a basic obligatory system of pension insurance funded on the pay-as-you-go principle and a voluntary, prefunded supplementary pension insurance.[36] The public pension insurance (the first pillar) continues to be of fundamental importance. It will be the basis for analysis of the gender aspects of these reforms, provided below.

---

[36] The supplementary insurance funds were created by Act No. 248/1994 Coll.

Gender-related Changes

Benefit Formula

The benefit formula established in 1995 is redistributive, providing a higher return on contributions to low income workers than to workers with higher earnings. This formula is beneficial for women as a group, since their average wages are significantly less than those of men. See section 1. Thus, the pension formula serves to compensate in part for gender inequalities on the labour market.

As described earlier, the formula has two parts. The first is a fixed sum that is stated by law and subject to increase by government decree, the last increase being in 1998. No periodic indexation of this amount is set down in law. Since then, it has equalled CZK 1,310. This sum constitutes a greater portion of the benefit of workers with below average earnings than of higher paid workers. The second part is earnings related, but it gives greater weight to low earnings. For workers retiring in 2002, the first CZK 7,100 of countable earnings toward a benefit is credited at 100 percent; countable earnings between CZK 7,100 and CZK 16,800 are credited at 30 percent; and countable earnings exceeding CZK 16,800 are credited at ten percent.[37] The gender impact of this formula can be observed by comparing the gender wage gap with the gender gap in pensions. In December 2000, the old-age pensions paid to women were 82 percent of the pensions paid to men, while their wages were on average about three quarters of men's average wage. Thus, the pension system served to offset approximately a third of the gender wage gap.

A second reform with a gender impact is the 1995 extension of the earnings assessment period. At the present time, only earnings after 1985 are used to calculate pension benefits.[38] Under the 1995 Pension Insurance Act, however,

---

[37] The so-called calculation base is arrived at in this manner. To this, the percentage portion of the pension is set at 1.5 percent for each year of insurance, with a minimum sum of CZK 770.

[38] Until 30 September 1988, pensions were calculated on incomes for the five or ten years prior to gaining the right to a pension; then to the end of 1995 the basis was the five years with the highest earnings over the period of ten years prior to gaining the right; and, from 1 January 1996, all the years after 1985 are taken into account.

this period will be gradually increased until the last 30 years of employment will be counted. If women continue to work fewer years than men, a longer assessment period can be expected to increase gender differences in benefits.

Finally, it should be noted that the updating of 'old' pension benefits for past inflation in the early 1990s benefited women pensioners disproportionately, given their longer life expectancies and greater prevalence among pensioners.

Pension Age

As previously described, the 1995 reform provides for a gradual increase in the pension age. The increase is larger for women and, as a result, the pension ages of men and women are becoming more similar. By 2007 when the change is fully phased in, men will be able to retire at age 62 and women with no children at age 61. As before the reform, women with children will be able to retire earlier on a schedule that reflects the number of children.

Under the old system, women generally worked five years less than men, and it has been estimated that this served to decrease the pensions of women compared to men by five to six percent (Klimentova, 1999). After 2007, the average difference in the years worked is estimated at two to three years.

The reduction – but not elimination – of the gap between the retirement ages has an ambiguous effect on women's economic well-being. The significantly different participation of men and women in caring for children is often stated as the reason for having different retirement ages. This inequality in time spent on child care creates double disadvantage for women, who have reduced earnings in the periods of parental leave as well as shorter work lives because of the earlier pension age for mothers. Both factors work to reduce the eventual pension.

Identical pension ages could address this problem but, at the same time, could create difficulties for those women in their 50s who have responsibility for the care for elderly parents or young grandchildren. This is a situation where the unequal division of family care obligations has a negative impact on the old-age security of women.

Survivors' Benefits

The change in survivors' benefits introduced by the 1995 Pension Insurance Act brought eligibility conditions for widowers' pensions into line with those for widows. While widowers' pensions had first been introduced in 1991, the eligibility conditions did not fully correspond until after 1996.[39]

Under the revised rules, a widow/widower is eligible for a pension based on the rights of her/his spouse if that spouse had received an old age pension or full or partial disability pension, or was eligible for either an old age or *full* disability pension, or who died as the consequence of a work-related injury. The pension is paid for one year after the death of the spouse but can be longer if the widow/widower:

a) cares for a dependent child, a seriously disabled child of any age, or an incapacitated parent (either his/her own or that of his/her spouse), or

b) is fully disabled, or has reached a set age – for women, 55 years, for men, 58 years (or the pension age, if this is lower).

If a survivor retires within 5 years after his previous entitlement for a survivor's pension expires, he or she again becomes entitled to this pension.[40] If the surviving spouse remarries, the right to the widow's/widower's pension expires and the individual receives a lump-sum equal to 12 monthly pension payments.

While providing equal protection for women and men under the law, the practical effect of these rules is to provide greater benefit to women who fulfil their traditional roles as family caregivers.

---

[39] The method of calculating the pension is identical in both cases. This amount is equal to the sum of the basic amount (equal to CZK 1,310 since 1998) and an amount which is equal to 50 percent of the amount of the pension to which the deceased person had the right at the time of his/her death.

[40] Up to the end of 1995, this period was two years.

Benefits in the Event of Divorce

Neither the former nor the current pension system provides divorced persons with rights to part of the pension of the former spouse, nor is there any right to a widow's/widower's pension in the event of death of their former spouse. Because it is usually women who take leave to bring up the children resulting from the marriage, the lack of pension benefits in the case of divorce works to the financial detriment of women.

Caring Credits

As described earlier, pension eligibility is based on years worked plus so-called substitute periods, which include periods of caring for a child up to the age of four years (age 18 if the child suffers from a long-term severe disability) or periods of caring for an incapacitated relative. The period of providing care is counted as a substitute period for pension purposes, though the care provider pays no contributions. This amounts to a cross-subsidy within the pension scheme for family caregivers and thus benefits women disproportionately.

Due to labour market conditions, the consequences of providing such care are often more serious in the case of an incapacitated person than a child (although both are fully credited as service periods). This is because care for an incapacitated family member is frequently provided by women approaching pension age.[41] The impact on her future pension depends on the degree to which this interrupts her working career, i.e. on her success in returning to the labour market. Return to work is difficult for many older women, and any periods of unemployment following such care could be reflected in a lower pension.

---

[41] It should be added that for the period of care of an incapacitated person, the carer has the right to means-tested allowances from the social assistance system (paid out of the state budget and not from insurance).

Impact of Other Periods out of Full Employment
(e.g. Unemployment, Part-time Work, Atypical Work)

As with child care, unemployment is treated as a substitute period in the Czech Republic and therefore credited for pension eligibility purposes though no contributions are made.[42] Given the higher unemployment rate among women, this provision works to their general benefit. However, since 1997, only 80 percent of the unemployment period is counted as a substitute insurance period, which leads to lower retirement benefits.

Voluntary participation in social insurance by certain groups, including housewives, enables the relatively small number of Czech women who do not work outside the home to obtain coverage in the event of old age or disability. However, the option for voluntary coverage has not been widely utilized.

Simultaneous Eligibility for Different Benefits versus Exclusiveness

If an individual is eligible for both an old-age pension and a full (or partial) disability pension, only the higher is paid. However, if an individual is eligible for an old-age or full or partial disability pension *and* a widow's/widower's pension, the higher pension is paid in full; and half the earnings-related part of the lower pension is paid (see the preceding subsection on the benefit formula). In December 2000, 30 percent of women pensioners and ten percent of men pensioners received old-age and survivor's pensions simultaneously. In the case of women, the lower pension supplements the first one by 20 percent, while widower's pension increases a man's own pension by only 10 percent. The average men's simultaneous old-age and widower's pension is, however, still higher than that of women. See Annex 1, Table A1.18. If the widow's pension is a women's sole source of income, she is in serious danger of poverty. However, because of the high economic activity of women, very few women draw only a widow's pension, and it can be assumed that even fewer men draw only a widower's pension.[43]

---

[42] This is provided for the first three years of unemployment.

[43] Klimentová found that, of women pensioners above 55 years of age, four percent draw only widow's pensions. 78 percent of these women were more than 70 years of age and half were more than 80 years of age.

Gender Differences in Contribution Compliance; Exclusion from Coverage

Participation in pension insurance is compulsory for all groups of persons – employers, employees and the self-employed – who fulfil the set conditions. All these groups are obliged to pay contributions under similar conditions. Some economically inactive persons participate in pension insurance but do not pay contributions, while others participate in insurance voluntarily. There is no information available on differential rates of compliance among firms that might hire larger numbers of men or women.

Slightly more women than men have supplementary pension insurance, as shown below in Graph 1. Participants tend to be in their late 40s and 50s. Generally contributions are very low, ranging around 2.5 percent of the average wage. No data are available on average contribution differences by sex.

Graph 1
Participants in voluntary pension coverage, Czech Republic (1999)

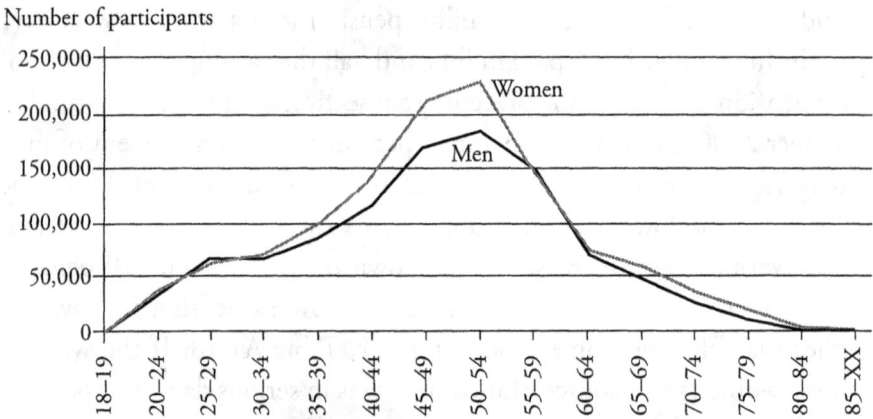

Number of participants

Source: www.mpsv.cz

Conclusion: Pension Options, Employment Choices, and Gender Relations

From a legal perspective, the reformed Czech pension system has become more gender neutral as a result of the reforms of the 1990s but still contains some gender-specific features. The major gender differences are that:

- A lower retirement age for women has been retained.
- Giving birth to a child reduces the mother's retirement age, regardless of whether or not she was the primary caregiver. A man who acts as the primary caregiver for his child(ren) receives no similar reduction.

At the same time, the reforms preserve some gender inequalities in the *consequences* of the pension system. Here the main source of inequality is that women's lower wages lead to lower pension benefits. However, a significant level of redistribution in favour of persons with low incomes, who are frequently women, is provided by the two-part structure of old-age pensions, including both the first (fixed) component and the manner of calculating the second component, which gives greater weight to lower earnings.

From a gender standpoint, the transformation of the pension system after 1990 brought about the following changes that mitigated gender inequalities:

- Adjustment of pensions eliminated the inequality in pensions issued at different times, which was reflected in inequalities based on age. Adjustment benefited older pensioners, among whom women predominate.
- The 1995 Pension Insurance Act introduced widower's pensions under the same conditions as widow's pensions, eliminating the inequality of widowers.
- The 1995 Pension Insurance Act enabled new groups of the population to participate in pension insurance on a voluntary basis, including housewives.
- The pension ages of men and women are becoming more similar as these ages are gradually increased. Beginning in 2007, the difference will be one year, but the impact of this change is reduced by the provision of lower retirement thresholds for women based on the number of children.

The transformation of the pension system after 1990 brought at least one change that could increase gender inequalities in future: the earnings assessment period is being extended and will reach 30 years in 2016 (in 2001 this period was 15 years), which could mean that periods of parental leave or care giving for other family members beyond the substitute periods will lower the amount of the eventual pension, especially in combination with the retention of early retirement for mothers. However, the eventual effect will depend on the future fertility rate, the average age of mothers giving birth, and a possible further increase in the retirement age.

Because of their higher average life expectancy, lower pension age, and the inclusion of periods of study and care for children in substitute pension periods for which no contributions need be paid, a woman may draw an old-age pension for a longer period than that during which she paid contributions.[44] This reflects a strong combination of advantages afforded women by the current Czech system. However, these advantages may be less pronounced in the future given the increase in retirement age and the decrease in fertility. In addition, they may be affected by future reforms of the system, i.e., changes in the benefit formula and/or a partial privatisation of pension benefits.

References

Cermakova, Marie (1997): *Rodina a menici se gender role – socialni analyza české rodiny (Family and Changing Gender Roles – Analysis of Czech Family)*, Prague: Institute of Sociology of the Academy of Sciences.

Ceska společnost a seniori (Czech Society and Seniors), 1997. Brno: Masaryk University Press.

Development of Main Economic and Social Indicators of the Czech Republic 1990–2000 (1.Q 2001), No.16, 2001. Prague: Research Institute of Labour and Social Affairs.

---

[44] 'Relations and Changes in Gender Differences in Czech Society in the 90s,' Prague, Institute of Sociology of AS CR, 2000, p.56.

Dlouhy, Jiri (1997): *Vzajemne vazby systemu dani a davek v České republice (Mutual relations in the system of taxes and allowances in the Czech Republic)*. Prague: Socioklub.

Equal Opportunities for Women and Men in the European Union: Annual Report 1998, 1999. Luxembourg: Office for Official Publications of the EC.

Fakta o socialni situaci v Ceske republice (Facts on the Social Conditions in the Czech Republic), 1997. Prague: Czech Statistical Office.

Ferge, Zsuzsa (1997): Women and Social Transformation in Central-Eastern Europe, *Czech Sociological Review*, Vol. V.

Fialova, Ludmila and Horska, Pavla (1995): *Soucasne a perspektivni promeny rodiny, manzelstvi a rodicovstvi (Present and Perspective Changes of Family, Marriage and Parenthood)*, Prague: Start.

Fialova Ludmila, Hamplova Dana, Kucera Milan and Vymetalova Simona (2000): *Predstavy mladych lidi o manzelstvi a rodicovstvi (Young People's Notions on Marriage and Parenthood)*, Prague: SLON.

Formy rodinneho zivota mlade generace (Family Life Patterns of the Young Generation), 1997. Prague: RILSA.

Havelkova, Hana (1995): Dimenze 'gender' ve vztahu soukrome a verejne sfery (Gender Dimension in the Relationship of Private and Public Sphere), *Sociologicky casopis*, No. 1.

Hirsl, Miroslav (1999): Jak se meni počet deti pobirajicich pridavek na dite (Changes in the Number of Children Receiving Child Allowance), *Socialni politika*, No. 10.

Hirsl, Miroslav (2001): Regionalni rozdily v podilu deti se socialnim prispevem (Regional differences in the ratio of children receiving supplementary social allowances), *Pohledy*, No. 1–2.

Historicka rocenka CSSR (Historical Yearbook of Czechoslovakia), 1985. Prague: SNTL-ALFA.

Human Development Report Czech Republic, 1999, Prague: UNDP, RILSA.

Klimentova, Jana (1999): Socialni a ekonomicka situace starsich zen, (Social and Economic Situation of Elderly Women), *Socialni politika*, No. 11.

Kucharova, Vera and Zamykalova, Lenka (1998): *Aktualni otazky postaveni zen v CR (Current Topics of Women's Status in C.R.)*. Prague: RILSA.

Kucharova, Vera and Tucek, Milan (1999): *Socialne ekonomicke souvislosti rodinneho chovani mlade generace v Ceske republice (Social and Economic Consequences of Younger Generation Family Behaviour in the Czech Republic)*, Prague: Narodohospodarsky ustav.

Kucharova, Vera, Nedomova, Alena and Zamykalova, Lenka (1999): *Predpoklady snatkoveho a rodinneho chovani mlade generace (Conditions of Nuptial and Family Behaviour of the Young Generation)*. Prague: RILSA.

Kucharova, Vera and Zamykalova, Lenka (2000): *Rovne prilezitosti muzu a zen na trhu práce (Equal Opportunities of Men and Women in the Labour Market)*. Prague: RILSA.

Labour and Social Affairs Statistical Yearbook 1996, 1997, 1998, 1999, 2000, 2001. Prague.

Labour Force Survey, Czech Statistical Office. Results are published quarterly and in time series.

Microcensuses of the incomes of shared-budget households 1992, 1996. Prague: Czech Statistical Office.

Mares, Petr (2000): Socialni politika a socialni kompetence jejich klientu (Social Policy and Social Cognisance of its Clients), *Sociologicky casopis*, No. 2.

Mares, Petr (2001): Zneuzivani vs. nevyuzivani socialnich davek – selhani cilenosti (Abuse vs. failure to utilize social allowances – failure of target principle). In Mares P. et al., *Dávky sociálního státu (Welfare State Benefits)*. Brno: MU.

Marikova, Hana (2000): *Promeny soucasne ceske rodiny. Rodina – gender – stratifikace (Changing Contemporary Family. Family – Gender – Stratification)*. Prague: SLON.

Navrhy na zajisteni motivace k praci a vydelecne cinnosti v ramci systemu poskytovani socialnich davek (Proposals for ensuring work and gainful activity motivation within the system of social benefits), 2001. Prague: Ministry of Labour and Social Affairs (working document).

Operational Programme for Human Resources Development in the Czech Republic, www.mpsv.cz.

O chudobe v ceske a slovenske spolecnosti (On Poverty in the Czech and Slovak Society), 1995. Brno: MU.

Souvislosti a zmeny genderovych diferenci v české spolecnosti v 90. letech (Relations and Changes of Gender Differences in the Czech Society in the 90s), 2000. Prague: Institute of Sociology of the Academy of Sciences.

Statistical Yearbook of the Czech Republic 2000, 2001. Prague: Czech Statistical Office.

Tomes, Igor (2001): *Sociální politika (Social Policy)*, Prague, Socioklub.

Trh práce v Ceske republice (Labour Market in the Czech Republic), 2000. Prague: Czech Statistical Office.

Tucek, Milan et al. (1998): *Ceska rodina v transformaci – stratifikace, delba roli a hodnotove orientace (Czech Family in Transformation – Stratification, Division of Roles and Value Orientations)*. Prague: Institute of Sociology of Academy of Sciences.

Tucek, Milan and Friedlanderova, Hana (2000): *Cesi na prahu noveho tisicileti (The Czechs on the Threshold of New Millenium)*. Prague: SLON.

Vecernik, Jiri (1998): *Obcan a trzni ekonomika (Market and People)*. Prague: Lidove Noviny.

Vecernik, Jiri and Mateju, Petr (1998): *Zprava o vyvoji ceske spolecnosti 1989–1998 (Report on the Development of Czech Society 1989–1998)*. Prague: Academia.

Women in Transition, 1999. Florence: UNICEF.

Zeny a muzi v cislech (Women and Men in Figures), 2000. Prague: Czech Statistical Office.

Research Data

Family Life Patterns of the Younger Generation, 1996, Research data of the Research Institute of Labour and Social Affairs.

Women and Men 1998, Research data of the Research Institute of Labour and Social Affairs (published in Kucharova, Zamykalova, 1998).

Family 2001, Research data of the Research Institute of Labour and Social Affairs.

Annex 1: Statistical Annex

Table A1.1 Economic activity rate (%)					
	1993	1995	1997	1999	2001, Q1
Men	71.3	71.5	71.1	70.6	69.4
Women	52.3	52.3	51.8	52.1	51.7
Total	61.4	61.5	61.1	61.0	60.2
Female ratio of total economically active	44.3	44.2	44.1	44.3	44.5

Note: Employed and unemployed persons (incl. armed forces) in % of population 15 years and older.

Source: *Main Economic and Social Indicators of the Czech Republic 1990–2000* (Q1, 2001), Research Institute of Labour and Social Affairs, Prague 2001.

Table A1.2
Age structure of the population

Year	Age group					
	0–14		15–59		60 and over	
	Men	Women	Men	Women	Men	Women
1980	23.4		59.8		16.8	
1990	21.0		61.1		17.9	
	22.3	20.1	63.2	59.1	14.5	20.8
1992	20.0		62.0		18.0	
	21.1	19.0	64.2	60.1	14.7	21.0
1994	18.8		63.2		18.0	
	29.9	17.9	65.3	61.1	14.8	21.0
1996	17.9		64.1		18.0	
	18.8	17.0	66.3	62.0	14.8	21.0
1998	17.4		64.5		18.0	
	18.4	16.5	66.8	62.4	14.9	21.0
2001	16.2		65.4		18.4	
	17.0	15.3	67.6	63.3	15.4	21.4
2010[1]	14.5		62.5		23.0	
2020[1]	14.4		58.6		27.0	

[1] Prediction of the Czech Statistical Office from 1997: middle of three alternatives.

Sources: *Výhled vývoje obyvatelstva České republiky do roku 2020.* 1998. Praha: ČSÚ (*Outlook for the Development of the Population of the Czech Republic up to 2020*: Czech Statistical Office); Kokta, J. 1999. *Aktuální demografická situace v ČR, MPSV (Current Demographic Situation in the Czech Republic*, Prague: Ministry of Labour and Social Affairs); *Employment and Unemployment in the Czech Republic as Measured by the Labour Force Sample Survey*, Czech Statistical Office (issued quarterly).

Table A1.3
Women and men aged 15–59 by their economic status (thousands and percentage)

	Employed		Unemployed		Inactive	
	Thousands	%	Thousands	%	Thousands	%
			WOMEN			
1993	2,011.6	68.2	115.8	3.9	821.8	27.9
1999	1,907.7	63.4	249.6	8.3	851.9	28.3
2001, Q1	2,024.0	60.7	231.7	6.9	1,076.4	32.3
Growth		–7.4		3.0		4.4
			MEN			
1993	2,632.0	81.4	90.1	2.8	509.8	15.8
1999	2,608.6	77.4	207.1	6.1	552.0	16.4
2001, Q1	2,590.4	76.7	200.9	5.9	586.4	17.4
Growth		–4.7		3.1		1.6

Source: Employment and Unemployment in the Czech Republic as Measured by the Labour Force Sample Survey, Czech Statistical Office (issued quarterly).

Table A1.4a
Structure of economically inactive women aged 15+

	1993	1995	1997	1999	2001 (Q1)
Pensioners (old age and disability)	59.4	60.9	60.9	63.4	63.9
Students	15.0	16.7	17.5	17.1	16.4
Parental leave	9.5	8.1	7.9	8.9	8.3
Caring for children and household	8.0	8.6	9.7	7.2	6.9
Having health problems	4.7	3.4	2.2	1.3	4.5
Other	3.4	2.3	1.8	2.1	

Table A1.4b
Structure of economically inactive men aged 15+

	1993	1995	1997	1999	2001 (Q1)
Pensioners (old age and disability)	61.4	62.9	63.2	65.1	64.7
Students	27.6	30.2	33.6	30.6	31.6
Having health problems	5.5	4.2	2.6	1.5	1.2
Parental leave	0.3	0.1	0.0	0.0	2.5
Caring for children and household	0.4	0.3	0.3	0.3	
Others	10.3	6.5	2.9	4.0	

Source: *Employment and Unemployment in the Czech Republic as Measured by the Labour Force Sample Survey,* Czech Statistical Office (issued quarterly).

Table A1.5
Unemployment rate (average)

	1990[1]	1993	1995	1997	1999	2000	2001 (Q1)
Men	0.7	3.4	3.4	3.9	7.3	7.9	8.1
Women	0.8	5.4	4.8	5.9	10.5	10.4	9.2
Total	0.7	4.3	4.0	4.8	8.7	9.0	8.9

[1] Different method of calculation (only the registered unemployed, which means that slightly lower rates are calculated).

Sources: *Men and Women in Figures,* 2000, Prague, CSO; *Main Economic and Social Indicators of the Czech Republic 1990–2000* (1.Q 2001), No.16, Research Institute of Labour and Social Affairs, Prague 2001.

Table A1.6
Employment by ISCO-88 classification (percentage)

	1993			2000		
	Male	Female	% F	Male	Female	% F
Legislators, senior officials and managers	5.8	2.5	25.3	8.0	3.6	25.7
Professionals	8.0	10.6	50.7	9.0	12.8	52.1
Technicians and associate professionals	14.3	22.6	55.3	15.1	23.4	54.2
Clerks	2.6	13.5	80.2	2.9	14.0	78.9
Service workers and shop and market sales workers	5.9	16.7	68.9	7.3	18.0	65.2
Skilled agricultural and forestry workers	2.2	3.1	52.3	2.1	1.9	40.2
Craft and related trades workers	33.5	9.3	17.8	30.4	7.5	15.9
Plant and machine operators and assemblers	17.8	7.4	24.5	16.8	7.6	25.7
Elementary occupations	7.1	14.1	60.9	6.3	11.2	57.7
Army personnel	2.6	0.0	1.4	2.0	0.0	1.6
Total	100.0	100.0	43.9	100.0	100.0	43.3

Note: 1993 – average, 2000 (Q3).

Source: *Employment and Unemployment in the Czech Republic as Measured by the Labour Force Sample Survey*, Czech Statistical Office (issued quarterly).

Table A1.7
Average net monthly wage of men and women

Year	Monthly wage (CZK)				Ratio in %	
	Female	Male	Total	Difference F–M	F/M	M/F
1984	2,515	3,652	3,171	–1,137	68.9	145.2
1988	2,801	3,968	3,486	–1,167	70.6	142.0
1996	7,320	9,339	8,490	–2,019	78.3	127.6
1997	8,278	10,725	9,590	–2,447	77.2	129.6
1998	8,488	11,645	10,200	–3,157	72.9	137.2
1999	9,069	12,285	10,785	–3,216	73.8	135.5

Sources: *Sample Surveys on Wages 1984, 1988,* Czech Statistical Office; *Men and Women in Figures,* 2000, Prague, CSO.

Table A1.8
Status in employment by CZ–ISCE in one (main) job (percentage)

	Male	Female	% F
1993			
Employees	84.0	90.2	46.3
Employers	3.8	1.4	22.1
Self-employed workers	8.0	4.4	30.7
Members of producers' cooperatives	3.9	3.6	42.0
Contributing family workers	0.2	0.4	62.5
2000			
Employees	80.1	88.7	45.9
Employers	5.7	2.3	23.7
Self-employed workers	12.9	7.1	29.5
Members of producers' cooperatives	1.2	0.9	36.2
Contributing family workers	0.2	1.1	78.8
2001 (Q1)			
Employees	79.9	88.6	46.2
Employers	5.4	2.1	22.8
Self-employed workers	13.2	7.4	30.2
Members of producers' cooperatives	1.2	0.9	35.9
Contributing family workers	0.2	1.0	77.8

Source: Employment and Unemployment in the Czech Republic as Measured by the Labour
Force Sample Survey, Czech Statistical Office (issued quarterly).

Table A1.9
State Social Support Benefits 1996 – 2000 (in thousands CZK)

Benefit	1996	1997	1998	1999	2000
Child allowance	12,194	12,495	11,493	12,474	12,748
Social allowance	6,244	6,224	6,273	6,251	6,199
Parental allowance	7,357	7,612	7,780	7,718	7,691
Birth grant	484	525	563	566	581
Maintenance allowance	34	25	23	19	15
Housing allowance	677	813	1,367	2,084	2,518
Foster care benefit	144	154	233	315	339
Transport allowance	839	938	946	994	1,045
Funeral grant	348	331	519	543	540
Energy prices compensatory allowance		67	277	236	106
Rent prices compensatory allowance		49	163	127	73
State social support benefits total	28,321	29,233	29,637	31,327	31,855
Gross domestic product (GDP)	1,447,700	1,432,800	1,401,300	1,390,600	1,433,800
GDP accounted for by state social support	1.96%	2.04%	2.11%	2.25%	2.22%

Source: *Labour and Social Affairs Statistical Yearbook 1996, 1997, 1998, 1999, 2000, 2001*, Prague.

Development of Main Economic and Social Indicators in the Czech Republic 1990–2000, No. 16, Prague 2001.

Table A1.10
Structure of State Social Support Benefits, 1996–2000 (percentage)

	1996	1997	1998	1999	2000
Child allowance	43.06	42.74	38.78	39.82	40.02
Social allowance	22.05	21.29	21.17	19.95	19.46
Parental allowance	25.98	26.04	26.25	24.64	24.14
Birth grant	1.71	1.80	1.90	1.81	1.82
Maintenance allowance	0.12	0.09	0.08	0.06	0.05
Housing allowance	2.39	2.78	4.61	6.65	7.90
Foster care benefit	0.51	0.53	0.79	1.01	1.06
Transport allowance	2.96	3.21	3.19	3.17	3.28
Funeral grant	1.23	1.13	1.75	1.73	1.70
Energy prices compensatory allowance		0.23	0.93	0.75	0.33
Rent prices compensatory allowance		0.17	0.55	0.41	0.23
State social support benefits – Total	100.00	100.00	100.00	100.00	100.00

Source: *Labour and Social Affairs Statistical Yearbook 1996, 1997, 1998, 1999, 2000, 2001*, Prague.

Development of Main Economic and Social Indicators in the Czech Republic 1990–2000, No. 16, Prague 2001.

Table A1.11
Trends in average monthly size of child allowance, social allowance,
parental allowance and birth grant in 1992, 1996 and 2000;
comparison with trends in wages (in CZK)

	Parental allowance	Child allowance	Social allowance	Birth grant	Average wage	Minimum wage
1992	1,200	200–1,720[1]	average per child: 243[3]	3,000	4,644	2,200
1996	2,112	198–650[2] average per child: 475	177–762[4] average per family: 984[3]	5,240	9,676	2,500
2000	2,695	237–784[2] average per child: 520	212–919[4] average per family: 1,084[3]	6,400	13,289	4,500

Note: Where a range is given, the values are set by law; the average values are calculated from the allowances actually paid out.

[1]   Paid out according to the number of children: CZK 200 for one child; CZK 1,720 for four or more children.

[2]   For those entitled, paid out according to the age of the child and depending on the family income (not paid out to families with incomes of more than three times the subsistence minimum).

[3]   According to the statistics of family budgets; the amounts per child were 262 in 1995 and 454 in 1999 (in: Hirsl, 2001).

[4]   For those entitled, paid out according to the age of the child and depending on the family income (not paid out to families with incomes over 1.6 times the subsistence minimum).

Sources: Data from the Ministry of Labour and Social Affairs; Statistics on Family Budgets of the Czech Statistical Office; *Trends in Economic and Social Indicators in CR 1990–2000*, No. 16, Prague, RILSA 2001; Hirsl 2001.

Table A1.12
Child care in nurseries and kindergartens

	Year				
	1990	1994	1997	1999	2000
Number of nurseries	1,043	235	133	122	118
Number of children in nurseries			4,233	3,481	3,417
Number of children aged 0–2	387,853	346,443	275,584	269.558	269,865
Number of children aged 1–2	258,498	240,539	183,319	180,356	179,243
	School Year				
	1990/91	1994/95	1996/97	1998/99	1999/00
Number of kindergartens	7,335	6,526	6,343	6,028	5,901
Number of children in kindergartens	352,139	338,722	317,153	302,856	290,192
Number of children per class	21.7	22.9	22.0	22.4	22.3
Number of children per teacher	11.0	12.2	11.5	12.0	11.8
Number of children aged 3–5	395,808	381,579	369,042	321,608	291,490
Share of children aged 3–5 in kindergartens (%)	89.0	88.8	85.9	94.2	99.5

Source: *Statistical Yearbook 2000*, Prague, CSO 2001; *Vital Statistics of the Czech Republic*, Czech Statistical Office.

Table A1.13
Structure of households and incomes (annual per capita)

	Households with children – total			Two-parent families	Single-parent families – head of household:					
					Female			Male		
	1988	1992	1996	1996	1988	1992	1996	1988	1992	1996
Average number of:										
• Members	4	4	4	3.76	2.73	2.80	2.79	2.79	2.98	2.91
• Economically active	2	2	2	1.64	1.06	1	0.90	1.16	1.17	1.08
• Children	2	2	2	1.76	1.49	1.45	1.48	1.39	1.35	1.36
(%)										
Share of social incomes	16.9	17.3	13.6	11.0	26.5	30.1	30.1	21.7	27.4	24.8
Share of child allowance	8.6	5.3	3.7	7.6	10.6	6.7	6.6	7.3	4.7	3.7
Share of low income families[1]	10.9	20.1	12.8	10.6	32.5	42.5	33.8	10.8	31.0	18.1

[1] Families with net income up to 1.29 times the subsistence minimum.

Source: *Women and Men in Figures*, 2000, CSO, pp.55, 61 (microcensuses).

Table A1.14 a
Indicators of relations between the household composition
and structure of incomes in 2000
(average figures; incomes per capita, per year, in CZK)

	Type of household					
	Low-income families with children[1]		Employed with children		Employed total	
	Number	%	Number	%	Number	%
Average number of:						
Members	3.73	—	3.57	—	2.81	—
Economically active members	1.01	—	1.64	—	1.60	—
Children (dependent)	2.12	—	1.64	—	0.96	—
Of which: aged 0–5	0.52	—	0.35	—	0.21	—
Others[2]	0.60	—	0.29	—	0.25	—
Incomes						
Gross incomes total	42,556	100.0	90,245	100.0	106,478	100.0
From employment and business	25,768	60.6	76,773	85.0	91,497	85.9
Social	14,347	33.7	8,718	9.7	10,089	9.5

[1] With total incomes not exceeding 1.4 times the subsistence level of the given household.

[2] Pensioners and economically inactive members.

Source: Household Budget Statistics, Czech Statistical Office, www.czso.cz.

Table A1.14 b
Indicators of relations between the household composition and structure of incomes
in 1999 (average figures per capita, per year, in CZK)

	Type of household							
	Low-income families with children[1]						Employed with children	
	Two-parent families				Single-parent families			
	2 children		3 children					
	Number	%	Number	%	Number	%	Number	%
Average number of:								
Members	4.0	—	4.98	—	2.82	—	3.57	—
Economically active members	1.33	—	1.27	—	0.59	—	1.65	—
Children (dependent)	1.99	—	2.98	—	1.82	—	1.63	—
Money incomes								
Gross incomes total	41,040	100.0	39,564	100.0	39,859	100.0	87,576	100.0
From employment and business	—	72.1	—	64.7	—	39.3	—	85.5
Social	—	26.3	—	32.2	—	46.7	—	9.0

Note: In 1999 the average total gross incomes in low-income families was CZK 40,647.

[1] With total incomes not exceeding 1.4 times the subsistence level of the given household.

Source: *Statistical Yearbook of the Czech Republic 2000, 2001*, CSO.

Table A1.15
Characteristics of women and households in selected types of households in 1988, 1992 and 1996

	Households with children (total)			Households with income below 50 % of average income			Single-parent families with a woman as head of household		
	1988	1992	1996	1988	1992	1996	1988	1992	1996
Number of members[1]	4	4	4	3.26	3.73	3.85	2.73	2.80	2.79
Number of dependent children[1]	2	2	2	1.52	1.87	1.97	1.49	1.45	1.48
Age of women (wives)									
up to 24[2]	8.9	9.3	7.8	17.4	16.0	12.9	6.6	6.4	6.4
25–34	36.5	35.0	36.1	31.9	49.6	52.4	26.4	24.8	29.5
35–44	42.1	40.5	37.5	11.8	23.2	25.8	45.9	44.8	39.3
45–54	11.0	14.1	16.6	2.0	6.8	6.8	14.8	18.5	19.8
55–64	1.2	1.0	1.6	6.2	3.5	1.4	3.8	3.2	2.0
65 +	0.3	0.1	0.2	30.8	0.9	0.7	2.4	2.2	2.9
Education of women (wives)[2]									
Without or unfinished education	0.0	0.1	0.0	0.0	0.3	0.3	0.2	0.1	0.0
Basic	24.3	16.3	14.0	53.2	36.3	31.5	30.6	25.9	19.3
Secondary vocational	33.4	37.7	35.6	27.5	39.7	43.6	29.5	30.5	33.8
Full secondary technical/general	33.6	36.0	39.7	15.4	20.9	21.3	31.4	35.9	37.9
University	8.6	10.0	10.6	3.4	2.7	3.2	8.3	7.6	9.1

Table A1.15 (continued)
Characteristics of women and households in selected types of households in 1988, 1992 and 1996

	Households with children (total)			Households with income below 50 % of average income			Single-parent families with a woman as head of household		
	1988	1992	1996	1988	1992	1996	1988	1992	1996
Structure of households[2]									
Two-parent nuclear family	74.5	71.8	71.0	66.8	56.8	60.4	—	—	—
Couple with/without children + other members	14.5	16.2	15.6	1.6	8.5	8.0	—	—	—
Single-parent family	11.0	12.0	13.4	24.6	30.5	27.6	—	—	—
Others	—	—	—	7.1	4.3	3.9	—	—	—
Share of families with income[2]									
Up to subsistence level	1.8	5.1	4.3	72.1	77.5	39.1	8.7	18.1	14.7
1.00–1.29 times subsistence level	9.1	15.0	8.5	27.9	22.6	53.9	23.8	26.4	19.1

[1] Average.
[2] Percentage.

Source: Ženy a muži v číslech (Women and Men in Figures), CSO 2000, pp.55–61.

Table A1.16 Population and vital statistics – per 1,000 inhabitants					
Year	Live births	Deaths	Marriages	Divorces	Natural increase
1950–54	19.6	11.0	8.9	1.2	8.6
1960–64	14.4	10.3	8.0	1.5	4.1
1970–74	17.0	12.5	9.6	2.4	4.5
1980–84	13.8	12.9	7.7	2.8	1.0
1985–89	12.8	12.5	7.9	3.0	0.3
1990	12.6	12.5	8.8	3.1	0.1
1992	11.8	11.7	7.2	2.8	0.1
1994	10.3	11.4	5.7	3.0	−1.1
1996	8.8	10.9	5.2	3.2	−2.1
1997	8.8	10.9	5.6	3.2	−2.1
1998	8.8	10.6	5.3	3.1	−1.8
1999	8.7	10.7	5.2	2.3	−2.0

Source: Population and Vital Statistics in the Czech Republic, Czech Statistical Office.

Table A1.17 Indicators of economic activity of people after (or about) retirement age					
	1993	1995	1997	1999	2001 (Q1)
Employment rate by age groups – women					
55–59	26.0	29.7	34.6	32.9	33.0
60–64	12.3	13.3	14.1	13.6	12.4
65+	3.9	3.4	2.9	2.9	2.0
Employment rate by age groups – men					
60–64	26.6	28.0	30.3	27.3	22.4
65+	9.4	9.1	8.7	7.2	6.4
Unemployment rate by age groups – women					
55–59	4.5	3.9	3.6	4.5	5.4
60–64	7.3	3.7	6.7	6.7	7.1
65+	5.4	3.8	3.5	7.0	3.0
Unemployment rate by age groups – men					
60–64	6.9	4.5	4.9	4.3	5.5
65+	5.3	4.4	3.5	4.3	4.5
Employed pensioners					
Women (thousands)	95.1	114.1	109.0	93.7	—
(%)	4.4	5.2	5.1	4.5	—
Men (thousands)	95.0	117.6	116.9	95.9	—
(%)	3.5	4.2	4.2	3.6	—

Source: Labour Force Sample Survey, Czech Statistical Office.

Table A1.18
Relations between men's and women's pensions in 2000

a	Average old-age pension – women	CZK 5,781
b	Average old-age pension – men	CZK 7,047
c	Average simultaneous old-age and survivor's pension – women	CZK 6,954
d	Average simultaneous old-age and survivor's pension – men	CZK 7,736
a/b	Ratio of the average old-age pension for women and men	82.0%
c/d	Ratio of the average simultaneous old-age and survivor's pensions for women and men	89.0%
c/a	Ratio of the average simultaneous pensions and simple old-age pensions for women	120.3%
d/b	Ratio of the average simultaneous pensions and simple old-age pensions for men	109.8%

Source: Statistics of the Ministry of Labour and Social Affairs.

Annex 2: Criteria and Calculation of Allowances

Child Allowance

Child allowances are provided at three levels depending on the income of the family in the previous calendar year. The amount is set as a multiple of the subsistence minimum for the personal needs of the child. A dependent child has the right to a monthly children's allowance as follows:

a) in the amount of 0.32 times the subsistence minimum for the personal needs of the child, if the income of the family did not exceed 1.1 times the subsistence minimum for the family;

b) 0.28 times the subsistence minimum for the personal needs of the child, if the income of the family exceeded 1.1 times the subsistence minimum for the family, but did not exceed 1.8 times the subsistence minimum for the family; and

c) 0.14 times the subsistence minimum for the personal needs of the child, if the income of the family exceeded 1.8 times the subsistence minimum for the family, but did not exceed 3.0 times the subsistence minimum for the family.

Families with an income greater than 3.0 times the subsistence minimum for the family do not have the right to the child allowance.

From 1 April 2000, the amount of the child allowances in the individual groups had the following values:

Age of the dependent child	Amount of the children's allowance for an income (in multiples of the subsistence minimum) of (in CZK)		
	Up to 1.1 SM*	1.1–1.8 SM	1.8–3.0 SM
From 0 to 6 years	541	474	237
From 6 to 10 years	605	530	265
From 10 to 15 years	714	625	313
From 15 to 26 years	784	686	343

* Subsistence minimum.

Social Allowance

The right to the social allowance is linked to care for a dependent child and to a set limit for the income of the family, which must be less than 1.6 times the subsistence minimum in the previous calendar quarter. Child allowances are included in the calculation of the family income in determining eligibility for the social allowance.

As the income of the family increases, the amount of the allowance is gradually decreased, so that the amount of the supplementary social allowance always reflects the specific income situation of the family. The supplementary social allowance reacts to changes in the social situation in the family, and its amount is also adjusted in response to the disability of a member of the family, or single parenthood.

The amount of supplementary social allowance for a child is dependent on the income of the complete family (in multiples of the subsistence minimum) and the age of the child. This chart shows the levels of benefits valid from 1 April 2000 and assumes no additional social situation exists in the family that would lead to an increase in the supplementary social allowance.

Age of the dependent child	Amount of the supplementary social allowance for a family income (in multiples of the subsistence minimum) in the previous quarter year (in CZK)		
	1.0 SM*	1.2 SM	1.4 SM
From 0 to 6 years	634	423	212
From 6 to 10 years	709	473	237
From 10 to 15 years	837	558	279
From 15 to 26 years	919	613	307

* Subsistence minimum.

Parental Allowance

A parent has the right to this allowance if s/he personally cares full-time for a child of up to four years of age, or for a child of up to seven years of age if the child suffers from a long-term disability. The parental allowance equals 1.1 times the subsistence minimum; thus, from 1 April 2000, the amount of the parent allowance equals CZK 2,695 a month.

Annex 3: Family Benefits

	Entitlements	Duration	Value	Paid by	Changes since 1989
Maternity benefit	270 insured days in last two years before delivery. Maternity benefit is provided to the mother and, only exceptionally, to the father (because of the mother's death, disability, or her inability to provide child care).	28 weeks, or 37 weeks in the case of a single mother.	69% of avarage gross income	Social insurance	Up to 1993, the amount was 90% of average net income.
Benefit for parent who takes care of a sick child (up to 15 years old)	270 insured days in last two years.	9 days, or 16 days in the case of a single parent	69% of avarage gross income.	Social insurance	Up to 1993, the amount was 90% of average net income.

	Entitlements	Duration	Value	Paid by	Changes since 1989
Birth grant	Birth grant is a universal benefit which is provided to the mother, and only exceptionally to the father (because of the mother's death).	One-time benefit	The amount of the birth grant depends on the number of children born: it equals four times the subsistence minimum for the personal needs of the child; if two children are born simultaneously, then the amount of the birth grant equals 5 times the subsistence minimum for these children; and, if 3 or more children are born simultaneously, 9 times the subsistence minimum for the personal needs of these children.	General taxes	Up to 1995, a one-time benefit of CZK 2,000.

	Entitlements	Duration	Value	Paid by	Changes since 1989
Child allowance	Mother or father or a dependent child, if child is older than 18 years and younger than 26 years.	The period up to the end of child's compulsory education and also up to the end of child's full-time university education or disability, but up to a maximum child's age of 26 years.	Income-tested benefit. The benefit is awarded to children depending on the size of the family's net income in the preceding calendar year and the size of the benefit depends on the child's age. The criterion for awarding the benefit and the base for calculating the size of the benefit is the subsistence minimum. See Annex 2 for details.	General taxes	Up to 31 October 1993, universal benefit whose size was dependent on the number of children in the family (i.e. the size of family). Up to 31 December 1995, universal benefit whose size was dependent on the children's age (the age structure of family).
Social allowance	Mother or father.	The period up to the end of child's compulsory education and also up to the end of the child's full-time university study or disability, but up to a maximum child's age of 26 years.	Income-tested benefit. The amount of the benefit depends on the size of the family's income in the preceding calendar quarter. The criterion for awarding the benefit and the base for calculating the size of the benefit is the subsistence minimum. See Annex 2 for details.	General taxes	This benefit was introduced in 1990 as the 'state compensatory allowance.' Between 1990 and 1995 the state compensatory allowance was universal.

	Entitlements	Duration	Value	Paid by	Changes since 1989
Parental allowance	It is paid out to a mother or father who takes care of a small child under fixed conditions (full-time care of a child, restriction of the carer's earnings), up to the child's fourth birthday.	The period up to the child's fourth birthday.	The base for calculating the size of the benefit is the subsistence minimum. See Annex 2 for details.	General taxes	Up to 1989 maternity allowance was provided to a mother caring for a child up to three years of age. From 1990 it was provided as a 'parental allowance' to a mother or father caring for a child up to three years of age. Since 10 January 1995 the parent allowance has been provided to a mother or father caring for a child up to four years of age.

Annex 4:
Sources of the Data Used in Tables A4.1 and A4.2 Below and Tables 1–8 in the Text

Data on the income situation of Czech households is collected by the Czech Statistical Office in the form of microcensuses of the incomes of shared-budget households, drawn up once every four years, and in the form of family accounts statistics, which are drawn up every year.

The most recent microcensus of the incomes of shared-budget households was the 1996 microcensus drawn up in March 1997 for household incomes in 1996. Since under Act no. 117/1995 Coll. the entitlement to and size of social benefits boosting the incomes of families with children changed at the start of 1996 (except for parental allowance which had changed on 1 October 1995), this latest previous data from the microcensus of household incomes were used to analyse the impact of the changes to social benefits on the income structure of families with children. The previous microcensus of the incomes of shared-budget households was the 1992 microcensus drawn up in March 1993 for household incomes in 1992.

The plan for the 1996 microcensus was to survey one percent of Czech households, which means 38,000 households in the Czech Republic, but in the end 28,000 were surveyed. The 1992 microcensus surveyed 0.5 percent of Czech households (16,000). For the samples to provide representative results, experts stipulated coefficients (weightings) for households to make them representative of the socio-demographic structure of all Czech Republic households (approximately 3,820,000 households).

Family accounts statistics represent much more detailed research into the income and expenditure of shared-budget households and are performed annually, although with a smaller sample of households (2,630 households, based on a quota selection). 1,400 households of people in employment, 350 farmers' households, 350 households of the self-employed and 530 pensioners' households are surveyed. Quota selection contains certain risks, however, the result of which is a levelling out of extremes (exclusion of high-income families). The numbers of households per social group in family accounts statistics are not entirely proportionate to their fraction of the population as a whole, which means that it is necessary to treat the results cautiously. As the latest available microcensus reports incomes from 1996, however, the family accounts statistics from 1999 were used to complement the analysis of the changes in the scope and size of social benefits in the incomes of families with children. Each comparison of the social benefits provided in 1996 and 1999 is a comparison of the data from the microcensus and family accounts.

Table A4.1
Types of families with children, in absolute and percentage terms

| | Family | | | | | |
| | Two-parent family | | Single-parent family | | Total | |
	Absolute	%	Absolute	%	Absolute	%
1992	1,153,423	89.24	139,116	10.76	1,292,539	100.00
1996	1,128,005	87.97	154,253	12.03	1,282,258	100.00
1999	942	89.37	112	10.63	1,054	100.00

Table A4.2

Number of families with children by economic activity of parents
in absolute and percentage terms

| | Two-parent family | | | | | | Single-parent family | | | | | | Total | |
| | Both parents EA | | One parent EA | | EA parent | | EI parent | | | | | | | |
	Absolute	%	Absolute	%	Absolute	%	Absolute	%	Absolute	%	Absolute	%	Absolute	%
1992	878,119	67.94	275,304	21.30	124,220	9.61	14,896	1.15					1,292,539	100.00
1996	858,277	66.93	269,728	21.04	138,167	10.78	16,086	1.25					1,282,258	100.00
1999	678	64.33	264	25.05	112	10.63	0	0.00					1,054	100.00

EA = Economically active
EI = Economically inactive

Annex 5:
Estimated Changes in the Net Costs of Employment and Education of Women at Various Income Levels

Introduction

Care for preschool children is provided mostly by nurseries (for children up to three years of age) and kindergartens (children aged three to five years). For school age children, after-school centres and clubs are provided free of charge at elementary schools. These are used by about 40 percent of pupils.[1]

While nurseries were widely available throughout the country under the socialist regime, today they are found only in larger cities. Their total numbers have fallen sharply, from 1,043 in 1990 to 118 in 2000. See Annex 1, Table A1.12. This results in part from the falling birth rate, which reduced the number of zero- to two-year-olds by 30 percent. Other explanatory factors include the introduction of parental leave and parental allowances which do not permit recipients to use child care facilities more than four days a month. In addition, some child care is being provided by unregistered individuals and organizations in the informal sector.

The number of kindergartens dropped far less than nurseries, by about one-seventh during the 1990s, and there was a commensurate drop in the number of children attending them.[2] This too is associated with a 30 percent decline in children of kindergarten age. While the network of kindergartens has been reduced and there are regional differences in availability, the number of children per class has remained constant at 22 over the entire period and the average number of children per teacher has increased slightly from 11.0 to 11.8.

While some churches have begun organizing kindergartens, today the vast majority – 98.6 percent – are managed by local councils. Since 1993 local

---

[1]   Information from the Ministry of Education, Youth and Sports, 2001.

[2]   Between 1990 and 1999, the number of children attending kindergartens decreased from 352,100 to 290,200, while the number of kindergartens decreased over the same period from 7,335 to 5,901 (*Statistical Yearbook 2001*).

councils have been permitted to charge up to 30 percent of their over-all non-investment costs as parent fees. Representative data on fees are not available. A few municipalities (in different regions) were asked by the authors to provide this information, and the reported fees ranged between CZK 150–250 monthly (CZK 300 in Prague). This amounts to US$ 4.00 to US$ 8.00 In addition, parents pay about CZK 400 monthly, or US$ 11.00, for meals. Thus there are two sources of the increase in the costs that parents pay for kindergartens – rising prices of meals and newly introduced fees.

Throughout the 1990s, the share of children aged three to five years attending kindergartens in the Czech Republic was close to 90 percent.[3] Those who attend kindergarten do so for a relatively long period, 2.7 years on average (Souvislosti, 2000, p.54).

According to a sociological survey carried out by the Research Institute of Labour and Social Affairs (Prague) in 2001 (*Family* 2001), about one-third of families with preschool-age children consider the fees for nurseries or kindergartens as having significant impact on the family budget. Consequently, many local councils provide a discount for low-income families; on the other hand, more luxurious and more expensive kindergartens, providing above-standard services, are being established.

A Model

Before constructing the model, we need to describe the basic characteristics of the economic and social environment.

- The economic activity rate of women at the age when they most often have a (the youngest) child of preschool age varies between 62 percent (women aged 20–24 years) and 77 percent (women 30–34 years).
- About 90% of children in the relevant population attend kindergartens. The costs of child care grew during the 1990s because kindergarten fees were introduced for the first time in 1993.

---

[3] In OECD countries the net rates of enrollment in preschool education by age in 1995 was as follows: aged three: 63 percent; aged four: 75 percent; aged five: 93 percent (*Education at a Glance – Indicators 1997*, OECD 1997).

- Fees have not so far been instituted at state secondary and tertiary educational institutions. Only a quarter of secondary schools and 35 percent of schools that provide lower tertiary education are private.[4] The first private schools providing higher tertiary education have been established only during the last two years[5].
- In the 1990s wage inequality grew markedly, and in 1996 income-tested family allowances were introduced. The share of family benefits in family incomes has increased insignificantly[6] in the majority of families. A relatively greater increase has occurred only in families with a greater number of children and having only one economically active member as well as in one-parent families. These are families with lower incomes per capita (less than half of the income of 'average' families with children) and with a higher share of social incomes (34 percent compared to 10 percent in 'average' families with children) as shown in Annex 1, Table A1.14b.

The following factors governed our choices in constructing the model:
- Average costs of child care in the Household Budgets Statistics are not adjusted for family types (e.g. number of children, whether children attend any child care facility, if a mother is employed), and thus we used the mode of fees found in a small survey, carried out in medium-sized cities;[7]

---

[4] Fees at private secondary schools range from about CZK 12,000 to about CZK 130,000 per school year, the average fee at private higher vocational schools was CZK 5,825 per school year in 2000 (information from the Institute of Information on Education, Prague). Estimated fees charged for some short-term training courses are CZK 3,000–10,000.

[5] Education is free in all state and church schools as well as in universities. Some fees are paid in private schools, but the state pays a per capita subsidy of some 70 to 100 percent of what a student in a state school costs. Scholarships are awarded to students from low-income families (from: *Education at a Glance – OECD Indicators 1996*, OECD 1996).

[6] The share of the most frequent benefits for families with children – child allowances – decreased, while the other benefits grew.

[7] Statistical representativeness could not be ensured, but most of the amounts reported were between CZK 150–220 (the majority about CZK 200) in 2000. In big cities such as Prague or Pilsen, the fee is higher, up to about CZK 300.

- Because of the prevalence of state schools in the Czech Republic, net child care costs as a percentage of education costs are calculated for two scenarios – when a mother studies at a state school (of any type), and when a mother attends a private higher vocational school. Many of these vocational schools are private, while the majority of universities are tuition-free state facilities. Data for private training courses are not reliable enough to be included in this study.
- Net child care costs are calculated as the difference between kindergarten fees and child care benefits.
- Particular benefits are provided under complex conditions, and their amount differs depending on earnings, other social benefits and the subsistence minimum of individual families. Therefore, we had to choose particular family types, as representative of Czech families and which could, at the same time, be described more precisely. Thus conditions for our model situations are:
  - mothers who have only one child in a kindergarten[8];
  - women earning the minimum wage who live in households with incomes at the level of the subsistence minimum;
  - women with average wages who live in households with an income level equal to 1.4 times the subsistence minimum; and
  - women with wages equal to 150 percent of the average wage who live in households with an income level equal to three times the subsistence minimum.[9]

Parental allowance is not included in this model because mothers/fathers receiving these allowances are allowed to have their children in a child

---

[8] Mothers of children of kindergarten age are more likely to be employed, and information about at least approximate fees at these facilities can be found, although they are not centrally registered.

[9] Income levels must be defined, because all state social support benefits are derived from the income level of the household; the thresholds we use here correspond with the thresholds according to which the amount of child allowance is determined. There are three levels of child allowance for each of four stated age groups of dependent children in our state social support scheme. See Annex 2.

care facility only three days a month. Should the parent wish to attend an educational course meeting one day a week (i.e. four times a month), s/he would not comply with this condition. The law does not permit any exceptions, even for the purpose of full-time study. An amendment which would permit a parent receiving parental benefits to have a child in a child care facility four days a month was introduced only in October 2001. Those who receive parental allowance may work part-time, but their monthly net earnings may not exceed the subsistence minimum.[10]

---

[10] Employed mothers/fathers with monthly net earnings higher than CZK 1,200 in 1992, CZK 1,920 in 1996 and CZK 2,190 in 2000 (i.e. the amount of the subsistence minimum for an adult person) are not eligible for parental allowances. In these years parental allowances were: CZK 1,200 in 1992, CZK 2,112 in 1996 and CZK 2,409 in 2000.

Table A5.1

Summary of net minimum wages, net average women's wages, selected social benefits and estimated school fees
(data per month, in CZK)

Year	1992			1996			2000		
Income group	Minimum wage	Average wage	150% average wage	Minimum wage	Average wage	150% average wage	Minimum wage	Average wage	150% average wage
Net earnings	1,914	3,090	4,635	2,175	7,276	10,914	3,915	9,734	14,601
Child allowances[1]	200	200	200	452	395	198	512	448	224
Social allowance	220	220	220	529	177	0	600	400	0
Allowances total	420	420	420	981	572	198	1112	848	224
Incomes total	2,334	3,510	5,055	3,156	7,848	11,112	5,027	10,582	14,825
Kindergarten fee[2] – X			0			150			200
Kindergarten fee + meals[2] – Y			160			450			680
State secondary school or state university fee – A			0			0			0
Private higher vocational school fee[3] – B	Did not exist					500			600

Table A5.1 (continued)
Summary of net minimum wages, net average women's wages, selected social benefits and estimated school fees (data per month, in CZK)

Year	1992			1996			2000		
Income group	Mini- mum wage	Average wage	150% average wage	Mini- mum wage	Average wage	150% average wage	Mini- mum wage	Average wage	150% average wage
Net child care costs – X	0	0	0	0	0	0	0	0	0
Net child care costs – Y	0	0	0	0	0.	252	0	0	456
Net child care costs X as a % of earnings	0	0	0	0	0	0	0	0	0
Net child care costs Y as a % of earnings	0	0	0	0	0	2.3	0	0	3.1
Net child care costs as a % of education costs – A/X, A/Y, B/X	0	0	0	0	0	0	0	0	0
Net child care costs as a % of education costs – B/Y	0	0	0	0	0	50.4	0	0	76.0

[1] One child three to five years of age.

[2] An estimate.

[3] Lower tertiary education.

Sources: Act No. 103/1988, Coll.; *Main Economic and Social Indicators of the Czech Republic 1990–2000* (Q1 2001), Research Institute of Labour and Social Affairs, Prague 2001; information pages of the Ministry of Labour and Social Affairs (www.mpsv.cz).

Chapter 4
The Gender Dimensions of Social Security Reform in Poland

*Bożena Balcerzak-Paradowska, Agnieszka Chłoń-Domińczak,
Irena E. Kotowska, Anna Olejniczuk-Merta, Irena Topińska,
and Irena Wóycicka (coordinator)*

1. Labour Market Transformation and Women's Employment and Life Choices

Polish women maintained a high level of labour force participation under the socialist regime: In 1960, 59 percent worked outside the home; in 1970, the portion was 62 percent; in 1978, 58.7 percent, and 1988, 57 percent. Women's access to paid work was facilitated by the labour-intensive economy, low productivity, and low wages. The socialist regime also supported their work ideologically by equating emancipation with employment. Yet the women's high level of economic activity coexisted with a traditional model of the family: the female role was perceived mainly as that of wife and mother, while the husband's main responsibility was to provide income. The easy availability of child care facilities made it possible for women to reconcile family responsibilities with paid work, but with a rising burden as shortages grew. Places in child care facilities became more difficult to secure; scarce consumer goods meant more time needed for shopping; and the lack of household services and products left working women without domestic support (Plakwicz, 1992, Kotowska, 1995, Titkow, 2001).

The effects of the transformation on women employed in these circumstances evolved over the 1990s. For a clear picture, it is useful to consider first the major changes in the economy and then their impact.

Economic development since 1989 can be divided into three periods: an initial recession brought on by rapid economic liberalization (so-called 'shock therapy'); several years of strong recovery and growth; and most recently an economic slowdown characterized by high unemployment.

- *Recession*: In 1990, Balcerowicz introduced his radical macroeconomic program. It featured withdrawal of state subsidies, tight monetary policy, liberal trade regulations, privatization, and labour market restructuring. During the first two years of the transition, there was a cumulative decline in GDP of 20 percent and rising unemployment. By December 1991, the number of unemployed exceeded 2.1 million and the unemployment rate reached 11.4 percent.[1]

- *Recovery*: A turnaround commenced in 1992, with rising GDP growth and declining inflation. By 1994, both wages and employment levels had also begun to increase. The recovery was marked by the rapid development of the private sector. Its robustness made Poland one of the fastest growing CEE countries.

- *Slowdown*: Since 1998, there has been a slowdown of growth and higher unemployment. GDP growth declined from 6.8 percent in 1997 to 4.8 in 1998 and then to only one percent in 2001. During 1998–2000, employment declined by 795,000.[2] In September 2001, the unemployment rate exceeded 16 percent.[3]

By 2000, the portions of the economically active among both men and women had been reduced by about 14 percent, each, compared to 1988. For men, the economic activity rate had dropped from 74 to 64 percent, whereas for women, it had dropped from 57 percent to 49 percent.[4]

The economically active population is of course comprised of two groups – the employed and those who are unemployed and seeking work. In terms of unemployment, women experienced greater hardship. In 1992, women's

---

[1]   Appendix 2, Table A2.3.

[2]   Appendix 2, Table A2.2.

[3]   Overall changes in the labour force and employment are shown in Appendix 2, Tables A2.1 and A2.2.

[4]   Appendix 2, Table A2.1.

unemployment rate was 15.2 percent, compared to 12.4 percent for men. In the late 1990s, the economic slowdown caused male unemployment to rise to 14.2 percent of the economically active population compared to 18.1 percent for women (2000 figures).[5] These rates include significantly higher levels of long-term unemployment among women – 52 percent compared to 36 percent for men (2000). It is important to note that in Poland, educational attainment does not protect women against unemployment to the same extent as men. While unemployment rates by women with tertiary education remained stable during most of the 1990s (5.2 percent), unemployment rates among men with tertiary education declined from 5.8 percent in 1992 to 4.3 percent in 2000. For women with post secondary and vocational secondary education, the unemployment rate increased from 14.7 percent in 1992 to 16.4 percent in 2000, while for men with the same education, it remained steady (10.7 to 10.6 percent). Married women have been hit harder than single women. This seems to be due to their continuing status as secondary wage earners and the greater demands of the market economy for labour mobility. For women between 30 and 44, the unemployment rate is more than twice as high among married women than single women (Kowalska, 2000).[6]

Women also have greater difficulties entering the work force and reentering it (Ingham, 2001; Sztanderska; 2000, Kotowska, 2001; Kowalska, 1996, 2000). This is evidenced in a significantly higher unemployment rate among women who are recent college graduates – in the first year after graduation, ten percentage points higher than that for men (Kowalska 2000). Once unemployed, women have a probability of labour force reentry that is about one fourth lower than that of men.[7]

Furthermore, women experience disadvantages in compensation levels and access to top jobs. Gender pay differentials continue to exist throughout the Polish economy, with the gap averaging about 20 percent (Kotowska 1997;

---

[5]   Appendix 2, Table A2.4.

[6]   Higher unemployment rates can be found among married women across the age spectrum except for age 20–24.

[7]   Labour force surveys show that women's probabilities of transition from unemployment to work were 0.290 in the period November 1997–November 1998 compared to 0.380 for men.

Ingham, Ingham 2001; Ingham, Węcławowicz, 2001). The gap is greatest among the highest paid workers, where it grew by 13 percentage points between 1985 and 1997.[8] There is an increasing feminization of some sectors – i.e. women are generally underrepresented in private sector and industrial jobs and overrepresented in the public sector and some low-paid service occupations, especially health care and education.[9] Only one third of parliamentary deputies, high-ranked officials, and managers are women; and only 2.8 percent are employers, compared to 4.9 percent for men.

The intractability of these disadvantages is increased by a certain social acceptance of men's stronger labour market position. In 1990s, a World Value Survey showed that 51.5 percent of Polish respondents agreed with the statement, 'If the number of jobs is not sufficient, men have a right over women to get one.' A 1994 survey confirmed this result (Siemieńska, 1997). Moreover, a rapid fertility decline in the 1990s was invoked by advocates of a conservative approach to women's and family issues as an argument against women working outside the home, further reinforcing this perspective (Siemieńska, 1997).[10]

2. Family Benefits

Family benefits underwent considerable change during the 1990s. The reforms were driven by several different motivations, which sometimes caused inconsistent policies or policy shifts over time. First, there was a need to decouple benefit eligibility from employment status. Poland had a tradition of Bismarkian social benefits linked to employment; but the massive unemployment and rising poverty in the early 1990s created a need for other bases for eligibility and ways of reaching target populations. Second, as previously noted, a large

---

[8]   The female/male wage ratio for a white-collar worker in the ninth decile declined from 70.6 percent in 1985 to 63 percent in 1991 to 56.1 percent in 1995, and rose modestly to 57.5 percent in 1997 (Kotowska, 1997, Appendix 2, Table A2.9).

[9]   The female–male wage ratio in October 1998 was 77.3 percent in the public sector and 82.3 percent in the private sector (Ingham, Ingham, 2001, p.59).

[10]   The total fertility rate declined from 2.078 in 1990 to 1.376 in 2000.

drop in the birth rate made demographic trends unfavorable for population maintenance. This motivated changes in social benefits which were designed to encourage larger families.[11] Third, social policy was shaped by shifting political ideologies. During 1997–2001, the AWS, the largest party in the Parliament and the one with closest links to the Catholic church, introduced measures to support larger families and increase maternity leave. In January 2002, under the new leadership of the SLD (post-communist) government, the Parliament reduced maternity leave, reduced benefits to the middle classes, and limited eligibility for many benefits to the lowest income groups. Fourth, the prospect of membership in the European Union created a new external pressure for gender equality in all public programs, including social benefit schemes. Finally, fiscal pressures created a need to cut government expenditures and, at the same time, the rise in poverty in the early 1990s created a need for anti-poverty measures. Given that none of the post-socialist governments in Poland has assigned a high priority to gender issues, these pressures were translated into significant cuts in benefits which are utilized by women.

Reflecting these motivations, the main thrust of the reforms was as follows:

- Some benefits which had been linked to employment in state enterprises were transferred to the state budget or placed under the jurisdiction of local governments;
- A new class of social assistance benefits was introduced to address rising poverty;
- Some benefits were expanded for multiple-child families;
- Child raising and child care benefits were made available to either parent on an equal basis; and
- Social spending was restricted by: i) converting universal benefits into means-tested ones; ii) reducing benefit adjustments (i.e., switching from wage to price indexing); and iii) tightening eligibility for income-tested benefits via a new and more restrictive standard, the 'social minimum.'

---

[11] In 1999 there was a real drop of 13,400 in population compared with 1998, when the natural increase was about 6,000. The urban population declined by 15,400. In 2000 the natural increase was about 10,300 while the annual drop amounted to 9,400. In cities, the population decline was greater, 30,500.

Changes in the Social Security Benefit Structure[12]

a) **Maternity Leave and Benefit**

The major changes made since 1989 are two-fold: (i) an increase in the length of maternity leave, followed two years later by a reduction, and (ii) an extension to fathers of the right to use a part of this benefit.

i) *Benefit duration* – Until 1999, there were no changes in maternity benefits. Then the Parliament under the AWS majority extended the duration of maternity leave and benefits as a means of promoting increased childbearing within the family by providing support for women in reconciling maternal and professional obligations. From 1 January 2000, maternity leave, and with it the period over which maternity benefits are paid, was extended from 16 to 20 weeks for the first and all successive births, and from 26 to 30 weeks for multiple births. As of 1 January 2001, maternity leave was further extended to 26 and 36 weeks, respectively.

These changes turned out to be short-lived. In January 2002, the new leftist government largely negated them as part of a larger effort to reduce social expenditures. Maternity leave and benefits were cut back to 16 weeks for the first birth, 18 weeks for the second and each subsequent birth, and 26 weeks in the case of multiple births.

ii) *Fathers' maternity benefits* – The right of a father to utilize part of a mother's maternity leave was also introduced on 1 August 2001. Under this reform, fathers can use two weeks out of the mother's 16 week leave or four weeks out of 18 weeks, as applicable. As yet, there are no statistics showing the division of maternity leave and benefits between father and mother.

---

[12] There are currently no maternity, family, or child care benefits that are universal in coverage. Some benefits are employment related (child care benefits), some are income-tested (family allowances), and some are both (child raising benefits). Maternity leave, child care leave, and child raising leave and their attendant benefits are all employment-linked. For details regarding the changes in social benefits during 1989–2001, see Appendix 1, Table A1.1.

Box 1
Maternity leave and benefit in Poland

Maternity leave and benefits are provided for qualified female workers who give birth to a child, adopt a child, or provide foster care. A portion of these benefits may be shared with the child's father. The length of maternity leave is 16 weeks (this can be divided into 14 weeks for the mother, two for the father) upon giving birth for the first time and 18 weeks (can be divided into 14 weeks for the mother and four for the father) for the second and each successive time, and 26 weeks in the case of multiple birth. Benefits amount to 100 percent of the employee's average wage for the three–month period preceding the leave.

Maternity benefits for individual farmers are payable for eight weeks. In this case, the amount of benefit is PLN 4 a day (US$ 1.00).

Financing source: Social insurance revenues, including contributions and state budget subsidies.

---

b) Child Care Leave and Benefit[13]

First introduced in 1954, the regulations on child care leave and benefit remained unchanged up to 1995. A revision in that year extended equal rights to these benefits to men and women. This reform was promoted by the Civil Rights Ombudsman, who maintained that the previous law discriminated against men. The proposal was the subject of a lively legislative debate, in which some argued that equal treatment for men and women would be costly since the benefits reflect the recipient's previous wages.[14] To offset this possible cost increase, the child care benefit was reduced from 100 to 80 percent of recipient wages.[15]

---

[13] In Poland, child care leave and benefit are not equivalent to child care leave and benefits in the other countries of this study, which might be better compared to the Polish child raising leave and benefit. See subsection c).

[14] The average wages paid to men are about 20 percent higher than the average wages of women.

[15] A similar adjustment was made in sickness benefits.

Box 2
Child care leave and benefit in Poland

The child care benefit is available to an employee taking a leave of absence from work in connection with care for a child. Such an absence may be taken for care for a sick child up to age 14 or for a healthy child up to age eight in the following cases:

- An unforeseen closure of a nursery school, kindergarten, or elementary school attended by the child; or
- The illness, childbirth, or stay at an in-patient health care institution of the spouse caring for the child on a permanent basis.[16]

Both parents have equal rights to this benefit.

The benefit amount is 80 percent of the employee's previous remuneration. The period of disbursement of the benefit is 60 days per year, regardless of the number of children.[17]

Financing source: Social insurance revenues, including contributions and state budget subsidies.

---

c) **Child Raising Leave and Allowance**

The main purpose of child raising leave is to provide job security for parents who take time off to care for young children.[18] First introduced in 1968, child raising leave consisted of one year of leave without pay. In 1972, the period of leave was increased to 36 months. It then went unchanged for

---

[16] Leave may also be taken for care for another sick family member living in the household.

[17] If the care is directed at another family member, the maximum benefit period is 14 days.

[18] These guarantees include:
- Stability of work relations. The employer can neither serve notice nor terminate the employment contract during the period from the date of application for child raising leave up to the date of its end. Termination may occur only in the case of specific conditions (as defined in the Labour Code, such as the liquidation of the work place).

24 years, until 1996 (see below). A complementary child raising allowance was introduced in 1981 to provide financial support during leave for low-income families. This allowance was means-tested, and therefore some parents are eligible for the former but not the latter. While the child raising leave may extend up to 36 months, the allowance may be collected only for 24 months.

A reform introduced in 1996 extended the right to take child raising leave to men (previously a father could take such leave only in restricted circumstances – e.g. upon the death or illness of the child's mother). This change was motivated by an effort to provide equal rights for men and women and, indirectly, to strengthen the position of women on the labour market.

The child raising allowance was first set as a percentage of the average wage in the national economy and, until 1996, was indexed to average wage growth. Since then, the allowance has been indexed according to changes in consumer prices. As wage growth exceeded price growth in Poland, the importance of this allowance as a component in family income has been systematically diminished.

In 1999, higher child raising benefits were extended to persons bringing up a third child and subsequent children. The objective of this change was to combat poverty among larger families, as well as to address the decline in the fertility rate.

- Return to work. The employer is obligated to accept the employee for work at a position equivalent to that which he or she occupied prior to the commencement of the leave, or any other position in line with the worker's qualifications for remuneration no lower than that due at the position occupied prior to the leave.
- The period of child raising leave is considered as a part of the period of employment with the given employer (who granted the leave) as well as part of the period of time taken into account in establishing rights to pensions.

Box 3
Child raising leave and allowance in Poland

Child raising leave may be taken for up to 36 months in order to care for a child up to age four. It may be extended for another 36 months if the child is disabled, chronically ill, or mentally retarded and requires care, but for no longer than the child's 18th birthday. Guarantees of job retention are extended to all recipients of this leave.

The child raising allowance is paid to a person who is on child raising leave and lives in a two-parent household in which per capita income does not exceed PLN 548 (the social minimum income in 2001). A single parent may receive the allowance if household per capita income does not exceed PLN 612. The allowance is generally paid over a period of 24 months (36 months for a single parent raising a child and for a person caring for more than one child born at a single birth). In 2001, the child raising allowance amounted to approximately 60 percent of the net minimum wage. A single parent raising a child and persons raising a third or subsequent child are entitled to a higher allowance.

Both parents have equal rights to child raising leave and allowance.

Financing source: State budget revenues.

---

d) Family Allowance

The family allowance was first established in 1947 and has been revised frequently over the years. Reform legislation enacted in 1994 (effective 1 March 1995) made the following changes:

- Family allowances are entirely financed out of state budgetary resources (previously they had been paid from social insurance funds);
- A means test was applied, restricting allowances to persons in families whose per capita income does not exceed 50 percent of the average wage in the national economy; and[19]
- The basis for adjustments of the allowance was shifted from wage increases to the consumer price index.

---

[19] This restriction disqualified 16 percent of otherwise eligible Polish families.

In 1997 the amount of the family allowance was made variable based on the number of children, thus providing higher benefits to larger families.

In 2002, as part of its effort to reduce state expenditures, the new government substantially restricted the income criteria for family allowances and introduced price indexation to replace the previous wage indexation.

Box 4
Family allowance in Poland

Family allowances are payable for children (and, in certain cases, a spouse) living in families whose per capita income does not exceed PLN 548 (the social minimum income, in 2001). Single parents receive the allowance if their per capita family income does not exceed PLN 612. The family allowance may be granted to farmers if their acreage is small, that is, less than two equivalency ha (4.9 acres) per family member.

Entitlement to the family allowance exists with respect to:

- A child aged up to 16, or up to 20 if continuing his or her education;
- A spouse if he or she is caring for a disabled child, is over 60 in the case of women and 65 in the case of men, or is disabled.

The basic allowance applies to the first and second child. It is increased to a higher amount for the third and every subsequent child. In 2001, allowances for two children amounted to 16 percent of the minimum wage; for three children, to 26 percent; and for four children, to 38 percent.

Financing source: State budget revenues.

---

e) Benefits from the Alimony Fund

Benefits from the alimony fund were introduced in 1974 to assist single parents (overwhelmingly women) who had been awarded alimony but whose former spouse declined to pay it. This benefit has been changed several times since 1989. Income-related criteria were first waived and later reinstated (1989 and 1999, respectively). A ceiling was placed on benefits, first at no more then 25 percent and later, 30 percent, of the average monthly earnings in the national economy. In 2002, eligibility for benefits was restricted to those with per capita family income of less than PLN 612, the social minimum for a one-person household.[20]

Box 5
Benefits from the alimony fund, Poland

Benefits from the alimony fund may be granted to a person who is unable to collect alimony awarded by a court and whose income per family member does not exceed 612 PLN (the social minimum for a two-person household in 2001). Benefits are paid at the level of the adjudicated alimony, up to a limit of 30 percent of the average monthly wage. In 1999, the maximum level of benefits paid represented about 72 percent of the net minimum wage.

Financing source: Benefits are financed from a combination of state budget revenues and repayments to the fund from alimony.

---

f) Social Welfare Benefits

In 1990, the government established a new social welfare system to assist low-income families with a wide range of problems, including homelessness, unemployment, orphanhood, disability, pregnancy and single parenthood, and incapacity in child raising or household management. Benefits are means-tested and financed from state and local budget revenues and calculated using the OECD equivalence scale for households.[21]

Two social welfare benefits have particular importance from a gender perspective:

i) *The guaranteed periodic benefit* is payable to a person who has exhausted his/her right to unemployment benefits and who is raising a child as a

---

[20] The benefit had previously been granted to a person whose income per family member did not exceed 60 percent of the average wage in the national economy.

[21] Under this scale, a coefficient of 1.0 is assigned to the first person in the household, 0.7 for the second and every successive person above the age of 15, 0.5 for the second and every successive person below the age of 15. The amount so established is adjusted applying the consumer goods and services price indicator. As of 1 June 2001, to qualify for social welfare benefits the level of income cannot be greater than PLN 447 per single-person household, PLN 406 for the first person in the family, PLN 285 for the second and successive persons aged over 15, and PLN 204 for family members below the age of 15.

single parent. The benefit is payable for a maximum of 36 months, but will cease in any case when the child completes elementary school or reaches age seven, whichever comes sooner.[22] The benefit amount equals the qualifying income criterion for social welfare benefits: As of 1 June 2001, this was PLN 447, or 88 percent of the net minimum wage. Benefits are paid at this level for the first 12 months, while for the next 24 months they are reduced to 80 percent of this initial amount, or about 70 percent of the minimum wage.

ii) Benefits for pregnant women and women raising children were introduced in 1993. The concept of the new benefit arose parallel to anti-abortion legislation, as a measure to help pregnant women from low-income families. A pregnant woman or a woman raising a child who satisfies the income criteria of the Act on Social Welfare may receive payments as follows:

- The benefit amount is calculated as the difference between the qualifying criterion for social welfare and the actual income of the woman. In 2001, an upper limit was set at PLN 406, representing 72.5 percent of the net minimum wage;
- Eligibility extends from birth to the fourth month of the life of the child;
- A one-time cash payment is made for every newborn child; and
- Benefits are adjusted according to the consumer price index.

Originally benefits were paid for 12 months, and the amount equaled 28 percent of average monthly earnings in the national economy. However, program expenditures dramatically exceeded the government's estimates; and it responded first in 1994 and again in 2001 with cuts in the duration of benefits and the amounts.

Starting in 2002, this benefit was transformed to the periodic maternal benefit, granted to the mother (or father) for the first four months of the child's life. The benefit amount is the difference between the income criterion in the Act on Social Welfare and the actual income of the applicant. It cannot exceed a set amount (PLN 406). There is also a one-time maternal benefit (PLN 195).

---

[22] Until the end of 2001, the benefit could be provided until the child was age 15.

Changes in the Scheme Expenditures, Use, and Benefit Levels

a) Expenditures

The share of spending on family benefits in total social expenditures declined throughout the decade, as shown in Figure 1.[23] The share of these benefits in the GDP rose at the beginning of the decade but has been declining since 1992 (Figure 2). This second pattern partly reflects changes in GDP due to the economic downturn and subsequent recovery.

Figure 1

Expenditure on benefits as percentage of social expenditure, Poland

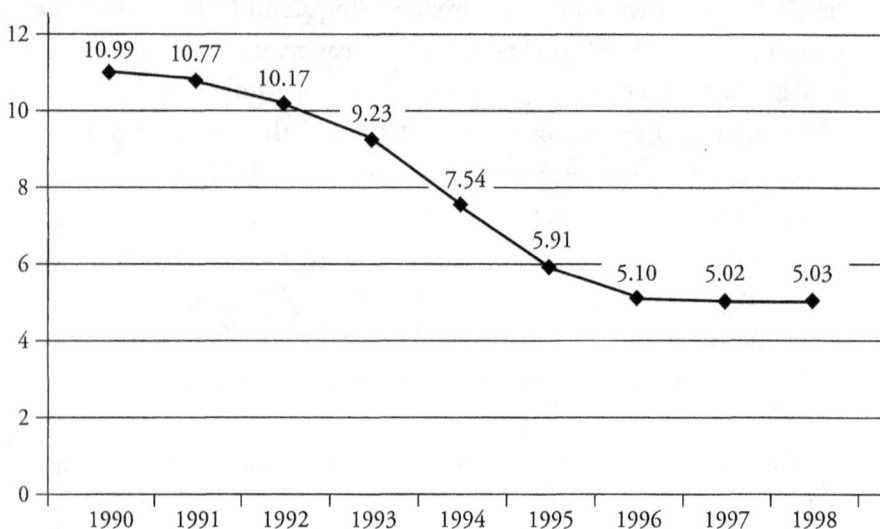

Source: Hagemejer, Liwiński, Wóycicka, 2002.

b) Number of Beneficiaries

There are several discernable patterns in the changes in scheme beneficiaries, including: i) a decline in the number of beneficiaries of employment-linked benefits (i.e. maternity benefits, child care benefits, and child raising benefits); ii) a decline in the number of family allowance beneficiaries; iii)

---

[23]   Also see Appendix 2, Tables A2.12a and A2.12b.

Figure 2
Expenditure on family benefits in Poland as a percentage of GDP

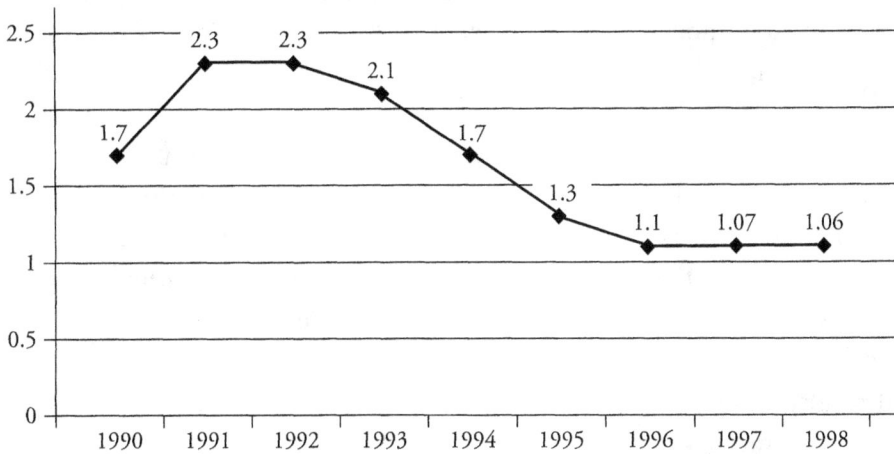

Source: Hagemejer, Liwiński, Wóycicka, 2002.

an increase in the number of recipients of alimony fund benefits; and iv) a rise and fall in the recipients of social welfare benefits.[24]

Benefits paid in connection with employment declined due to a combination of the net loss of jobs since 1998, better control placed on some benefits, and the dramatic decline in birth rates (a 30 percent decline in the annual number of births between 1990 and 1999). In addition, some studies find a growing reluctance on the part of workers, overwhelmingly women, to use such benefits for fear of losing their jobs.[25] The extent of

[24]   Appendix Table A1.11.

[25]   Surveys conducted by the Center for Women's Rights (2000) and the Institute of Labour and Social Studies (Balcerzak-Paradowska 2001) suggest a growing reluctance on the part of women to make use of such benefits as child care leave and child raising leave, due to fear of losing employment. There are cases where women returning from child raising leave are soon laid off. The research also shows that some employers even require that young female job applicants provide medical certification that they are not pregnant, and there are cases in which signing a declaration waiving entitlement to child care leave is a prerequisite for a woman being hired (Center for Women's Rights 2000 studies).

reduction was dramatic, in the range of 30–60 percent, depending on the scheme. Between 1990 and 2000, the annual number of days for which maternity benefits were paid declined from 47.8 million to 30.5 million; the annual number days of child care benefits declined from 22 million to 6.5 million; and the annual number of employees receiving child raising allowance declined from 282,000 to 164,000.[26]

The number of family allowances declined by about 30 percent, from 10.8 million in 1990 to 7.3 million in 2000. This was due primarily to the drop in the birth rate and the means testing of the allowance in 1995.

In contrast, the number of benefits paid from the alimony fund increased dramatically, from 116,000 in 1990 to 436,000 in 2000. This was due to the waiving of the income criterion between 1989 and 1999, described earlier, as well as to the decline in the economy and the growth of unemployment, which increased the number of those unable to meet their alimony obligations.

Finally, the number of beneficiaries of social welfare first grew, peaking for most programs around 1998, followed by a decline. The decline does not correspond to an improvement in economic conditions in Poland but rather to its growing fiscal problems. In terms of the need for social welfare, there was clearly no decrease: income below the limit set by the Act on Social Welfare was earned by 13.3 percent of the total population in 1997, 12.1 percent in 1998, and 14.4 percent in 1999. In addition, the number of unemployed who lost their eligibility for unemployment insurance increased from 1.08 million in December 1995 to 2.1 million in 1999. At the same time, however, there was a fall in the numbers of people benefiting from guaranteed benefits for single parents raising children (from 58,740 in 1998 to 55,680 in 2000), as well as benefits for expectant mothers and those raising children (from 130,343 in 1998 to 125,393 in 2000). This was the result of the lowering of amounts earmarked for social welfare benefit payments administered by state and local governments. This latter factor has had the greatest impact on limiting numbers of beneficiaries.

---

[26] See Appendix Table A1.11.

c) Benefit Levels

In terms of their levels, the benefits under examination can be classified into two main categories:

- Those in which the amounts paid are *based on the personal remuneration* received by the beneficiary, i.e., maternity and child care benefits. In this case, an increase in average remuneration results in an increase in the average level of such benefits. While maternity benefits remained at 100 percent of personal remuneration, child care benefits declined to 80 percent; and

- Those in which the level of payment is set *in line with standards* (pursuant to legal regulations) that are periodically updated in accordance with price increases. All remaining benefits in this study are now set in this way: child raising benefits, family allowances, the ceiling on benefits from the alimony fund (individual benefits are dependent on adjudicated alimony levels), and social welfare benefits. Growth in benefit levels has been slower for this category than for the former one. Furthermore, the ratio between these benefits and the minimum and average wages (substitution rate) has generally been falling, though with some fluctuations. See Annex 2, Tables A2.13a and A2.13b.

Child Care Institutions: Cost and Availability

Before 1989, child care institutions were organized and managed by units of the state administration and by state enterprises. Places in kindergartens were in great demand because of the relatively high employment level of mothers and because in the 1970s attendance at pre-school or kindergarten became mandatory for children beginning at age six. The number of places in child care institutions was always insufficient in relation to needs.[27] However, there was far less parental demand for nurseries. Some children of nursery age were taken care of by mothers on child raising leave or by other members of the family (grandmothers). In 1989, 34 percent of the children aged three to six were attending kindergarten, while only 4.4 percent of the children up to age two were enrolled in nurseries.

---

[27] In 1980, there were 124 children attending kindergarten per 100 places.

After 1989, local governments (*gminas*) were made responsible for operating nurseries and kindergartens. Under this arrangement, kindergartens could be public or non-public, with the latter eligible to receive payments from the *gminas* for up to 50 percent of the per child costs of public kindergartens.[28] Almost immediately, *gminas* began to experience a financial squeeze due to falling revenues and rising costs. Revenues contracted due to the general crisis in public finance. Between 1990 and 1997, state and local government revenues for child care declined from 0.46 to 0.39 percent of GDP (or by 17 percent), while revenues for nurseries declined from 0.10 to 0.03 percent of GDP (70 percent).[29] At the same time, the operating costs of these institutions increased due to elimination of state subsidies on basic goods and diseconomies of scale in operations, with the latter due mostly to reduced enrollment brought about by the declining birth rate.

Between 1990 and 1999, the number of kindergartens dropped by nearly a third (from 12,308 to 8,733) and the number of nurseries, by about two thirds (from 1,412 to 469).[30] This decline did not, however, result in a shortage of kindergarten places, as the portion of children of kindergarten age who were actually enrolled increased over the decade, from 32.8 to 39.1, and the number of children attending per 100 places increased from 96 to 99. Rather, the reduction in available slots served to offset the reduced number of kinder-garten-aged children.

Though there is no greater scarcity of places, *gminas* did pass their higher operating costs on to parents in the form of higher charges. While the data is spotty, it appears that parents are paying 30–40 percent of the costs of kindergartens and nursery schools.[31] These are paid in the form of increased

---

[28] A kindergarten must provide the minimum educational program set by the Minister of Education; parents do not pay for this.

[29] Appendix 2, Table A2.25.

[30] Appendix 2, Table A2.26. At the same time, the number of pre-school sections at primary schools declined by a third (from 13,565 to 10,152).

[31] A 1994 study shows that payments made by parents amounted to 20 percent of the income of infants' day nurseries and to 40 percent of the income of kindergartens (Balcerzak-Paradowska and Golinowska, 1994). Another study in progress in 2001 shows that payments made by parents averaged 30 percent of the costs of both types of institutions ('Market and Social Changes in Poland in the 1990s and Chances and Risks for Children and Youth Development' directed by Professor Anna Olejniczuk-Merta, in progress in 2001).

fees for meals, charges for services beyond the minimum educational program, and requirements for contributions to parents' committee funds.[32] Their effect on the budgets of women who work outside the home will be considered in Part (d) of the following section.

Impact of the Changes at the Household Level

How were these changes in social expenditures reflected in family budgets? Data to address this question are presented here in five parts. The first traces changes in maternity, family, and child care benefits as a percentage of household income over the period 1988–99. Second, the current importance of these benefits is considered for different population groups. Third, the portion of social benefits of all types received by women is compared with that received by men. The fourth part considers the impact of increased child care costs on family budgets and, in particular, their effect on work incentives/disincentives for women with various income profiles. The final section considers the impact of the reforms on the division of household work and child care.

---

[32] According to the 1991 survey by Olejniczuk-Merta, average payments made by parents to pay for meals equalled PLN 50.54 per month. Payments for meals vary greatly: from less than PLN 10 (when a child is covered by special reductions of costs) to PLN 250. If a child attends a kindergarten and does not use any additional services, parents make monthly payments of approximately PLN 180, which is 38 percent of the minimum wage (net). Additional activities involve added fees (all in PLN): foreign language lessons – 22.19; sports activities – 19.14; music classes – 13.48; speech therapy – 17.14. Excursions on average cost 38.71, trips to cinemas and theatres, 37.21. Costs of additional activities are covered in full or in a major part by parents: foreign language lessons – in 100 percent of cases; music classes – in 83 percent of cases; corrective gymnastics – in 40 percent of cases; dance classes – in 100 percent of cases; speech therapy – in 25 percent of cases; excursions – in 70 percent of cases; trips to cinemas, theatres, etc. – in 90 percent of cases. Other expenditures are usually covered by the parents' committee's funds, in rarer cases from budgets of kindergartens.

a) Longitudinal Changes, 1988–1999

The effort to trace social spending changes over time is impeded by a lack of data, as well as by the frequency of policy changes during the period examined and the resulting shifts in spending categories. In addition, changes in household sampling techniques and concepts make some data incompatible. Thus, these findings should be treated cautiously. The analysis is based on data from household budget surveys (HBS).[33] Tendencies are presented for 12 years, 1988–1999, in Annex 2, Table A2.20. The main patterns are as follows.

Table 1				
Share of selected social benefits in household income, Poland*				
	1988	1992	1993	1999
Household income	100	100	100	100
Total social benefits	23.08	32.73	31.71	31.02
Maternity	0.14	0.12	NA	0.10
Family & nursing allowances**	4.16	4.15	3.42	1.24
Child raising benefit	0.16	0.31	0.37	0.20

* Data for 1988 and 1992 are not fully comparable to data for 1993 and 1999 due to methodological changes.

** Nursing allowance, which covers assistance to the elderly or very ill, has been added here because the main statistical sources do not permit this allowance to be broken out from the other benefits.

Source: See Annex 2, Table A2.20.

---

[33] Household budget surveys are conducted every year by the Central Statistical Office (Główny Urząd Statystyczny, GUS). Each year the sample contains over 30,000 households, or over 100,000 individuals. Since 1993, the sample has been representative of virtually the whole population, excluding foreigners or people living outside 'standard' households (in dormitories, for instance). Before 1993, the survey also excluded households of the self-employed, policemen, and military personnel, so its representativeness was lower.

As can be observed in Table 1, the share of benefits that support women was a very small portion of all the social benefits received by households at the beginning of the transition; and it is considerably lower now than then – 1.54 compared to 4.46 percent (sum of last three rows). The largest benefit, family and nursing allowances, underwent the greatest decline. At the end of the 1980s, these allowances represented more than four percent of net household income. By the end of the 1990s, their share had dropped to 1.24 percent.

The share of maternity benefits in household income was also lower at the end than at the beginning of the decade. On the other hand, the child raising benefit rose in the beginning of the 1990s but declined later. In both cases, it is hard to say how much of the decline was attributable to the demographic changes and how much to the reforms.

It is noteworthy that changes in the income share of all social benefits taken together are different from that of the benefits examined here. At the beginning of the transition, there was an increase of the share of social benefits such as pensions and unemployment support, followed by a stabilization. In 1988–1990, the total of all social benefits constituted about 23–26 percent of household income, whereas in 1992 it had risen to nearly 33 percent. This indicates that the policy towards women-supporting benefits was more restrictive than the one towards pensions, giving less protection to women and families with children than to the elderly. Pensions were reduced less due to budget cutbacks than family and child care benefits.[34]

b) Distribution of Benefits

The share of benefits varies quite significantly according to the type of household, as illustrated in Table 2 and shown in more detail in Annex 2, Table A2.14. Households living on social benefits are the main benef-iciaries, and receive far more than the others in relative terms. For them, these benefits represent over nine percent of disposable income; family

---

[34] Under the new pension reform, however, pensions are predicted to decline in the coming decades.

Table 2

Social benefits per capita in Poland, by socioeconomic category of household, 1998

Income and benefits	Socioeconomic category of household[a]							
	Worker/employee	Farmer-worker	Farmer	Self-employed	Pensioner (receiving retirement pensions)	Pensioner (receiving disability pensions)	Living on social benefit[b]	Total
Disposable income	100.00	100.00	100.00	100.00	100.00	100.00	100.00	100.00
	Percent (disposable income = 100)							
Social benefits received by household								
Total social benefits	10.7	18.3	20.9	7.2	86.3	79.7	50.5	31.7
Total benefits for women and families[c]	1.76	2.49	1.39	0.92	0.51	1.41	9.34	1.60

Source: Appendix 2, Table A2.14.

All items: net, in current prices; in cash and in kind (when applicable).

a Households have been grouped according to the main source of income (compare: GUS)

b Including households living on temporary jobs.

c Includes maternity benefits, family allowances, nursing allowances, child raising benefits, social assistance benefits for pregnant women, and benefits from the alimony fund.

allowances alone constitute almost four percent; benefits from the Alimony Fund, over two percent; and child raising benefits, almost two percent. For this group of households, only the maternity benefit is completely unimportant. Maternity benefits, which are work-related, are also negligible in farmer households, and – for obvious demographic reasons – in pensioner households. Social assistance benefits for pregnant women are virtually absent in all households except those living on social support in general.

As shown in Table 3, the share of benefits received is closely related to the level of per capita household income. For all benefits except maternity, the higher the income, the lower the share of benefits. Even the nursing allowance, which is not income tested, follows this pattern. The decline of the benefit share is most visible for family allowance. It drops from nine percent in the first income decile group to zero in the tenth group. On the other hand, the child raising benefit reveals the weakest decline in its share with increasing household income.

Family size and status strongly affect the amount of benefits received, as shown in Table 4. Although the share of all social benefits is highest in single person households, the share of women/family support benefits is the highest for single-parent and multiple-child families.[35] This is mainly because of the high share of family allowances in disposable income, but also the share of child raising benefits is quite high for these two groups.

---

[35] In 1995, 14 percent of Polish families were headed by a single female, and one percent were male-headed single parent families. Calculations are the authors' based on *Demographic Yearbook*, 2000, CSO, p.93.

Table 3
Social benefits in Poland per capita, by income decile, 1998

| Income and benefits | Income decile[a] number | | | | | | | | | | |
	1	2	3	4	5	6	7	8	9	10	Total
	Percent (disposable income = 100)										
Disposable income	100.0	100.0	100.0	100.0	100.0	100.0	100.0	100.0	100.0	100.0	100.0
Social benefits received by household											
Total social benefits	55.4	33.3	31.0	29.5	32.9	33.8	35.1	37.8	36.0	22.0	31.7
Total benefits listed below:	12.03	6.50	4.13	3.05	2.17	1.37	0.88	0.56	0.40	0.15	1.60
Maternity benefits	0.2	0.1	0.1	0.2	0.2	0.1	0.1	0.0	0.1	0.1	0.1
Family allowances	8.9	4.4	2.5	1.9	1.3	0.8	0.5	0.2	0.1	0.0	1.0
Nursing allowances	1.0	0.5	0.4	0.3	0.3	0.2	0.1	0.1	0.1	0.0	0.2
Child raising benefits	1.0	0.9	0.6	0.4	0.2	0.2	0.1	0.1	0.1	0.0	0.2
SA benefits for pregnant women	0.2	0.1	0.1	0.0	0.0	0.0	0.0	0.0	0.0	0.0	0.0
Benefits from Alimony Fund	0.8	0.5	0.4	0.2	0.2	0.2	0.1	0.1	0.1	0.0	0.1

Source: See Appendix 2, Table A2.15.

All items: net, in current prices; in cash and in kind (when applicable).

[a] Deciles for persons, according to the per capita disposable income.

Table 4
Social benefits in Poland per capita, by family type, 1998

Income and benefits	Single person	Parents + 1 child	Parents + 2 children	Parents + 3+ children	Single parent with children	Other hhlds with children	Other hhlds without children	Total
Disposable income	100.0	100.0	100.0	100.0	100.0	100.0	100.0	100.0
				Percent (disposable income = 100)				
Social benefits received by household								
Total social benefits	61.8	12.0	7.9	13.4	25.3	26.0	50.0	31.7
Total benefits listed below:	0.08	1.02	2.01	5.64	7.55	2.32	0.48	1.60
Maternity benefits	0.0	0.2	0.2	0.1	0.0	0.1	0.0	0.1
Family allowances	0.0	0.4	1.4	4.5	2.3	1.4	0.2	1.0
Nursing allowances	0.1	0.1	0.2	0.5	0.4	0.2	0.1	0.2
Child raising benefits	0.0	0.3	0.2	0.4	1.0	0.3	0.1	0.2
SA benefits for pregnant women	0.0	0.0	0.0	0.0	0.1	0.0	0.0	0.0
Benefits from Alimony Fund	0.0	0.0	0.0	0.1	3.7	0.2	0.1	0.1

Source: See Annex 2, Table A2.16.

All items: Net, in current prices; in cash and in kind (when applicable).

c) Social Benefits Received by Women and Men

It may be interesting to look at the various social benefits paid to men and women to see which gender adds more benefits to household income. For this analysis, only those benefits for which recipients may be reasonably identified by sex have been chosen: pensions, unemployment, and social assistance benefits (permanent and temporary).[36]

As shown in Table 5, women and men on average bring almost the same portions of benefits to the household: women 51 percent and men, 49 percent. There are, however, marked differences if one looks at separate benefits. Women are the main recipients of survivors' pensions (receiving almost 90 percent of such pensions), as well as of social assistance (over 70 percent). Women receive less than men, however, in retirement and disability pensions.

This overall pattern changes slightly with household type. In farmer households, for instance, women are not major recipients of social assistance, but they receive more than men in the form of retirement pensions.

The share of various benefits received by women does not vary much according to the household's income level, as shown in Table 6. However, some fluctuations in the share of benefits received by women may be seen as one moves from the lower to the higher income deciles. See Table 6. Unemployment benefit is the only one showing a certain regularity: the share received by women increases with the household income level. However, there is no income-related pattern with respect to other benefits: no matter what income decile is considered, women remain major recipients of survivors' pensions and social assistance, while their shares in disability and retirement pensions are below parity.

Family type influences the share of benefits received by women but only to a degree. As shown in Table 7, single-person households reveal a different pattern than the others. Here women are major recipients of retirement

---

[36] Unfortunately, HBS information on household members receiving family or nursing allowance is unreliable, so these benefits – which can be received by either men or women – cannot be considered. On the other hand, there is no need to examine who received maternity benefits or benefits for pregnant women (only in 2001 did men become eligible for maternity benefits).

Table 5
Social benefits in Poland received by women by socioeconomic category of household, 1998

	Socioeconomic Category of Household[a]							
	Worker/ employee	Farmer-worker	Farmer	Self-employed	Pensioner (receiving retirement pensions)	Pensioner (receiving disability pensions)	Living on social benefit[b]	Total
	Percent (benefit of household = 100)							
Benefits received by women (total)	53.3	54.4	55.5	57.5	45.9	58.9	57.5	51.1
Retirement pensions	59.6	55.3	60.4	61.8	44.5	83.0	48.7	47.6
Disability pensions	44.8	49.4	52.6	48.9	67.4	41.5	57.0	46.8
Survivor pensions	76.1	80.6	58.8	79.8	70.0	95.6	45.5	88.8
Unemployment benefits	59.1	53.0	47.9	68.7	42.5	47.3	42.5	51.8
Permanent SA benefits	74.1	59.3	43.0	78.0	62.3	66.3	83.6	71.6
Temporary SA benefits	80.7	94.9	78.8	93.2	80.3	59.7	76.3	76.3

Source: See Appendix 2, Table A2.17.

All items: net, in current prices; in cash and in kind (when applicable).

a   Households have been grouped according to the main source of income (compare: GUS)
b   Including households living on social benefits.

Table 6
Social benefits in Poland received by women, by income decile, 1998

Income Decile[a] Number

	1	2	3	4	5	6	7	8	9	10	Total
	Percent (benefits received by household = 100)										
Benefits received by women (total)	50.3	51.8	51.2	51.5	51.7	53.1	53.2	51.1	50.0	49.4	51.1
Retirement pensions	57.6	53.6	50.1	50.6	48.3	50.3	50.8	48.8	45.1	43.9	47.6
Disability pensions	42.7	40.3	45.8	44.9	48.5	49.5	48.6	43.7	50.0	48.4	46.8
Survivor pensions	82.9	88.1	82.0	80.8	78.9	86.3	87.9	89.3	93.3	93.9	88.8
Unemployment benefits	33.8	49.0	52.7	48.7	65.6	55.1	56.4	62.4	64.0	60.7	51.8
Permanent SA benefits	66.3	82.3	80.1	74.7	68.7	66.5	53.9	55.6	77.8	100.0	71.6
Temporary SA benefits	76.1	83.7	71.7	81.6	82.0	87.9	67.7	85.9	35.2	9.0	76.3

Source: See Appendix 2, Table 18.

All items: net, in current prices; in cash and in kind (when applicable).

[a] Deciles for persons, according to the per capita disposable income.

Table 7
Social benefits in Poland received by women, by family type, 1998

	Single person	Parents + 1 child	Parents + 2 children	Parents + 3+ children	Single parent with children	Other households with children	Other households without children	Total
					Percent (benefits received by household = 100)			
Benefits received by women (total)	79.3	36.0	40.6	39.5	81.1	55.8	43.7	51.1
Retirement pensions	78.1	23.9	24.1	20.6	74.0	55.9	39.7	47.6
Disability pensions	64.6	35.8	34.7	28.7	80.2	49.7	46.5	46.8
Survivor pensions	98.8	88.9	88.1	87.1	96.9	76.3	80.2	88.8
Unemployment benefits	53.7	55.7	61.8	50.8	100.0	48.9	45.7	51.8
Permanent SA benefits	84.1	63.5	59.6	70.6	91.1	71.2	64.7	71.6
Temporary SA benefits	46.2	76.0	69.3	79.9	95.4	78.3	71.3	76.3

Source: See Appendix 2, Table A2.19.

All items: net, in current prices; in cash and in kind (when applicable).

pensions (their share is almost 80 percent) – a reflection, no doubt, of women's longer life expectancy. On the other hand, households consisting of single women receive less than men in temporary social assistance.

d) Net Costs of Employment for Women with Different Earnings Profiles

The above section, 'Child Care Institutions: Cost and Availability' showed that the portion of institutional child care costs which parents must pay as fees rose significantly during the 1990s, to approximately 30–40 percent of total fees. This section assesses these costs in relation to the wages of women with different earnings profiles. Ideally, such a comparison would show how child care fees changed as a percentage of wages over time. This is not possible in Poland, however, due to a lack of fee data, which is not collected systematically.[37] Thus, the evaluation will consider the portion of wages which these fees consume in a single year, 2000.

Based on a recent survey of nursery schools and kindergartens in various sized cities as well as villages, we estimate that the average kindergarten fee for one child amounted PLN 180 per month and the fee for a day nursery, PLN 60 per month.[38] To evaluate employment costs for women with different wage profiles, we compared these child care costs with women's net wages (Table 8).

---

[37] While exact figures are not available, we estimate that the ratio of the average child care fee to the average wage increased between 1992 and 1996 by zero to two percent, and by a further three to five percent between 1996 and 2001. In these same periods, the proportion of the incomes of child care institutions being paid by parents is estimated to have grown by one to two percent, and two to three percent respectively (estimate by Professor Anna Olejniczuk-Merta, 2002).

[38] The cost of child care is set by each *gmina* and thus varies by locality. The survey on which this estimate is based was carried out as part of the research project, 'Market and Social Changes in Poland in the 90s and Chances and Risks for Children and Youth Development' directed by Professor Anna Olejniczuk-Merta, Institute of Commerce and Consumption, Warsaw.

	Kindergarten		Nursery	
	One child	Two children*	One child	Two children*
Child care costs as percentage of:				
Net minimum wage	38	76	13	25
Women's net average wage	19	37	6	12
Women's net wage, highly-qualified specialist	9	18	3	6

Table 8
Child care fees as percentage of net wage in 2000, Poland

Source: *Statistical Yearbook*, Warszawa, 2001, and author's calculation.

* These calculations do not take into account discounts for the second child which are offered by some institutions, so this figure may be lower in reality.

As can be observed, the cost of kindergarten for average earners is relatively high when there is more than one child of three to six years old in the family – at least 37 percent of net wages. These costs become extremely high for a woman with low qualifications who earns the minimum wage in the economy: If a woman has two children aged three to six years old, the costs of kindergarten could consume more than 75 percent of her net wage. For a woman earning low and average remuneration, the costs of nursery school are more affordable but still significant.[39] These costs seem easy to cover from wages only if low and average earners have only one child in care.

Some kindergartens have a policy of reducing or annulling payments for children from low-income families or from families with many children. Among kindergartens covered by the 2001 survey, 40 percent offer such discounts frequently and 20 percent, rarely. Approximately 20 percent of the children in the institutions surveyed benefit from this policy of fee reductions.

---

[39] While there are no exactly comparable data, a 1992 study reported that child care costs represented about 15–20 percent of average wages (Balcerzak-Paradowska and Golinowska, 1994).

These calculations seem roughly in line with the responses of parents surveyed as part of the 1991 study. Forty-five percent reported that payments for kindergartens are moderate expenses in their family budgets, while 18 percent considered these payments as major expenses which required them to forego addressing other needs. The remaining 36 percent did not consider such fees a significant expense. Nursery fees were a moderate expense for 51.6 percent of the surveyed families and a serious expense for 13 percent. Unfortunately, there are no comparable data for those who do not send their children to kindergarten or nursery school, so we can only speculate about their reasons for this choice.

It is difficult to estimate the adequacy of child care benefits in relation to these costs. The family allowance in 2000 was PLN 40 per child month, so would cover 75 percent of the average cost of one child in a nursery, but less than 25 percent of the average cost of one child in a kindergarten, for those families which were eligible for this benefit. Families that meet the income criteria entitling them to receive social welfare benefits can get special cash benefits to cover the cost of services provided by nurseries or kindergartens, but the scale of such assistance is not known. Child raising benefits are paid to those on child raising leave from employment, so cannot be used to pay for child care.

In sum, child care costs – and their incentive effect on employment – seem to depend heavily on the age of the child. Nursery costs are low, and do not pose a barrier even to women earning low wages, especially if there is only a single child in care. However, child care costs for low and average income women with children in the three to six year age group become high, and may deter such women from entering or re-entering the labour market. Social assistance benefits to cover child care costs may be available for women with very low incomes, and some child care institutions offer discounts to low-income families. Family allowance is insufficient to cover kindergarten costs.

e) **Impact on the Gender Division of Household and Care Work**
Neither the economic changes nor the policy reforms which took place during the transition produced equality in the gender division of household and care work, both of which remain mostly women's responsibilities.

However, some increases in the percentage of men engaging in such activities can be noted.

According to the most recent Time Use Study carried out as a pilot survey by the Central Statistical Office (1996), the mean time spent on household work by women was nearly double that of men, that is, nearly five hours per day for women compared to two and a half hours for men.[40] Moreover, a higher percentage of women than men were involved in household work, 94 percent compared to 80 percent.

A comparison of these figures with a similar survey undertaken in 1984 shows that the situation 1996 represents modest progress toward equality.[41] Two comparisons are of interest. First, the percentage of both genders involved in household work increased from 1984 to 1996; it increased more for men than for women. Specifically, the percentage of men rose from 63.7 to 83.5 while that of women, from 96.6 to 98.1.[42] Second, the mean time spent on such work increased for men and declined for women. The mean average household work time for men rose from 2 hours and 10 minutes to 2 hours and 36 minutes per day, while for women the mean decreased from 5 hours 9 minutes to to 4 hours 50 minutes per day. These findings seem to indicate an increasing involvement of men in household work, which may in part be due to increased unemployment and perhaps also to some shifts by gender in household responsibilities. However, the latter hypothesis requires additional investigation.

It is noteworthy that although child care leave and child raising leave and benefits have been available equally to men and women since 1996, there are no statistics available on their use by men and women. The failure to collect and publish data on this issue may in itself indicate that the

---

[40] The nationally representative sample consisted of 2,484 persons aged ten years and over who were investigated by use of the questionnaire based on EUROSTAT recommendations (*Time Use Survey 1996*, CSO, 1998). The respondents were asked about their activities during one working day and one weekend day in October.

[41] The different methods used in these surveys as well as different classifications of daily activities do not allow for detailed comparisons between them. Thus, only these general observations can be offered.

[42] *Time Use Survey for 1996*, CSO, 1998, p.140.

reforms were driven more by the EU accession process than by a policy of encouraging greater equality in the gender distribution of caring activities. Moreover, there is no evidence, even anecdotal, that men are using these benefits.[43]

Wider Economic and Social Impacts of Reform

Beyond the quantifiable impacts of the reforms on household incomes and budgets, it is also important to consider their effects on the broader environment in which women and men live and work. This is necessarily a speculative exercise, since broad social and economic changes typically have complex causes. Nevertheless, there are grounds for considering two possible influences.

The first is the creation of so-called welfare traps for low-income women with limited skills. While the development of social assistance and the means-testing of family and child care benefits have the advantage of targeting assistance toward those most in need, this approach may also discourage women from taking up employment. This seems a particular risk with the guaranteed benefit which is available to unemployed single parents under the social welfare system.[44] Close observers perceive that a significant number of women who receive this benefit consider it 'rightfully theirs.' Taking up employment would mean foregoing it, and, at 88 percent of the net minimum wage, the loss could be very significant in relation to possible earnings. Though it is difficult to document, the availability of this benefit may be leading some women who would otherwise try to work to remain in the social welfare system.

Second, in combination with several other factors, the reforms may be contributing to low birth rates. As shown in section 2 ('Changes in the Social Security Benefit Structure'), women were far less protected from the economic hardship of the early 1990s than other groups such as the elderly. While the

---

[43] Similarly, there is no statistical evidence of the use of maternity leave and benefits by men, introduced in 2000.

[44] See subsection (f), (i) of this section.

government expanded spending on early retirement and disability benefits in order to absorb excess unemployment and avoid massive poverty among older workers, its approach to the social benefits which are of special importance to women was mostly to trim and curtail them. The reduction in these supports occurred at the same time that women's position on the labour market weakened.[45] Thus, women were disadvantaged in two realms simultaneously. Though this impact is also hard to quantify, this double hit may have led some to delay or forego childbearing.

Conclusions: Gender Impact of the Reforms of Family Benefits

Women's position on the labour market changed dramatically at the beginning of the 1990s. While both genders suffered losses due to rising unemployment, the higher rates experienced by women left them in a worse position than men. Government policies regarding women and family ranged from passive to harmful. As a result, public support for the reconciliation of parental and work responsibilities has been weakened considerably. This occurred at the same time that labour market conditions deteriorated in ways that made it far more difficult to combine work and family responsibilities.

Rather than explicitly supporting women and family, the governments of the 1990s directed social policy reforms at the lowest income groups in order to combat growing income differentiation and poverty. The recipients of family benefits are now almost entirely persons with low incomes; the types of benefits targeted at the poorest have been expanded (within the framework of social welfare); income criteria have been introduced to determine eligibility for most preexisting benefits (except the employment-related maternity and child care benefits); and the income limits have recently been lowered, further restricting the numbers eligible to receive them. The policy towards benefits that support women has been far more restrictive than that towards pensions.

---

[45] This was evidenced by women's higher unemployment rate, greater difficulty entering and reentering the labour market, and the rising gender wage gap for white collar workers. See Section 1.

Although the share of social benefits in the households has remained relatively stable, the share of women and family supporting benefits has decreased.

Although significant progress has been made since 1989 with respect to equal rights for men and women to make use of family-oriented benefits (child care, child raising, and maternity benefits and leave), there is no evidence that men are claiming these benefits. The traditional family model remains strong despite the fact that most families have two breadwinners, and domestic work and child raising remain mostly women's tasks.[46] The strong competition for jobs and the greater loss of family income if men take child care leave mean that there is no financial incentive for them to make use of this benefit. There are, however, some indicators of change in the division of household work between men and women, especially in the younger generation.

The means testing of social benefits created work disincentives for women, as did the rising costs of child care. There are indications that those receiving guaranteed temporary benefits (three years) have little incentive to seek paid work, especially if they have limited skills. Due to the relatively high costs of kindergartens, the employment costs for low- and middle-income women with more than one child are high.

The opportunity costs of child care periods (child raising benefits) increased significantly in the transition period and are progressive with income. Women with higher remuneration lose more than those whose earnings are low. Men, who on average have higher remuneration than women, lose the most.

Women's opportunity costs of marriage and child bearing have also increased and may be one factor in the dramatic decline in fertility. Postponement of child bearing and marriage, and reduction in the number of children desired by couples, can be seen as adjustments to the new harsher labour market conditions.

---

[46]   However, as previously noted, there are some indicators of changes in the division of household work between men and women, especially in the younger generation.

3. Pension Benefits

In Poland, social insurance for the risks of old age, disability, and survivorship consists of three systems that cover different groups of society. The largest in terms of the number of insured persons and beneficiaries covers employees and self-employed persons (approximately 12 million insured persons and over seven million pensioners). The second system covers farmers (approximately 1.5 million insured persons and two million pensioners), and the third covers the uniformed services, including soldiers, policemen, etc. (financed from the state budget, approximately 0.4 million pensioners).

In the years 1989–2000, the social insurance system underwent numerous reforms. In 1990, a new act on social security for farmers was adopted, which changed the benefits formulae, as well as the organization and financing of this insurance. In 1992, a new act came into force which changed the formulae for old-age, survivors', and disability pensions for employees and the self-employed. These changes provided a stronger link between benefit levels on the one hand and years of work and compensation levels on the other, while at the same time introducing a new redistribution factor in the benefit formula.

However, the most far-reaching reform to date was the reform of old-age pensions for employees and the self-employed adopted by the parliament in 1998 and implemented in 1999. This reform was necessary because the system existing in 1998, with its high replacement rate and low retirement age, was not financially sustainable. In the short term, this system required large annual subsidies from the state budget. In the long run, demographic projections indicated growing deficits due to a graying of the Polish population and an increase of the elderly dependency ratio.

The main aim of the reform was long-term financial sustainability of the old-age pension system. This was to be achieved through a decrease of wage replacement rates and an increase of the retirement age. In addition, it was assumed that a partial shift from pay-as-you-go financing to pre-funding of pensions would help to achieve this aim.[47]

---

[47] For a detailed description of the changes in the laws on the old-age and survivors' pensions, see Appendix 1, Table A1.2.

Box 6
1998 reform of the old-age pension system in Poland
for employees and the self-employed

The main features of the reform were:

- Workers' contributions were divided between two old-age pension pillars: the pre-existing public, pay-as-you-go scheme and a new system of privately managed individual savings accounts. This splitting of contributions was mandatory for workers under age 30 and optional for those aged 30–50, while those over 50 remained in the preexisting public system.

- The new private pillar is pre-funded, with the savings invested and managed by private pension funds. The government guarantees a minimum rate of return, if other measures to ensure good returns fail. There is still no law in place specifying how savings in individual pension accounts will be converted to annuities at the time of retirement.

- The public scheme was transformed from a defined benefit (DB) scheme with substantial redistribution toward low-income workers to a Notional Defined Contribution (NDC) scheme in which benefits will be based on each worker's own contributions. The amount of the pension will be calculated by dividing the accumulated contributions paid by the average statistical life expectancy of the worker's age cohort at retirement age (gender neutral life tables will be used in this calculation). Thus, benefits will decline automatically in response to increased life expectancy (unless the individual keeps working and delays retirement). Individual accounts will be established to record each worker's contributions. Past contributions will be adjusted at the rate of the increase in the Consumer Price Index plus 75 percent of the real growth of wages which are subject to contributions. This reform applies to all those who were 50 or younger on the date the reform came into force; others will continue to be covered by the preexisting DB system.

- Beginning in 2007, all early retirement entitlements will be eliminated (special provisions enabling early retirement to continue for a relatively narrow group of occupations is foreseen).

Changes in the Pension System with a Gender Impact

Benefit Formula

Under the pre-reform pension formula, a pension consisted of two parts: a constant element corresponding to 24 percent of the average wage, and an earnings-related element, which depended on the wage level and work history of a pensioner. The constant element was equal to about a third of the pension for an average wage earner. Its weight in pensions of low-income earners with shorter tenure was higher than in the case of those with higher incomes and longer tenure. As women tend to have lower wages and shorter average tenure than men, this element caused their pensions to be higher on average than if they had been calculated according to purely actuarial criteria.

In both the first and second pillars of the new pension system, benefit levels depend on the sum of contributions paid during working years and life expectancy at retirement. The gender wage gap in Poland is approximately 20 percent, and women's retirement age is five years earlier than that of men.[48]

---

[48] Average monthly wages of men and women in October 1999.

Table 9

Average gross wages and salaries in PLN

	Total	Men	Women	Women (men=100) %
Total	1,800	1,991	1,592	80
Legislators, senior officials and managers	3,975	4,414	3,273	74
Professionals	2,293	2,813	1,999	71
Technicians and associate professionals	1,831	2,265	1,619	71
Clerks	1,635	1,681	1,619	96
Service workers and shop sales workers	1,218	1,419	1,087	77
Skilled agricultural and fishery workers	1,284	1,310	1,188	91
Craft and related trades workers	1,586	1,700	1,083	64
Plant and machine operators and assemblers	1,674	1,720	1,441	84
Elementary occupations	1,111	1,243	1,026	83

Source: GUS (2000), authors' calculations.

Both factors are reflected in the retirement pensions, to the detriment of women.

According to the simulations done for this study and presented in Section 4, the average old-age pension for women under the old system (with retirement age at 60) was 75 percent of the average man's pension (with retirement at 65). The simulation shows that, under the new system, the average woman's pension would drop to approximately 55 percent of the average man's, taking into account the differences in the retirement age.[49]

Retirement Age

Although the reform did not introduce any changes in the retirement age, which remains 60 for women and 65 for men, the elimination after 2006 of the formerly broad early retirement entitlements will mean a rise in the actual retirement age for men from 59 to 65 and for women from 56 to 60. With the larger increase for men, the gap between men's and women's pensions will widen. On average, women will have smaller accumulations in both the first and second pillars than men, and the accumulated amount of contributions paid will be divided by longer remaining average life expectancies, due to women's earlier retirement age. Before, the difference between the retirement ages of men and women was reflected in benefit levels but to a considerably smaller degree, due to a redistributive benefit formula which benefited those with shorter work careers.

---

[49] According to ZUS statistics, today the average old-age pension for a woman amounts to just 66 percent of that for a man (ZUS, 1999). The difference between the simulation results, as explained above, and this statistic probably results from different *actual* retirement ages and the differential availability of pension privileges for men versus women. Neither of these factors was taken into account in the simulation. The difference may also be partially explainable by variations between the general population and the insured population.

Caring Credits

Until 1991, periods of child raising leave were treated as equal to contributory years in calculating pension benefits. After 1991, employment years were taken into account in the benefit formula at a rate of 1.3 percent of the individual assessment base (average earnings) for each such year, and caring periods at only 0.7 percent, thus reducing the future pension that a care provider would eventually receive compared to the previous formula.[50]

Under the 1998 reform, any period of contribution, no matter how short or how little is earned, will be counted for pension purposes; but there are no longer any periods for which pension credits are earned without payment of contributions. Thus, the impact of caring credits on a woman's benefit depends entirely on whether contributions are paid and, if so, at what level.

The 1998 reform law also stipulates that contributions for caring periods are paid from the state budget and, regardless of a care provider's previous earnings, are calculated on the basis of the minimum wage in the national economy.[51] This state budget contribution is an explicit subsidy from general revenues, replacing the indirect cross subsidies within the pension system with that existing prior to the reform. The use of the minimum wage makes these credits far less advantageous for middle- and high-income persons than the previous system.

Furthermore, taking into consideration the gender wage gap, the new system does not create any incentives for men to take child care leave.

The reforms also restricted the duration of child care periods that can be counted for purposes of earning a pension. Prior to 1992, child care periods were treated in the same manner as periods of work for purposes of satisfying the duration-of-work requirement for a pension. In 1992, a limit was placed on such periods so that they, along with certain other noncontributory periods, could not exceed one third of a person's total work history. This regulation is

---

[50] Appendix 1, Table A1.2.

[51] The reform has not changed the situation of persons on maternity leave but has worsened the situation of those who are taking child care leave. While the contributions for periods of maternity leave are paid by the state budget on the basis of the parent's former wage, child care leave periods are no longer covered by social insurance.

incorporated into the new old-age pension system for purposes of establishing eligibility for the minimum old-age pension.

Sex-differentiated Annuity Rates in Private Savings Scheme

Under the new Notional Defined Contribution (NDC) system in the public pension pillar, gender neutral life expectancy tables will be used to compute annuities at retirement. This means that women's greater average life expectancy will not result in lower benefit levels.

As explained previously, no legislation has yet been enacted with respect to the provision of annuities by the mandatory private second pillar of the pension system. There have been no decisions made on the type of entities (public or private) that will provide annuities or on the regulations regarding the benefits to be provided, i.e. whether annuities will be calculated, as the private companies favor, using sex-differentiated life expectancy tables. These decisions will be crucial in determining women's future material well-being in retirement in Poland.

If the benefit formula for the second pillar would allow for the use of separate life expectancies, the gap between women's and men's projected replacement rates is estimated to increase by 5.5 percent at retirement age 60 and by more than eight percent at retirement age 65.[52]

Benefits in the Event of Divorce

Before 1999, a divorced person had no right to any part of the old-age pension of her (his) former husband (wife).[53] Under the reform, funds accumulated in the second pillar private pension funds, to the extent that these constituted common property of the spouses, are subject to division in the case of a divorce or annulment of a marriage.[54] A portion of these funds are then transferred to the private pension account of the other spouse. (A similar rule applies in the event of death of one of the spouses.)

---

[52] See simulation in Section 4.

[53] However, a divorced spouse could receive a survivor's benefit under certain conditions. See Appendix 1, Table A1.2.

[54] On the basis of the regulation of the Civil Code.

A regulation promulgated pursuant to the new law also stipulates that a former spouse can only obtain benefits out of the accumulated capital in her (his) pension fund account if s/he is entitled to an old-age pension. If the person is not so entitled, it is possible for him/her to receive the entire accumulated capital after reaching retirement age. While this rule makes sense generally as a way of ensuring that the components of the pension system work together it disadvantages female surviving divorcees who, as will be explained subsequently, may receive a survivor's benefit as early as age 50. The regulation needs to be revised to correct this inequity.

Impact of other periods out of full employment or partial employment

The portion of registered unemployed women who are ineligible for unemployment benefits is about ten percentage points higher than for men (in 2000, 83 percent versus 73 percent, see Annex 2, Table A2.29).[55] Payments of social insurance contributions are made only for those unemployed who receive unemployment benefits, so these payments reflect the underlying gender disparity in eligibility. Under the new pension system, future pension benefits are directly related to contributions. Therefore, periods of unemployment without benefits (and consequently without state contributions to the pension system) will mean lower eventual pension income.

At the same time, the reform benefited those who work part-time, among whom women are disproportionately represented.[56] Under prior law, pension participation was mandatory for persons working half-time and for a period of at least two weeks. Under the reform, mandatory social security insurance was extended to include any work that is less than full-time, and regardless of its duration.[57] Since more women than men have part-time and sporadic employment, the new law should improve the coverage of women. However, the potentially positive impact of these changes may not be achieved if the requirement for coverage stimulates higher levels of work 'off the books.'

---

[55] Unemployment benefits are paid for the first year of unemployment to those who worked for at least last 365 days before becoming unemployed.

[56] Ten percent of women and eight percent of men are part-time employees (GUS, 2000).

[57] That is, any type of work performed under employment contract or commission.

At the same time, the reform credits periods of part-time employment as a proportion of full-time employment for purposes of the minimum pension. Given the minimum number of years of work required for the minimum pension (20 for women, 25 for men), this is a more restrictive treatment than the previous one. Since women are employed on a part-time basis more often than men, the new restriction falls more heavily on them.

Simultaneous Eligibility for Different Benefits vs. Exclusiveness

Apart from a few narrow exceptions, the Polish social insurance system does not permit simultaneous receipt of two benefits. However, in cases of concurrent eligibility, the insured person always has the right to choose the most advantageous benefit. In combination with the rule described earlier on the distribution of second pillar savings in the event of divorce or death of a wage earner, this rule disadvantages widows since, as explained earlier, they can only access this capital if they themselves are old-age pensioners or they have reached the retirement age. As stated earlier, this rule is unfair and needs to be changed.

Coverage

Today in Poland virtually all men who are 69 or older receive an old-age, disability, or survivor's pension. Coverage is considerably lower among women: approximately 16 percent of those age 69 or older have no income whatsoever from social insurance (Hagemejer, Liwiński, Wóycicka, 2001).

The pension reform should contribute to increased coverage of women since, as explained previously, it abolished the minimum periods of work which were required for pension coverage. Thus, even the shortest periods of employment or child care will give entitlement to a pension.[58]

---

[58] In terms of compliance with the contribution requirement, Social Insurance Institution (ZUS) data show that the lowest compliance rates are found among firms undergoing economic reconstruction, such as railways and the coal and steel industry, where male employees predominate.

Survivors' Pensions

The 1998 reform did not introduce any changes in the eligibility criteria for survivors' pensions. A widow (widower) of an insured person who has reached age 50 (65) at the time of her/his spouse's death may receive a pension if (i) the deceased spouse was a pensioner or satisfied the eligibility criteria for a pension at the time of his/her death, and (ii) the surviving spouse is caring for a dependent child under 16 years of age, or is disabled.[59] The amount of the pension is calculated as a percentage of the old-age benefit if the spouse was retired at the time of death or as a percentage of the disability pension if s/he was still working.

While these eligibility rules remain unchanged, the reform will cause the adequacy of a survivor's pension to differ greatly depending on whether the spouse died during his or her working years or in retirement and on the survivor's age. This difference will occur because (i) the reform reduced retirement pension benefits but left disability pensions unchanged, and (ii), as explained previously, second pillar savings can only be paid to survivors who are receiving a retirement pension or have reached retirement age. Other survivors will receive only a pension based on the spouse's first pillar savings.[60]

The previous problem arises from the rules on simultaneous eligibility for two benefits, described earlier. Although a widow (widower) has a right to part of the capital accumulated by her (his) spouse in the fully-funded pillar, current regulations do not allow a survivor's pension to be combined with an annuity from the second pillar. This effectively blocks a person receiving a survivor's benefit from accessing these savings.

As the first new old-age pensions will begin to be paid in 2009, a new regulation should be adopted to allow survivor's to access second pillar savings and to receive a second pillar survivors pension. This change is vital to ensure that widows (widowers) will not be worse off under the reform.

---

[59] A divorced spouse can also receive survivors benefits if s/he meets one of these conditions and was receiving alimony.

[60] However, a surviving spouse can inherit a portion of the deceased spouse's second pillar savings.

Conclusions: Pension Options, Employment Choices and Gender Relations

In the reformed old-age pension system, the impact of factors which differentiate the situations of men and women is much greater than in the previous system. Among these factors, the main disadvantages for women are:

- The new pension formula more directly reflects gender differences in earnings;
- Child care periods and periods of caring for an ill family member will be assessed for pension purposes at the level of the minimum wage;
- The continuing earlier retirement age for women means a lower retirement benefit, even with gender neutral life-expectancy tables; and
- Women's greater risk of long-term unemployment means lower contributions to the public NDC system and private pension funds, both of which will be directly reflected in lower benefits.

Alongside these disadvantages, the new system also promotes gender equity in certain ways, namely:

- Spouses have a right to part of the funds accumulated in the second pillar in the event of divorce or death;
- The minimum period of covered work required for pension eligibility is abolished. This will benefit women with brief contribution periods due to long-term family care or unemployment. They will no longer have to pass a threshold in order to receive a benefit based on the limited contributions they do make to the pension system.

Based on the preceding analysis, we offer the following recommendations:

- Retirement ages for men and women should be equalized. The continuing existence of unequal retirement ages in the new NDC system will strongly disadvantage women. This is because, unlike the old benefit formula, the new one i) takes account of average remaining life expectancy at retirement, and ii) provides no redistribution toward low-income workers. In combination with a gender wage gap, these features are a recipe for poverty in old age for women. While public opinion on this issue still favors an earlier retirement age for women, support for equalizing the ages is growing.[61] Thus, public education is needed to bring home the point that the current system embodies a combination of features that is highly disadvantageous for women.

- New regulations are needed to allow those who are eligible for a survivor's benefit but not of retirement age to access their spouse's second pillar savings. When a new law is drafted specifying how savings in individual pension accounts will be converted to annuities at the worker's retirement, it should allow for payment of survivors' pensions financed from second pillar savings. This too is vital to prevent poverty among widows who may receive a survivor's pension before retirement age.

- The draft law on annuities from the second pillar should mandate the use of gender neutral life expectancy tables. This is justified by the fact that the second pillar, though privately managed, is nevertheless part of the social security system and has public purposes. The most basic of these is to prevent poverty by providing benefits which support a decent standard of living. Given the continuing gender wage gap in Poland and the total absence of redistribution toward low earners in the new pension system, the use of gender-specific life tables will thwart this public policy objective. To operate this pillar entirely on private industry principles would relegate a large portion of Polish women to poverty in old age.

---

[61] A CBOS poll in March 2002 found that 54 percent of those surveyed favored an earlier retirement age for women even at the cost of a lower pension benefit. In October 1999, 78 percent had answered 'yes' to a similar question. The percentage of those favoring equal retirement ages had grown over the same period from 19 to 28 percent. CBOS, Warsaw, March 2002.

4. Simulation: Pension Reform and Women's Old-Age Security

This section presents simulations of the impact of the 1998 pension reform on the future pension benefits of men and women. Five main conclusions can be drawn from these simulations:

- The projected replacement rate in the new pension system will be considerably lower than in the old one;
- The replacement rate for men retiring at age 65 is projected to be almost twice as high as that for women retiring at age 60;
- The pension increases significantly with the age of retirement. This creates financial incentives to retire later;
- Use of gender neutral life expectancies in the pension formula reduces the difference in pension size that would otherwise occur; and
- Lifetime earnings exert a stronger influence on pension size in the new pension system, while the old system favored those with higher earnings at the end of their working careers.

In order to assess the impact of wage and tenure on pensions, several simulations were prepared assuming different work and earnings profiles for women and men. For comparison, the simulated value of a pension under the non-reformed pension system is also presented. However, one must bear in mind that such a comparison is artificial, as the old pension system was not financially sustainable.

Assumptions Used in the Simulation

The economic assumptions used for the simulation are presented in Table 10.[62] They are based on a consistent set of economic variables (wage growth, rate of return) as well as existing law on indexation rules for the NDC system.[63]

---

[62] For a discussion of the methodology, see Castel and Fox (2000).

[63] Assumptions are consistent with assumptions used for simulations in Agnieszka Chłoń-Domińczak, 'The Polish Pension Reform of 1999,' in: Elaine Fultz (ed.), *Pension Reform in Central and Eastern Europe, Vol. 1, Restructuring with Privatization: Case Studies of Hungary and Poland* (Budapest: ILO, 2002).

Table 10
Economic assumptions used for Polish projection

Year	Notional accounts indexation	Second pillar rate of return	Wage growth
2000	1.139	1.147	1.146
2005	1.061	1.086	1.051
2010	1.051	1.068	1.045
2015	1.034	1.051	1.040
2020	1.025	1.034	1.034
2025	1.027	1.034	1.037
2030	1.029	1.034	1.038
2035	1.029	1.034	1.038
2040	1.026	1.034	1.038
2045	1.024	1.034	1.038
2050	1.023	1.034	1.038

Source: *Social Budget Model,* The Gdansk Institute for Market Economics.

Additionally, to eliminate the impact of demographic variables on the simulation results, we assumed the life expectancies forecast for 2050 in all the calculations. This had a strong influence on the results, since life expectancy at retirement age is expected to increase by over 20 percent. See Table 11.

The two basic scenarios used in the simulations are drawn from current statistical data and embody typical male and female characteristics. In the female profile, we assumed lifetime earnings at the level of 86.0 percent of average wage in the economy and total tenure of 36.2 years (the current average tenure counted for an old-age pension, plus the difference between legal retirement age of 60 and current actual retirement age of 55.9). Similarly, for men, we assumed earnings at the level of 112.9 percent of average wage and average tenure of 42.4 years (in effect, we assumed that the tenure of future pensioners will increase by the same number of years as the actual retirement age).

Age	Life expectancy (gender neutral)		% increase in projected life expectancy (in 2050 compared to 2001)
	2001	2050	
60	19.87	24.40	22.8
61	19.13	23.55	23.1
62	18.41	22.71	23.4
63	17.70	21.88	23.7
64	17.00	21.07	24.0
65	16.31	20.27	24.3
66	15.64	19.49	24.6
67	14.98	18.73	25.0
68	14.33	17.97	25.4
69	13.69	17.23	25.8
70	13.07	16.50	26.2

Table 11
Polish life expectancies at retirement ages

Source: The Gdansk Institute for Market Economics.

Results of the simulation

Table 12 presents the results of the simulation. The pension amount reflects both mandatory pillars of the pension system – pay-as-you-go and funded. The pension formula applied to both pillars is the same – the value of accumulated pension rights or capital is divided by gender neutral life expectancy at retirement age.[64]

---

[64] During the debate on the 1998 pension reform, the Security Through Diversity campaign used more generous assumptions in simulating second pillar benefits. These no longer seem justified given the more recent economic performance in Poland. In addition, the projections made at that time failed to incorporate assumptions of increased life expectancy. See Chłon in Fultz (2002).

Table 12
Projected replacement rates in old and new systems,
% of average wage in the Polish economy

Age	Typical female		Typical male	
	New system	Old system	New system	Old system
60	22.4	64.8	30.4	79.5
61	23.6	65.8	32.0	80.8
62	24.8	66.8	33.8	82.2
63	26.2	67.8	35.6	83.5
64	27.6	68.8	37.6	84.9
65	29.2	69.8	39.6	86.2
66	30.8	70.8	41.8	87.6
67	32.5	71.8	44.1	88.9
68	34.3	72.8	46.6	90.3
69	36.2	73.8	49.2	91.6
70	38.3	74.8	52.0	93.0

Source: Authors' calculations.

As one can observe, there are significant differences between pensions for the male and female profiles, as well as between the old and the new systems. The replacement rate for women retiring at age 60 is projected at 22.4 percent of average wage in the economy, and the replacement rate for men retiring at age 65, at 39.6 percent of this average wage. Thus, a man's pension may be almost twice as high as a woman's. For the same profiles in the old system, replacement rates were more than two times higher (for both men and women), and the typical female who retired at age 60 received a pension that was nearly three-fourths that of a typical man retiring at age 65.

What explains this growing gap between men's and women's pensions? The increased importance of retirement age in the new system explains about half of it. In the old system, the difference in the retirement age mattered only from the viewpoint of working tenure – men had longer tenure on average than women. In the new scheme, however, the pension formula also takes into account life expectancy at retirement. Each additional year of age means a 1.2 to 1.9 percentage point increase in the wage replacement rate, compared to one percentage point for each year of age in the former pension system. Thus, a person retiring later has a relatively higher pension. The other half of the gap is explained by the average wage differential between women and men, since wages have greater weight in the new pension formula.

Additional insights can be gained from comparing the relative sizes of the pensions men and women would receive based on gender neutral life expectancy tables with those they would receive under gender-specific tables. In requiring that the pay-as-you-go pillar of the new pension system use the former, the reform law provides some redistribution in favor of women – women, who live longer, and men, who have shorter lives, have the same life expectancy factors used for pension calculation. This means an increase of female pensions (and decrease of male ones) compared to a purely actuarial calculation. The rules governing distribution in the funded pillar are not known, because the annuities law has not yet been enacted.[65] In the baseline scenario, it is assumed that in the funded pillar the same rules will be applied for calculation of a benefit as in the pay-as-you-go pillar. If, however, the annuities law allows for using separate life expectancies, differences in pension size between men and women would further increase. Table 14 presents simulated values for retirement pensions assuming the hypothetical scenario that gender-specific life expectancies are used in the first and second pillars. As can be seen, the gap between women's and men's pensions is higher by 5.5 percentage points at the retirement age of 60 and by more than eight percentage points at the retirement age of 65, compared to those presented in Table 13. In the case of using separate life expectancies for second pillar pension calculation, the difference would be smaller than presented in Table 14, but still it would mean deepening the pension gap between men and women.

---

[65] The draft annuity law proposed by the Buzek government included a provision that pension benefits may take into account the sex of the pensioner. However, during the first reading of this bill in parliament, this provision was heavily criticized by all political parties and was withdrawn. The Miller government has not yet presented any legislation on this subject. Thus, currently it is difficult to predict the final decision regarding the funded part of the pension system.

Table 13
Projected replacement rates in the new Polish system for gender-specific life tables
(% of average wage in the economy)

Retirement age	Women	Men
60	20.34	33.89
61	21.40	35.83
62	22.52	37.89
63	23.71	40.09
64	24.96	42.42
65	26.29	44.89
66	27.70	47.51
67	29.21	50.27
68	30.81	53.22
69	32.51	56.37
70	34.34	59.77

Source: Authors' calculation.

In the new pension system, there is no redistribution among income groups, as benefits are directly linked to lifetime contributions. In the old system, such redistribution occurred mainly through application of the constant element in the formula. As explained earlier, the pension consisted of two elements: (i) a constant one, equal to 24 percent of average wage, and (ii) an individual-related element, depending on the wage and tenure of a pensioner. The constant element was equal to about a third of a pension for an average wage earner. Its weight in pensions of people with lower earnings and shorter tenure was higher than in those of persons with higher earnings and longer tenure. As women have lower wages and shorter tenure than men, the constant element meant that their pensions were relatively higher. The diminishing role of the constant element as work years increased meant that, with higher retirement ages, the pensions of women represented a slightly smaller proportion of the pensions of men (Table 14, third column).

Table 14
Women's pension as percentage of men's pension

Retirement age	New system	Old system
60	73.6	81.6
61	73.6	81.4
62	73.6	81.3
63	73.6	81.2
64	73.6	81.0
65	73.6	80.9
66	73.6	80.8
67	73.6	80.7
68	73.6	80.6
69	73.6	80.5
70	73.6	80.4

Source: Authors' calculations.

By contrast, the relation between pensions of men and women is constant in our simulation of the new pension system and results entirely from differences in wages and tenure. Elimination of income redistribution means that income differences during working years are transformed into similar differences in pension size.

Sensitivity Analysis

In order to test the robustness of our projection, we changed some of the assumptions which underlie it and observed how these changes affect the results. We prepared two projections with alternative assumptions, one with a different distribution of wages over an individual's work career and a second with a different assumption on tenure. In the first alternative, wages increase over time and, in the second, tenure is shortened. The results are presented in Table 15.

Table 15
Projected Polish pensions in old and new systems: sensitivity analysis
(percent of pension in base scenario)

Age	Increasing wage curve		Shorter tenure	
	New system	Old system	New system	Old system
60	94.42	110.99	72.54	72.22
61	95.46	112.76	71.75	70.93
62	96.50	114.54	70.98	69.68
63	97.53	116.28	70.23	68.50
64	98.57	118.14	69.49	67.28
65	99.88	120.92	68.58	65.61
66	100.91	122.83	67.88	64.46
67	101.78	124.34	67.30	63.56
68	103.06	127.02	66.46	62.10
69	103.82	128.08	65.97	61.48
70	104.56	128.79	65.51	61.04

Source: Authors' calculations.

The first two columns represent a working career in which wages increase from 56 percent of the average wage at the age of 20 to 132 percent at age 60. This pattern is based on current female wage statistics. Since the old pension formula counted only the last ten years before retirement, it rewarded people with this distribution of wages compared to a flat earnings profile.[66]

In the new system, for retirement ages from 60 to 65, pensions are slightly lower under the alternative scenario compared to the baseline (i.e. the percentages in the first six rows of column one are all below 100). After 65, however, the pension would surpass the baseline amount (as in row seven). This gradual increase reflects the accumulation of contributions as individuals work for longer periods. The analysis presented in Table 15 shows an interesting

---

[66] Technically, the highest average salary from ten consecutive years chosen from the last 20 years of employment. Usually, however, the last ten years are higher and therefore are the only ones counted.

feature of the new pension system: as more and more earnings are taken into account, persons with longer working careers and flat earnings profiles are less disadvantaged than in the old system; and persons who pay roughly the same amount of contributions over their careers can expect similar pensions, no matter how concentrated or dispersed their earnings may be.

The second alternative scenario assumed tenure of 25 years at age 65 (11 years shorter than in the baseline scenario). Not surprisingly, this shorter working career causes a lower pension in both the new and old systems. What is interesting is that the pension reduction resulting from shorter tenure is slightly lower in the new pension system (i.e. column three figures are larger than those in column four). This means that the old pension system was more restrictive for persons with shorter working careers than the new one. However, one has to take into account that the replacement rate is also much lower in the new scheme. Thus, the reduction in pension size resulting from a shorter working career can lead to inadequate benefits.

Transition Between Old and New Systems

The preceding projections assume that an individual is covered by either the new system or the old one. However, the pension reform included some transitional provisions for those age cohorts which started their working careers before the introduction of the reform but who were 49 or younger when it was enacted. These individuals are provided with initial 'notional capital' in the NDC system – that is, they are credited on the records of the new scheme with an amount of past contributions which represents the value of their accrued pension rights under the old system as of the end of 1998. Initial capital will represent a significant part of the pensions of the oldest cohorts covered by the reform, heavily influencing their replacement rates.

In addition, the reform law provides special transition rules for women retiring in years 2009–2013 (the first five cohorts covered by the new pension system). This was necessary because otherwise there would have been a significant difference in pension size between the last cohort of women retiring in the old system and the first cohort of women retiring in the new system. Like other workers who were between age 30 and 50 at the time of the reform, these women were given a choice to join the new mixed system or not. For those who decided not to do so, pensions will be calculated according to a mixed old-new system formula (with decreasing weight given to the old formula).

The results of the simulation of replacement rates for different cohorts are presented in Figure 3. Again, in order to eliminate the influence of changing demographics, projected life expectancies as of 2050 are used. The simulation presents both replacement rates (as a percentage of last salary) for a female retiring at the age of 60 (lower series) and at the age of 65 (upper series), and both in case of joining the prefunded pillar and remaining in the pay-as-you-go system. As one can see, the replacement rates are gradually reduced from around 50 to 30 percent (with an exception for the value of mixed pensions for cohorts retiring in years 2009–2013 which are higher) for those retiring at age 60 and from 65 percent to 40 percent for those retiring at age 65. The sharper downward slope of the top line means that the year-to-year reductions in replacement rates are larger at the beginning of the reform. This will create larger differences in the pension sizes of close age cohorts who stayed in the public system than will be the case in future years.

Figure 3
Simulated replacement rates for Polish birth cohorts 1949–1974
Female retiring at age 60 (lower series) and age 65 (upper series)

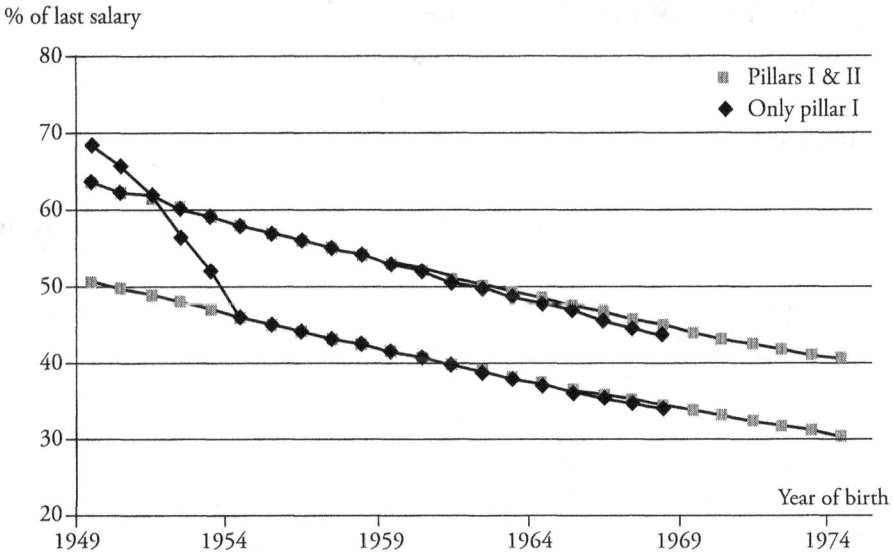

% of last salary

Legend: ■ Pillars I & II; ◆ Only pillar I

Year of birth

Source: Authors' calculations.

In sum, the pension reform is expected to have a significant impact on women's pensions, as well as on those of men. The greatest impact is a reduction in replacement rates. Benefits from the two mandatory pillars of the new pension system are going to be reduced compared to those under the old system. As transitional rules are applied, the reduction will be steepest in the early years but greater for the younger cohorts. In addition, pension reform also means elimination of redistribution toward low-income workers. As women usually have lower earnings and shorter working careers, the difference between the pensions of men and women are going to increase. Moreover, preexisting differences in retirement age will cause greater differences in pension size, as benefits are adjusted to life expectancy at retirement age. In the future, pension policy should be aimed at reducing differences in pension size, in particular by equalizing the retirement age.

References

Balcerzak-Paradowska, B. (ed.) (2001): 'Sytuacja kobiet i mężczyzn na rynku pracy w Polsce. Równość szans?' (The situation of men and women on the labor market in Poland. Equal opportunities?). *Studia i Monografie IPiSS* (Institute of Labor and Social Studies Studies and Monographs), Warsaw.

Balcerzak-Paradowska, B. (ed). (2000): 'Wpływ procesu prywatyzacji na położenie kobiet. Raport z badań' (The Impact of the Privatization Process on the Situation of Women. Study report). Warsaw: Center for Women's Rights.

Castel, P. and Fox, L. (2000): *Gender Dimensions of Pension Reform: the Former Soviet Union,* World Bank.

Domański H. (1994): 'The Decomposition of Social Stratification in Poland', *Polish Sociological Review,* no. 4, pp.335–358.

Domański, H. (2001): 'Social Mobility in Six East European Nations,' in: M. Ingham, H. Ingham and Domański, H. (eds.): *Women on the Polish Labor Market,* Central European University Press, pp.111–145.

Hagemejer K. (1999): 'The Transformation of Social Security in Central and Eastern Europe,' in: K. Müller, Ryll, V. and Wagener, V. (eds.): *Transformation of Social Security: Pensions in Central-Eastern Europe,* Physica-Verlag.

Hagemejer, K., Lliwiński, J. and Wóycicka, I. (2003): *Poland: Social Protection in Transition*. Geneva: ILO, Social Protection Sector, Financial, Actuarial and Statistical Service Branch.

Ingham, M. and Ingham, H. (2001): 'Gender and Labor Market Change: What Do the Official Statistics Show?,' in: M. Ingham, Ingham, H. and Domański, H. (eds.): *Women on the Polish Labor Market*, Central European University Press, pp.41–76.

Ingham M. and Węcławowicz, G.: 'Gender and Earnings: A Regional Approach,' in: M. Ingham, Ingham, H. and Domański, H. (eds.): *Women on the Polish Labor Market*, Central European University Press, pp.239–269.

Jóźwiak, J., Kotowska, I.E. and Kowalska A. (2000): 'Demographic Processes, the Labor Market and Education,' in: *Economic and Social Effects of Education* (in Polish). Warsaw: Institute for Problems of Contemporary Civilization, 2000, pp.87–120.

Kotowska, I.E. (1995): 'Discrimination against Women in the Labor Market in Poland during the Transition to a Market Economy,' *Social Politics*, vol. 2, no.1, pp.76–90.

Kotowska, I.E. (1997): 'Equality of Women and Men in the Labor Market,' in: R. Siemieńska (ed.): *Problems of Occupational Equality by Gender*, (in Polish). Warsaw: Scholar Publishing Company, pp.85–106.

Kotowska, I.E. (1999): 'The Second Demographic Transition and its Determinants,' in: I.E. Kotowska (ed.): *Demographic Changes in Poland in the 1990s from the Perspective of the Second Demographic Transition*, (in Polish). Warsaw: Warsaw School of Economics-SGH, Warsaw.

Kotowska, I.E. (2001): 'Demographic and Labor Market Developments in the 1990s,' in: M. Ingham, Ingham, H. and Domański, H. (eds.): *Women on the Polish Labor Market*, Central European University Press, pp.77–110.

Kotowska, I.E. and Kowalska, A. (2001): 'Labor Market,' in: M. Lubiński (ed.), *Poland: International Economic Report* 2000/2001, pp.98–108.

Kowalska, A. (2000): 'Women in the Polish Labor Market,' *Studia Demograficzne*, 2/138, pp.71–100.

Kowalska, A. (1996): *Females, Economic Activity and Their Position in the Labor Market, (in Polish)*. Warsaw: Central Statistical Office.

Liwiński, J., Socha, M.W. and Sztanderska, U. (2000): 'Education and the Labor Market,' (in Polish), in: *Economic and Social Effects of Education*. Warsaw: Institute for Problems of Contemporary Civilisation, Warsaw 2000, pp.27–85.

Kurzynowski, A. (1995): 'Aktywność zawodowa kobiet' (The professional activity of women), in Golinowska S. and Balcerzak–Paradowska, B. (ed.), *Rodziny w Polsce. Raport IPiSS* (Families in Poland. Institute of Labor and Social Studies Report), Warsaw.

Milanovic, B. (1997): *Income, Inequality and Poverty during the Transition from Planned to Market Economy*. Washington DC: World Bank.

Mills, M. (2001): 'Does Globalization Impact Family Formation? The Influence of Irregular Work Schedules in the 24 hour Economy', paper presented at EAPS European Population Conference, Helsinki, June 2001.

Panek, T., Podgórski, J. and Szulc, A. (1999): *Poverty: a Theory and Measurement Practice*, (in Polish). Warsaw: Warsaw School of Economics-SGH.

Pailhé, A. (2000): 'Family Responsibilities and Discrimination on the Labor Market,' Workshop on Gender Relations, Family and Work organized under 'Network for Integrated European Population Studies', Fifth Framework Program, with the financial support of the European Commission, Zahradky Castle, Czech Republic, September 2000.

Plakwicz, J. (1992): 'Between Church and State: Polish Women's Experience,' in: C. Corrin (ed.), *Superwomen and the Double Burden: Women Experience of Change in Central and Eastern Europe and the Former Soviet Union*. London: Scarlett Press.

Puhani, P. (1995): 'Labor Supply of Married Women in Poland. A Microeconometric Study Based on the Polish Labor Force Survey,' Discussion Paper No. 95–12, Zentrum für Europäische Wirtschaftsforschung GmbH, Labor Economics, Human Resources and Social Policy Series.

Racław–Markowska, M., Środoń, M. and Rymsza, M. (2000): 'Samotne matki jako klienci programów socjalnych' (Single mothers as welfare program recipients), paper for the XI National Convention of the Sociological Association, Rzeszów–Tyczyn, 2000.

Rutkowski, J. (1995): 'Changes in the Wage Structure during Economic Transition in Central and Eastern Europe,' World Bank, Data Report Series, Paper No. 1, May 1995.

Rutkowski, J. (1996): 'High Skills Pay Off: The Changing Wage Structure during Economic Transition in Poland,' *Economics of Transition*, vol. 4(1), pp.89–112.

Rutkowski, J. (1997): *Low Wages Employment in Transitional Economies of Central and Eastern Europe*, MOCT-MOST, No. 1.

Siemieńska, R. (1997): 'Values and Attitudes Conditioning the Females Presence in the Labor Market,' in: R. Siemieńska (ed.), *Problems of Occupational Equality by Gender*, (in Polish). Warsaw: Scholar Publishing Company, pp.61–83.

Steiner, V. and Kwiatkowski, E. (1995): 'The Polish Labor Market in Transition,' Discussion Paper no. 95–03, Zentrum für Europäische Wirtschaftsforschung GmbH, Labor Economics, Human Resources and Social Policy Series.

Sztanderska, U. (2000): 'Structural Mismatches on Selected Labor Markets,' (in Polish), in: Socha, M. and Sztanderska, U.: *Structural Determinants of Unemployment in Poland*, Warsaw, pp.196–273.

Sztanderska, U. and Liwinski, J. (2000) 'Women in the Polish Labor Market in the 1990s'(in Polish) in: *The Impact of Privatization on the Situation of Women: Polish Women in the Period of the Transitioning Economy*. Warsaw: Center for Women's Rights.

Titkow, A. (2001): 'On the Appreciated Role of Women,' in: M. Ingham, Ingham, H. and Domański, H. (eds.): *Women on the Polish Labor Market*, Central European University Press, pp.21–40.

Wóycicka, I. (ed.) (2002): *Poland in the Light of the International Development Goals*. Warsaw: United Nations Development Program.

Annex 1

Table A1.1.
Changes in Social Benefits over the Years 1989–2001

No.	Benefit	Year of introd.	Provisions of law in force in 1989	Significant changes over the years 1989–2001	Legal basis for change
1.	Maternity leave and benefits	1924	Length of leave: • 16 weeks on the birth of a first child; • 18 weeks on the birth of a second child and all successive children; • 26 week in the case of a multiple birth. Level of benefit – 100% of the employee's remuneration for the last three months prior to the leave (Act of 26 June 1974 – The Labor Code, *Journal of Laws* No. 24, item 141; Act of 17 December 1974 on Social Security Cash Benefits in Relation of Sickness and Maternity, *Journal of Laws* No. 47, item 280).	Leave over the periods of: 1 January–31 December 2000 • 20 weeks upon giving birth for the first and each successive time; • 30 weeks in the case of a multiple birth. From 1 January 2001: • 26 weeks upon giving birth for the first and each successive time; • 36 weeks in the case of a multiple birth. Level of benefit – 100% of the employee's remuneration for the last three months prior to taking leave. Expansion of right to a part of maternity leave and benefit to child's father.	Act of 19 November 1998 Amending the Labor Code, *Journal of Laws* No. 99, item 1152 (in force as of 1 January 2000). Act of 24 August 2001 Amending the Labor Code and the Act on Social Security Cash Benefits Relation of Sickness and Maternity (*Journal of Laws* No. 99, item 1075)

No.	Benefit	Year of introd.	Provisions of law in force in 1989	Significant changes over the years 1989–2001	Legal basis for change
		1977	Maternity leave and benefits for individual farmers: Length of leave in 1989: 14 weeks on the birth of a first child 16 weeks on the birth of a second and all successive children Level of benefit – 1/30 of the state pension/minimal pension/ for each day	(As explained in the text, maternity benefits were cut again on 1 January 2002 to 16 weeks for the first birth and 18 weeks for the second and each subsequent birth.) Length of leave since 1991: 8 weeks upon the birth of any child Level of benefit: 1/30 of the minimum pension for each day	Act of 20 December 1990 on Social Insurance of Individual Farmers (*Journal of Laws* No. 7, 1991, item 24; in force as of 1 January 1991)

Table A1.1 (*continued*)
Changes in Social Benefits over the Years 1989–2001

No.	Benefit	Year of introd.	Provisions of law in force in 1989	Significant changes over the years 1989–2001	Legal basis for change
2.	Child care benefits	1954	A female worker has the right to leave of absence from work to care for: • A child aged up to eight in the event of an unforeseen closure of the nursery school, kindergarten, or school attended by the child, illness, childbirth, or stay at an in-patient health care facility of the spouse caring for the child on a permanent basis; Duration of leave: • 60 days per year. Level of benefit – 100% of the employee's remuneration (Act of 26 June 1974 – The Labor Code, *Journal of Laws* No. 24, item 141; Act of 17 December 1974 on Social Security Cash Benefits in Relation of Sickness and Maternity, *Journal of Laws* No. 47, item 280).	An expansion of entitlement to include the child's father. Duration of leave – no change. Level of benefit – 80% of the employee's remuneration.	Act of 3 February 1995 Amending the Act on Social Security Cash Benefits in Relation of Sickness and Maternity (*Journal of Laws* No. 16, item 77).

No.	Benefit	Year of introd.	Provisions of law in force in 1989	Significant changes over the years 1989–2001	Legal basis for change
3.	Child raising leave and allowances	Unpaid child raising leave – 1968; Child raising allowance – 1981.	A female worker has the right to child raising leave and guarantees of: • Stability of employment relations; • A return to work to an equivalent position; • Inclusion of the leave period in the total period of employment. Length of leave: • 36 months (up to the child's fourth birthday); • Increased length in the case of a disabled child. The right to a child raising allowance is granted to a person whose income per one family member is not greater than 25% of the average remuneration in the national economy. • Level of allowance: Basic – 25% of the average remuneration in the national economy; Preferential – 40% of the average remuneration in the national economy for single–parent women raising children.	Level of child raising allowance is established as an amount adjusted by the percentage of growth of the average remuneration. Expansion of rights to the child raising leave (and benefits) to encompass both parents. Level of child raising allowance is established as an amount adjusted in accordance with the consumer goods and services price indicator. Expansion of rights to the preferential allowance level to persons raising a third and each successive child (as of 1 January 2000).	Enactment of the Council of Ministers of 28 April 1992 Amending the Enactment on Child Raising Leave (Journal of Laws No. 41, item 179). Enactment of the Council of Ministers of 28 May 1996 Amending the Enactment on Child Raising Leave (Journal of Laws No. 60, item 27). Act of 25 June 1999 on Cash Social Welfare Benefits in the Case of Sickness and Maternity (Journal of Laws No. 60, item 636).

Table A1.1 (*continued*)
Changes in Social Benefits over the Years 1989–2001

No.	Benefit	Year of introd.	Provisions of law in force in 1989	Significant changes over the years 1989–2001	Legal basis for change
			• Period of allowance disbursement: – Basic – 24 months; – Preferential – 36 months for single-parent women raising children; – 72 months for persons raising a disabled child. (Enactment of the Council of Ministers of 17 July 1981 on Child raising Leave, *Journal of Laws* No. 19, item 97, with subsequent amendments).		

No.	Benefit	Year of introd.	Provisions of law in force in 1989	Significant changes over the years 1989–2001	Legal basis for change
4.	Family allowances	1947	Family allowance entitlement is granted for: • A child aged up to 16, or if that child is continuing his or her education – up to 24 years of age (25 if that is the last year of study); • The spouse satisfying one of the following criteria: – a disabled person without income; – a woman aged at least 50 or a man aged at least 65 – without income; – the raising of a child up to 8 years of age or care for a disabled person. The right to family allowance was dependent on the level of income per family member.	Waiving of income-related criteria in granting rights to the family allowance. The family allowance was set at a fixed amount (no adjustment indicator). The lowering of the age of a child continuing his or her education for which there is entitlement to a family allowance from 24 (25) to 20 years of age. The granting of rights to family allowances to the unemployed and college students. Change in the principles and terms for granting family allowances: • Linking the right to a family allowance with the income level per family member (50% of the average monthly remuneration in the national economy);	Enactment of the Minister of Labor, Wages, and Social Welfare of 10 April 1989 on Family and Nursing Benefits (*Journal of Laws* No. 23, item 125). Enactment of the Minister of Labor, Wages, and Social Welfare of 19 May 1992 Amending the Enactment on Family and Nursing Benefits (*Journal of Laws* No. 54, item 325). Enactment of the Minister of Labor, Wages, and Social Welfare of 22 January 1993 Amending the Enactment on Family and Nursing Benefits (*Journal of Laws* No. 7, item 37; unified wording in: *Journal of Laws* No. 10, item 495).

Table A1.1 (continued)
Changes in Social Benefits over the Years 1989–2001

No.	Benefit	Year of introd.	Provisions of law in force in 1989	Significant changes over the years 1989–2001	Legal basis for change
			Level of allowance – 8% of the average remuneration in the national economy. An identical allowance was disbursed in the case of each child. Family allowances were disbursed from social security funds (Enactment of the Minister of Labor, Wages, and Social Welfare of 23 January 1984 on Family and Nursing Benefits (*Journal of Laws* No. 4, item 21, with subsequent amendments).	• Allowance level was established as an amount (PLN 21 – 3% of the average remuneration); • Family allowance was subject to adjustment applying the consumer goods and services price indicator; • Criteria granting rights for a family allowance for a spouse (aged over 60 for women and 65 for men; disability; the raising of a disabled child); • Allowances became social welfare benefits financed using budgetary resources. The level of the family allowance was differentiated depending on the number of children: • At the basic level for the first and second child; • At an increased level for the third, fourth, and every successive child.	Act of 1 December 1994 on the Principles and Terms for Granting Rights to Family and Nursing Benefits (*Journal of Laws* of 1995 No. 4, item 17, in force as of 1 March 1995). Act of 27 June 1997 Amending the Act on Family and Nursing Benefits and Amending Other Acts (*Journal of Laws* No. 93, item 569).

No.	Benefit	Year of introd.	Provisions of law in force in 1989	Significant changes over the years 1989–2001	Legal basis for change
5.	Benefits from the alimony fund	1974	Entitlement to benefits is granted to persons who are unable to collect alimony payments adjudicated by a court of law who: • Satisfy income criteria; • Level of benefits – up to the level of adjudicated alimony. Act of 18 July 1974 on the Alimony Fund (*Journal of Laws* of 1991 No. 45, item 200, with subsequent amendments).	The waiving of the following criteria: • Income qualifying for benefits; • Establishing the upper limit of benefits at 25% of the average remuneration in the national economy. Increasing the upper limit to 30% of the average remuneration in the national economy. Introduction of an income criterion to qualify for benefits (60% of the average remuneration as calculated for retirement purposes).	Act of 6 July 1989 Amending the Act on the Alimony Fund (*Journal of Laws* No. 35, item 191). Act of 29 November 1990 Amending the Act on the Alimony Fund (*Journal of Laws* No. 90, item 528). Act of 7 October 1999 Amending the Act on the Alimony Fund (*Journal of Laws* No. 90, item 1000).

Table A1.1 (continued)
Changes in Social Benefits over the Years 1989–2001

No.	Benefit	Year of introd.	Provisions of law in force in 1989	Significant changes over the years 1989–2001	Legal basis for change
6.	Benefits for pregnant women and women raising children	1993		A woman holds the right to benefits whose income per person does not exceed the lowest retirement pension. Forms of benefits: • Cash benefit amounting to 28% of the average remuneration disbursed starting with the fourth month of pregnancy to the sixth birthday of the child; • One-time cash benefit amounting to 15% of the average remuneration in the national economy. A shortening of the period of time over which the cash benefit is disbursed (from the eighth month of pregnancy to the fourth month of the child's life). A lowering of the level of the one-time family benefit to 14% of the average remuneration in the national economy.	Enactment of the Council of Ministers of 5 October 1993 Regarding the Scope and Form as well as Procedure for Granting Pregnant Women and Women Raising Children Social Welfare and Legal Aid (*Journal of Laws* No. 97, item 44). Enactment of the Council of Ministers of 29 March 1994 Changing the Scope and Form for Granting Pregnant Women and Women Raising Children Social Welfare and Legal Aid (*Journal of Laws* No. 44, item 172).

No.	Benefit	Year of introd.	Provisions of law in force in 1989	Significant changes over the years 1989–2001	Legal basis for change
				Changes to the principles of establishing income-related criteria for qualifying for benefits and the level of cash benefits (specified amount).	Enactment of the Council of Ministers of 8 October 1994 Changing the Scope and Form for Granting Pregnant Women and Women Raising Children Social Welfare and Legal Aid (*Journal of Laws* No. 123, item 577).
				Cash benefits are the difference between the amount that serves as the criterion for qualifying for benefits (as in the Act on Social Welfare) and the actual income of the entitled person. Adjustment of benefits in line with the consumer goods and services price indicator.	Enactment of the Council of Ministers of 29 October 1999 (*Journal of Laws* No. 88, item 983).
				The granting of one additional cash benefit for the seventh month of pregnancy.	

Table A1.1 (*continued*)
Changes in Social Benefits over the Years 1989–2001

No.	Benefit	Year of introd.	Provisions of law in force in 1989	Significant changes over the years 1989–2001	Legal basis for change
7.	Social welfare benefits	1990		Entitlement to benefits is dependent on the simultaneous satisfaction of two conditions: • Low income; • Existence of a hardship living condition. Income criterion = level of lowest retirement pension.	Act of 29 November 1990 on Social Welfare (*Journal of Laws* No. 87, item 506).
	Period benefits			Level of period benefit = 28% of the average remuneration. Introduction of the possibility of differentiating the period benefit depending on the circumstances of the qualified person up to a maximum of 28% of the average remuneration. Changes to income-related criteria differentiated in line with family structure.	Act of 1 August 1992 on Social Welfare (*Journal of Laws* No. 64, item 321). Act of 14 June 1996 on Amendments to the Act on Social Welfare and the Act on Employment and Fighting Unemployment (*Journal of Laws* No. 100, item 459).

No.	Benefit	Year of introd.	Provisions of law in force in 1989	Significant changes over the years 1989–2001	Legal basis for change
				Changes in the principles for establishing the level of the period benefit – the difference between the income criterion for the given family and its actual income.	
8.	Guaranteed period benefit	1997		The following persons are entitled to the benefit: • Those who lost their right to unemployment benefits; and • Are raising a child as a single parent (up to the age of 15). Period of disbursement and level of the benefit: • First 12 months – at a level equal to the income criterion of a single person; • For the next 24 months – 80% of the above stated amount. Social Security payments shall be made over the period of disbursement of the benefit (if the entitled person has made Social Security payments towards retirement for at least five years).	Act of 6 December 1996 Amending the Act on Employment and Fighting Unemployment and Amending Certain Other Acts (*Journal of Laws* No. 93, item 569, in force as of 1 January 1997).

Table A1.2.
Old-age and survivors' pension in 1989-2000

	Before 1992	1992–1998	New system
Old-age pension			
1. Benefit formula	$P = PLZ\ 3000 + 0.5*PW + 0.01*(L-20)*PW$ P – old-age pension PW – basis of pension assessment (remuneration in the last period) L – years of insurance	$P = 0.24W + W*I*0.013*L + W*I*0.007*A$ P – pension W – national average wage for previous quarter I – individual wage index, not higher than 250% L – total length of service A – additional years accepted for insurance benefits (see table row 5)	$L = C/LE$ L – pension C – total of contributions paid indexed by 0.75% actual growth of the payroll fund in the economy, LE – life expectancy – in the first pillar gender neutral
2. Insurance period required to obtain pension	Men: 25 years, Women: 20 years	Men: 25 years, Women: 20 years	Any period, to acquire the minimum benefit rights : Men: 25 years, Women: 20 years
2. Retirement age	Men: 65, Women: 60, or Earlier retirement: Men: 60, with 35 years of service, Women: 55, with 30 years of service	Men: 65, Women: 60, or Earlier retirement: Men: 60, with 35 years of service, Women: 55, with 30 years of service	Men: 65, Women: 60, From 2007. Earlier retirement abolished

	Before 1992	1992–1998	New system
3. Rights to the benefit in the case of a divorce	None	None	Only in the second pillar
4. Sex-differentiated annuity rates in private savings schemes	None	None	1. In the first pillar – life expectancy tables – gender neutral 2. In the second pillar – no applicable legal regulations
5. Caring and out-of-work periods accepted as insurance periods and impacting entitlement or level of benefits	1. Periods accepted for benefit assessment as service years: • Not longer than 6-year period of child care over a child up to 4 years of age – up to 3 years for each child and a total of up to 6 years – regardless of the number of children • Not longer than 6-year child care period over a disabled child up to 4 years of age or any other disabled family member. • Maternity and childcare allowance. • Periods of receiving unemployment benefits	1. Contributory periods (accepted for benefit assessment as service years): • Caring periods (up to 35 days) and maternity allowance 2. Non-contributory periods (periods accepted for benefit assessment to a lesser degree than service years, cannot last longer than 1/3 of contributory periods): • Not longer than 6-year period of child care over a child up to 4 years of age – up to 3 years for each child and a total of up to 6 years – regardless of the number of children	1. Periods accepted in the insurance periods required for minimum pension entitlement: • Not longer than 6-year period of child care over a child up to 4 years of age – up to 3 years for each child and a total of up to 6 years – regardless of the number of children • Not longer than 6-year childcare period over a disabled child, • Periods of care for a war invalid, • Periods of care allowances

Table A1.2 (continued)
Old-age and survivors' pension in 1989–2000

Before 1992	1992–1998	New system
	• Not longer than 6-year child care period over a disabled child, • Periods of care for a war invalid, • Periods of care allowances 3. Contribution payments: • For persons receiving regular allowance from social services in respect of care over a disabled child or other family member requiring permanent care. 4. Early retirement: • For persons indicated in 3. above. 5. Other: • Periods of receiving unemployment and training allowance (change of professional qualifications) – through payment of contributions from the state budget for the said period.	2. Periods for which contributions are paid: • Periods of receiving regular allowance or guaranteed periodical allowance from social services by persons caring for a child requiring permanent care or for a seriously ill family member. Contribution for these persons is paid out of the state budget and the lowest remuneration in the economy is the basis of its assessment. • Periods of receiving maternity allowance. Contribution financed out of the state budget – the allowance amount constitutes the assessment basis, • Periods of child raising leave – caring for a child not longer than 6 years of up to the age of 4, limit of three years 3 for each child. Contribution assessment basis: minimum remuneration. • Periods of child raising leave – caring for a disabled child, not longer than 6 years up to the age of 4; limit of three years, 3 for each child. Contribution assessment basis: minimum remuneration.

	Before 1992	1992–1998	New system
			3. Other: • Period of receiving unemployment allowance, training allowance (to change professional qualification)
Simultaneous eligibility for different benefits	The right to receive a higher benefit or one selected by the insured	The right to receive a higher benefit or one selected by the insured	The right to receive a higher benefit or one selected by the insured

2. Survivors' pensions

	Before 1992	1992–1998	New system
1. Eligibility criteria	– Age: Widow – 50 years old, – Widower – 65 years old a) When wife (husband) was pensioner or insured person who at the moment of death fulfilled eligibility criteria for old-age or disability pension and b) When s/he is over 50 (65) years old at the moment of husband's (wife's) death and cares for child below 16 years old, or c) When s/he is over 50 (65) years old and disabled, d) Divorced, when a) and b) or c) and s/he had rights to alimonies.	Same as in the previous column	Same as in the previous column

Table A1.2 (*continued*)
Old-age and survivors' pension in 1989–2000

	Before 1992	1992–1998	New system
2. Benefits formula	Level of benefit – percent of the actual or hypothetical old-age or disability pension of the deceased spouse	Level of benefit – percent of the actual or hypothetical old-age or disability pension of the deceased spouse	Level of benefit – percent of the actual or hypothetical old-age or disability pension of the deceased spouse. Widower (widow) shall have the right (as inheritance) to savings accumulated in the second pillar but not to annuities in the case that they are not old-age pensioners.

Annex 2: Statistical Tables

List of Tables

Table A2.1
Labor force and labor force participation rates

Period	Labor Force		
	Total	Males	Females
	Labor force (in thousands)		
1988*	18,452	10,070	8,382
1992**	17,529	9,481	8,048
1995	17,004	9,199	7,804
1998	17,162	9,283	7,878
1999	17,214	9,307	7,907
2000	17,300	9,397	7,902
	Labor force participation rates (in %)		
1988*	65.3	74.3	57.0
1992**	61.7	70.0	54.2
1995	58.4	66.5	51.1
1998	57.3	65.3	50.0
1999	56.6	64.3	49.7

* Economically active by Population Census 1988.
** For the years 1992, 1995, 1998, 1999 and 2000 Labor Force Survey.

Source: Kotowska, Kowalska, *Labour Force Survey in Poland, IV. Quarter 2000*, Central Statistical Office, Warsaw, 2001.

Period	Total	Males	Females
	Employment (in thousands)		
1992b	15,135	8,308	6,827
1995	14,771	8,089	6,682
1998	15,335	8,421	6,914
1999	14,573	8,100	6,473
2000	14,540	8,066	6,474
	Employment rates (in %)		
1992**	53.3	61.4	46.0
1995	50.7	58.5	43.7
1998	51.0	58.9	43.9
1999	48.0	55.9	40.7
2000	47.4	55.2	40.3

Table A2.2
Employment and employment rates*

* Employment rate defined as a percentage of employed persons among those aged 15 and over.

** For the years 1992, 1995, 1998, 1999 and 2000 Labor Force Survey estimates for the IV quarter.

Source: *Labour Force Survey in Poland, IV. Quarter 2000*, Central Statistical Office, Warsaw, 2001.

Table A2.3
Some indicators of registered unemployment 1990–2000 (as at the end of the year)

Year	Unemployment (in thousands)	Unemploy- ment rate	Percentage of long-term unemployment[*]		
				Males	Females
1990	1,126	50.9	6.1	—	—
1991	2,156	52.6	11.4	—	—
1992	2,509	53.4	13.4	40.6	49.2
1993	2,890	52.2	15.4	39.6	49.6
1994	2,838	52.7	15.7	38.4	49.4
1995	2,629	55.1	14.6	30.5	42.9
1996	2,360	58.3	13.0	32.8	47.0
1997	1,826	60.4	10.3	32.7	51.8
1998	1,831	52.2	10.4	27.0	49.9
1999	2,350	55.6	13.0	27.9	47.2
2000	2,702	55.2	15.0	35.5	52.1

[*] Data by gender are reported since 1992.

Source: Registered unemployment in 1994, Central Statistical Office, Warsaw, 1995.
Registered unemployment in 2000, Central Statistical Office, Warsaw, 2001.

Table A2.4
Unemployment rate by gender*

Year	Males	Females
1992	12.4	15.2
1993	13.6	16.5
1994	12.3	15.7
1995	12.1	14.4
1996	9.9	13.4
1997	8.7	12.0
1998	9.3	12.2
1999	13	18.1
2000	14.2	18.1

* As of IV quarter.

Source: *Labour Force Survey in Poland, IV Quarter 2000*, Central Statistical Office, Warsaw, 2001.

Table A2.5
Registered unemployment flows by gender, 1992–2000 (in thousands)

Flows	1992	1993	1994	1995	1996	1997	1998	1999	2000
					Males				
Inflow to unemployment	830	1,084	1,145	1,270	1,186	1,093	1,140	1,395	1,340
Outflow from unemployment	681	872	1,184	1,433	1,381	1,353	1,103	1,113	1,172
Balance	149	212	−39	−163	−195	−260	37	282	168
					Females				
Inflow to unemployment	730	887	949	1,101	1,039	959	988	1,167	1,136
Outflow from unemployment	525	719	962	1,147	1,113	1,231	1,020	931	951
Balance	205	168	−13	−46	−192	−272	−32	236	185

Source: Kowalska, 2000. *Registered Unemployment in 2000*, Central Statistical Office, 2001 and own calculations.

Table A2.6
Employment rates by gender and education, IV quarter 1992 and 2000 (%)

Education	Females		Males	
	1992	2000	1992	2000
Tertiary	76.3	75.5	78.0	77.8
Post-secondary and vocational secondary	64.0	57.8	73.7	69.2
General secondary	45.3	38.4	47.6	44.3
Basic vocational	54.3	47.3	72.4	65.4
Primary and incomplete primary	28.7	16.4	42.2	28.1

Source: *Labour Force Survey in Poland, IV Quarter 2000*, Central Statistical Office, Warsaw, 2001.

Table A2.7
Unemployment rates by gender and education, IV quarter 1992 and 2000 (%)

Education	Females		Males	
	1992	2000	1992	2000
Tertiary	5.2	5.2	5.5	4.3
Post-secondary and vocational secondary	14.7	16.4	10.7	10.6
General secondary	17.7	21.0	13.1	16.6
Basic vocational	21.7	24.6	14.6	16.6
Primary and incomplete primary	12.7	21.2	12.7	19.5

Source: *Labour Force Survey in Poland, IV Quarter 2000*, Central Statistical Office, Warsaw, 2001.

Table A2.8
Estimates on transition probabilities between work and unemployment based on LFS data

Period	Estimates of transition probabilities from work to unemployment		Estimates of transition probabilities from unemployment to work	
	Men	Women	Men	Women
November 1994–November 1995	0.039	0.029	0.402	0.308
November 1995–November 1996	0.031	0.029	0.400	0.270
November 1996–November 1997	0.026	0.023	0.460	0.291
November 1997–November 1998	0.023	0.019	0.380	0.290

Source: A. Kowalska, 2000, p.89.

Table A2.9
Female–male ratio for selected characteristics of gross wages
of full-time employed, 1985–1997

Employees		Decile 1	Median	Mean	Decile 9
1985	Blue-collar	76.9	66.7	65.2	62.9
	White-collar	78.6	72.7	70.8	70.6
1991	Blue-collar	76.9	72.9	70.5	64.0
	White-collar	83.6	75.2	70.2	63.0
1995	Blue-collar	85.5	70.0	68.9	62.1
	White-collar	86.5	71.3	64.9	56.1
1997	Blue-collar	86.6	70.1	69.6	63.1
	White-collar	88.2	71.6	65.2	57.5

Source: Own calculations based on data from 'Earnings Distribution in the National Economy as of September 1994,' CSO, Warsaw, 1995.
'Earnings Distribution in the National Economy as of September 1995,' CSO, Warsaw, 1996.
'Earnings Distribution in the National Economy as of September 1997,' CSO, Warsaw, 1998.

Table A2.10
Average gross wages by education, 1999 (in PLN)

Education	Males	Females	Female–male ratio (in %)
Total	1,990.93	1,591.92	79.96
Tertiary	3,354.38	2,207.01	65.79
Post-secondary	2,029.26	1,583.48	78.03
Vocational secondary	2,001.2	1,559.95	77.95
General secondary	2,018.91	1,667.27	82.58
Basic vocational primary and incomplete	1,624.28	1,131.23	69.65
Primary	1,547.99	1,130.67	73.04

Source: Table 8 in 'Structure of Wages and Salaries by Occupation in October 1999,' CSO, Warsaw, 2000 and own calculations.

Table A2.11
Social benefits in 1989–2000 (coverage)

Year	Maternity benefits for employees and individual farmers/number of benefits (in thousands)	Child care benefits/number of benefits (in thousands)	Child raising allowances/number of persons	Family allowances for employees, individual farmers and beneficiaries of social assistance/average monthly number of benefits (in thousands)	Benefits from alimony fund	Social welfare benefits			
						Periodic benefits/number of families	Guaranteed period benefits/number of families	Benefits for pregnant women and women raising children	Benefits for children
1989	48,572	2.9323	197,400	5,243.0[b]	115,044	—	—	—	—
1990	47,782.3	2.2273	281,700	10,378.4	115,724	—	—	—	—
1991	34,281.1	2.0560	391,000	10,353.2	141,270	190,470	—	—	—
1992	38,694.1	1.6170	362,000	10,258	201,375	351,030	—	—	—
1993	38,370.3	1.6572	303,000	10,324.9	263,096	927,065	—	81,037	a
1994	35,602.8	1.5978	254,000	10,120.7	308,600	715,147	—	309,800	252,642
1995	33,501.8	1.2713	221,000	8,173.3	340,600	802,730		218,540	177,950
1996	33,409	10,712.4	194,400	8,007.5	358,400	734,827	—	153,480	129,350
1997	31,972.9	1,0259	181,500	7,846.1	373,800	720,073	51,290	140,490	114,724

Table A2.11 (continued)
Social benefits in 1989–2000 (coverage)

Year	Maternity benefits for employees and individual farmers/number of benefits (in thousands)	Child care benefits/number of benefits (in thousands)	Child raising allowances/number of persons	Family allowances for employees, individual farmers and beneficiaries of social assistance/average monthly number of benefits (in thousands)	Benefits from alimony fund	Social welfare benefits			
						Periodic benefits/number of families	Guaranteed period benefits/number of families	Banefits for pregnant women and women raising children	Benefits for children
1998	29,157.8	10,264.2	173,060	7,435.1	393,600	844,555	58,740	130,343	105,980
1999	26,728	8,252.8	171,970	6,872.4	421,290	582,730	55,680	126,430	100,213
2000	30,454.8	6,583.1	163,900	7,380.7	435,700	491,390	55,680	125,393	101,886

[a] Family allowances for the beneficiaries of the social assistance since 1995.

[b] In the year 1989 – average monthly number of families.

Sources: *Poland: Social Protection in Transition*. By K. Hagemajer, J. Liwinski and Wócycka, I., ILO, Social Protection Sector, Financial, Acriarial and Statistical Service Branch. Geneva, 2001; ZUS (2001). Information concerning the scope of benefits from Social Security Fund.

Table A2.12a
Social benefits in 1989–2000. Expenditure (net) (in millions PLN)

Year	Maternity benefits for employees and individual farmers[a]	Child care benefits[a]	Child raising allowances	Family allowances for employees and individual farmers	Benefits from alimony fund	Social welfare benefits		Benefits for pregnant women and women raising children
						Periodic benefits	Guaranteed period benefits	
1989	10,715	7,400	31,620	238,053.2	859	—	—	—
1990	70,872	371,03,9	60,700	853,700	4,046	10,660	—	—
1991	124,910	73,487	186,015	155,300,0	39,440	53,362.1	—	—
1992	156,439.8	800,85.9	235,810	2,127,400	92,010	129,418.4	—	—
1993	208,975.7	112,142.3	282,810	2,217,700	153,615	426,892.1	—	18,920
1994	254,591	142,651.2	316,390	2,253,900	258,700	351,764.7	—	257,865.1
1995	310,962.7	136,369.8	374,061	2,150,800	383,400	550,658.8	—	126,518.4
1996	387,658.2	143,330.7	433,800	2,360,700	409,200	596,570	—	74,138.5
1997	463,829.8	170,388.6	487,400	2,66,3500	540,100	705,116.1	86,788.3	75,272.5
1998	534,663.6	208,076.1	512,138.2	2,943,100	648,124.7	765,623.3	187,947.3	79,709.2
1999	565,780	184,731.7	536,709.2	3,219,111	825,853.9	404,005.8	172,481.9	96,606
2000	734,759.8	159,174.7	619,139.3	3,567,198	1,010,345.3	289,291.5	136,682.2	94,528.1

— Benefits did not exist; [a] For years 1990–2000, author's own calculations; [b] Family allowance for the beneficiaries of social assistance since 1995.

Source: K. Hagemejer, 2001; ZUS, 1995; *Social Security Annual (1990–1995)*, ZUS (2001), Information concerning the scope of benefits from Social Security Fund and Alimony Fund,' data of the Social Assistance Department of the Ministry of Labor and Social Policy.

Table A2.12b
Social expenditure in 1990–1998 (related to total social expenditure)

Year	Total social expenditure (in mln PLN) = 100	Maternity benefits	Childcare benefits	Child raising allowances	Family allowances	Benefits from alimony fund	Periodic benefits	Guaranteed benefits	Benefits for pregnant women
1990	9,424	0.75	0.39	64	9.06	0.04	0.11	—	—
1991	18,792	0.66	0.39	0.98	8.26	0.2	0.28	—	—
1992	27,722	0.56	0.28	0.85	7.67	0.33	0.48	—	—
1993	36,979	0.56	0.3	0.76	6	0.41	1.15	—	0.05
1994	50,711	0.5	0.28	0.62	4.44	0.51	0.69	—	0.5
1995	67,914	0.45	0.2	0.55	3.16	0.56	0.81	—	0.18
1996	85,587	0.45	0.16	0.5	2.75	0.47	0.69	—	0.08
1997	102,640	0.45	0.16	0.47	2.59	0.52	0.68	0.08	0.07
1998	115,902	0.46	0.17	0.44	2.53	0.55	0.66	0.16	0.06

Sources: Own calculations based on data in Figure 1. Level of total social expenditure, Poland (K. Hagemejer, 2001).

Table A2.13a
Social benefits in 1989–2000, average amount

Year	Maternity benefits in PLN (daily)	Child care benefits in PLN (daily)	Child raising allowances			Family allowances in PLN (monthly)	Benefits from alimony fund		
			In PLN (monthly)	Related to average wage (in %)	Related to minimum wage (in %)		In PLN (monthly)	Related to average wage (in %)	Related to minimum wage (in %)
1989	0.25	0.25	13.34	6.4	35.1	3.78	0.51	2.4	13.4
1990	1.54	1.67	17.95	17.4	40.8	13.16	2.1	2	4.8
1991	3.2	3.57	39.64	22.6	56.6	23.81	15.3	8.7	21.8
1992	5	5.88	54.2	22.2	50.2	32.17	33	13.5	30.5
1993	6.98	8.25	77.78	24.3	55.5	34.68	45	14	32.1
1994	9.3	11.02	103.8	24.4	54.1	36.13	57.96	13.6	30.2
1995	12.05	13.22	141.04	25.1	57.8	43.96	72.3	12.9	29.6
1996	15.02	16.47	185.9	26.2	62.8	47.33	88.3	12.4	29.8
1997	18.59	20.18	223.78	25.5	62.8	55.17	107.8	12.3	29.9
1998	23.39	24.34	246.61	24.4	61.6	63.92	130.56	12.9	32.6
1999	27.89	27.7	260.08	18.7	49.2	76.36	155.63	11.2	29.9
2000	31.54	29.85	314.83	20.4	56.2	75.3	182.38	11.8	32.6

Sources: Own calculations based on data: ZUS (1995) Social Security Annual 1990–1995, Warsawa, ZUS (2001) Information.

Table A2.13b
Social benefits in 1989–2000, average amount

Year	Periodic benefits			Guaranteed periodic benefits[a]		
	In PLN (monthly)	Related to average wage (in %)	Related to minimum wage (in %)	In PLN (monthly)	Related to average wage (in %)	Related to minimum wage (in %)
1989	—	—	—	—	—	—
1990	31.1	30.2	77.7	—	—	—
1991	53.8	30.6	76.8	—	—	—
1992	69.5	28.5	64.3	—	—	—
1993	84.6	26.4	60.4	—	—	—
1994	92.5	21.7	48.1	—	—	—
1995	121.8	21.7	49.9	—	—	—
1996	143.4	20.2	48.4	—	—	—
1997	196.5	22.4	54.6	275	31.3	76.4
1998	198.7	19.6	49.7	316	31.3	79
1999	194.4	14	37.4	384	27.6	73.8
2000	191.5	12.4	34.2	401	26	71.6

Table A2.13b (*continued*)
Social benefits in 1989–2000, average amount

Year	Guarantee periodic benefits[b]			Benefits for pregnant women and women raising children		
	In PLN (monthly)	Related to average wage (in %)	Related to minimum wage (in %)	In PLN (monthly)	Related to average wage (in %)	Related to minimum wage (in %)
1989	—	—	—	—	—	—
1990	—	—	—	—	—	—
1991	—	—	—	—	—	—
1992	—	—	—	—	—	—
1993	—	—	—	*	*	*
1994	—	—	—	90.56	21.3	47.2
1995	—	—	—	114.96	20.5	47.1
1996	—	—	—	128.06	18	43.3
1997	220	25.1	61.1	147.37	16.8	40.9
1998	252.8	25	63.2	169.52	16.7	42.4
1999	307.2	22.1	59.1	194.27	14	37.3
2000	320.8	20.8	57.3	205.05	13	36.6

[a] Normatively maximum amount; [b] Normatively minimum amount.

Source: Own calculations based on data of ZUS (1995), *Social Security Annual 1990–1995*, Warsawa, ZUS (2001). Information concerning the scope of benefits from Social Security Fund and Alimony Fund, Warsawa.

Table A2.14

Social benefits per capita, by socioeconomic category of household in Poland, 1998

Income and benefits	Socioeconomic category of household[a]							
	Worker/ employee	Farmer-worker	Farmer	Self-employed	Pensioner (receiving retirement pensions)	Pensioner (receiving disability pensions)	Living on social benefit[b]	Total
	PLN, per month							
Disposable income	545.91	419.02	406.47	654.74	613.65	452.39	298.60	522.52
Social benefits received by household								
Total social benefits	58.31	76.88	85.02	47.09	529.58	360.56	150.87	165.79
Total benefits listed below:	9.60	10.44	5.65	6.04	3.14	6.37	27.90	8.35
Maternity benefits	0.75	0.51	0.04	0.48	0.11	0.15	0.00	0.47
Family allowances	6.01	7.66	4.41	3.61	1.16	3.46	11.07	5.07
Nursing allowances	0.88	0.85	0.47	0.65	0.97	1.36	2.58	0.94
Child raising benefits	1.11	1.12	0.57	1.18	0.42	0.53	5.73	1.04
SA benefits for pregnant women	0.06	0.02	0.10	0.00	0.05	0.08	1.35	0.09
Benefits from Alimony Fund	0.79	0.28	0.05	0.12	0.44	0.77	7.16	0.74

Table A2.14 (continued)
Social benefits per capita, by socioeconomic category of household in Poland, 1998

Income and benefits	Socioeconomic category of household[a]							
	Worker/ employee	Farmer-worker	Farmer	Self-employed	Pensioner (receiving retirement pensions)	Pensioner (receiving disability pensions)	Living on social benefit[b]	Total
	Percent (disposable income = 100)							
Disposable income	100.0	100.0	100.0	100.0	100.0	100.0	100.0	100.0
Social benefits received by household								
Total social benefits	10.7	18.3	20.9	7.2	86.3	79.7	50.5	31.7
Total benefits listed below:	1.76	2.49	1.39	0.92	0.51	1.41	9.34	1.60
Maternity benefits	0.1	0.1	0.0	0.1	0.0	0.0	0.0	0.1
Family allowances	1.1	1.8	1.1	0.6	0.2	0.8	3.7	1.0
Nursing allowances	0.2	0.2	0.1	0.1	0.2	0.3	0.9	0.2
Child raising benefits	0.2	0.3	0.1	0.2	0.1	0.1	1.9	0.2
SA benefits for pregnant women	0.0	0.0	0.0	0.0	0.0	0.0	0.5	0.0
Benefits from Alimony Fund	0.1	0.1	0.0	0.0	0.1	0.2	2.4	0.1

Table A2.14 (*continued*)

Social benefits per capita, by socioeconomic category of household in Poland, 1998

	Socioeconomic category of household[a]							
	Worker/employee	Farmer-worker	Farmer	Self-employed	Pensioner (receiving retirement pensions)	Pensioner (receiving disability pensions)	Living on social benefit[b]	Total
Memo								
Sample No. of HHs in category	12,749	2,659	1,765	2,011	7,453	4,190	930	31,756
Sample No. of HH members in category	43,300	12,049	7,241	7,205	14,932	9,103	2,681	96,510

Source: *Polish Household Budget Survey, 1998*, and author's computations.

* Computed as a difference between benefits received by a household and benefits received by women.

All items: net, in current prices; in cash and in kind (when applicable).

[a] Households have been grouped according to the main source of income (compare: GUS).
[b] Including households living on temporary jobs.

Table A2.15
Social benefits per capita, by income decile in Poland, 1998

Income and benefits	Income decile[a] number										
	1	2	3	4	5	6	7	8	9	10	Total
	PLN, per month										
Disposable income	120.47	244.81	306.54	363.37	420.03	481.38	552.40	642.70	781.88	1,311.38	522.52
Social benefits received by household											
Total social benefits	66.68	81.51	95.06	107.07	138.32	162.90	193.68	242.86	281.35	288.35	165.79
Total benefits listed below:	14.49	15.92	12.67	11.10	9.12	6.61	4.85	3.63	3.14	1.98	8.35
Maternity benefits	0.22	0.24	0.35	0.79	0.68	0.34	0.43	0.30	0.63	0.69	0.47
Family allowances	10.68	10.66	7.78	6.81	5.43	3.66	2.52	1.57	1.06	0.50	5.07
Nursing allowances	1.19	1.26	1.33	1.01	1.07	0.95	0.80	0.75	0.57	0.44	0.94
Child raising benefits	1.21	2.19	1.86	1.56	1.03	0.89	0.61	0.46	0.42	0.19	1.04
SA benefits for pregnant women	0.19	0.27	0.17	0.03	0.06	0.02	0.08	0.03	0.05	0.00	0.09
Benefits from Alimony Fund	1.00	1.30	1.17	0.89	0.83	0.74	0.41	0.52	0.41	0.16	0.74

Table A2.15 (*continued*)
Social benefits per capita, by income decile in Poland, 1998

Income and benefits	Income decile[a] number										Total
	1	2	3	4	5	6	7	8	9	10	
	Percent (disposable income = 100)										
Disposable income	100.0	100.0	100.0	100.0	100.0	100.0	100.0	100.0	100.0	100.0	100.0
Social benefits received by household											
Total social benefits	55.4	33.3	31.0	29.5	32.9	33.8	35.1	37.8	36.0	22.0	31.7
Total benefits listed below:	12.03	6.50	4.13	3.05	2.17	1.37	0.88	0.56	0.40	0.15	1.60
Maternity benefits	0.2	0.1	0.1	0.2	0.2	0.1	0.1	0.0	0.1	0.1	0.1
Family allowances	8.9	4.4	2.5	1.9	1.3	0.8	0.5	0.2	0.1	0.0	1.0
Nursing allowances	1.0	0.5	0.4	0.3	0.3	0.2	0.1	0.1	0.1	0.0	0.2
Child raising benefits	1.0	0.9	0.6	0.4	0.2	0.2	0.1	0.1	0.1	0.0	0.2
SA benefits for pregnant women	0.2	0.1	0.1	0.0	0.0	0.0	0.0	0.0	0.0	0.0	0.0
Benefits from Alimony Fund	0.8	0.5	0.4	0.2	0.2	0.2	0.1	0.1	0.1	0.0	0.1

Table A2.15 (continued)
Social benefits per capita, by income decile[a] in Poland, 1998

| Income and benefits | Income decile[a] number | | | | | | | | | |
	1	2	3	4	5	6	7	8	9	10	Total
						Memo					
Sample No. of HHs in ccategory	2,084	2,190	2,422	2,677	2,949	3,311	3,569	3,870	4,168	4,516	31,756
Sample No. of HH members in category	9,651	9,651	9,651	9,648	9,615	9,690	9,647	9,653	9,652	9,650	96,510

Source: Polish Household Budget Survey, 1998, and author's computations.

*   Computed as a difference between benefits received by a household and benefits received by women.

All items: net, in current prices; in cash and in kind (when applicable).

[a]   Deciles for persons, according to the per capita disposable income.

Table A2.16
Social benefits per capita, by family type in Poland, 1998

Income and benefits	Single person	Parents + 1 child	Parents + 2 children	Parents + 3+ children	Single parent with children	Other hhlds with children	Other hhlds without children	Total
				PLN, per month				
Disposable income	804.46	610.36	470.37	314.98	438.41	419.10	629.02	522.52
Social benefits received by household								
Total social benefits	497.13	73.02	37.01	42.18	110.96	108.83	314.74	165.79
Total benefits listed below:	0.68	6.24	9.46	17.77	33.12	9.73	3.03	8.35
Maternity benefits	0.00	1.15	0.72	0.36	0.00	0.43	0.23	0.47
Family allowances	0.02	2.69	6.59	14.02	10.10	5.87	1.19	5.07
Nursing allowances	0.63	0.59	1.03	1.58	1.95	0.94	0.71	0.94
Child raising benefits	0.00	1.57	0.99	1.32	4.38	1.35	0.49	1.04
SA benefits for pregnant women	0.00	0.06	0.03	0.10	0.51	0.18	0.07	0.09
Benefits from Alimony Fund	0.03	0.17	0.09	0.38	16.18	0.96	0.34	0.74

Table A2.16 (*continued*)
Social benefits per capita, by family type in Poland, 1998

Income and benefits	Single person	Parents + 1 child	Parents + 2 children	Parents + 3+ children	Single parent with children	Other hhlds with children	Other hhlds without children	Total
Disposable income	100.0	100.0	100.0	100.0	100.0	100.0	100.0	100.0
				Per cent (disposable income = 100)				
Social benefits received by household								
Total social benefits	61.8	12.0	7.9	13.4	25.3	26.0	50.0	31.7
Total benefits listed below:	0.08	1.02	2.01	5.64	7.55	2.32	0.48	1.60
Maternity benefits	0.0	0.2	0.2	0.1	0.0	0.1	0.0	0.1
Family allowances	0.0	0.4	1.4	4.5	2.3	1.4	0.2	1.0
Nursing allowances	0.1	0.1	0.2	0.5	0.4	0.2	0.1	0.2
Child raising benefits	0.0	0.3	0.2	0.4	1.0	0.3	0.1	0.2
SA benefits for pregnant women	0.0	0.0	0.0	0.0	0.1	0.0	0.0	0.0
Benefits from Alimony Fund	0.0	0.0	0.1	0.1	3.7	0.2	0.1	0.1

Table A2.16 (*continued*)
Social benefits per capita, by family type in Poland, 1998

Income and benefits	Family type						
	Single person	Parents + 1 child	Parents + 2 children	Parents + 3+ children	Single parent with children	Other hhlds with children	Other hhlds without children	Total
				Memo			
Sample No. of HHs in category	5,452	11,343	18,210	12,580	2,239	17,896	28,789	96,510
Sample No. of HH members in category	5,452	3,781	4,552	2,304	851	3,627	11,189	31,756

Source: Polish Household Budget Survey, 1998, and author's computations.

* Computed as a difference between benefits received by a household and benefits received by women.

All items: net, in current prices; in cash and in kind (when applicable).

Table A2.17
Social benefits received by women, by socioeconomic category of household in Poland, 1998

Social benefits received by women	Socioeconomic category of household[a]							
	Worker/ employee	Farmer- worker	Farmer	Self- employed	Pensioner (receiving retirement pensions)	Pensioner (receiving disability pensions)	Living on social benefit[b]	Total
	PLN, per capita, per month							
Benefits received by women (total)	31.08	41.79	47.19	27.08	243.11	212.47	86.74	84.79
Retirement pensions	9.04	15.22	25.03	9.77	214.10	16.28	2.81	43.30
Disability pensions	8.08	12.36	15.40	7.98	20.83	90.52	4.78	18.81
Survivor pensions	4.25	5.28	1.76	2.87	2.73	94.57	1.88	12.31
Unemployment benefits	1.71	1.49	0.32	1.07	0.67	1.64	12.89	1.68
Permanent SA benefits	0.39	0.39	0.44	0.31	0.59	1.13	11.75	0.80
Temporary SA benefits	0.52	0.42	0.32	0.24	0.29	1.13	15.12	0.90

Table A2.17 (continued)

Social benefits received by women, by socioeconomic category of household in Poland, 1998

Social benefits received by women	Socioeconomic category of household[a]							
	Worker/ employee	Farmer-worker	Farmer	Self-employed	Pensioner (receiving retirement pensions)	Pensioner (receiving disability pensions)	Living on social benefit[b]	Total
	Percent (benefit of a household = 100)							
Benefits received by women (total)	53.3	54.4	55.5	57.5	45.9	58.9	57.5	51.1
Retirement pensions	59.6	55.3	60.4	61.8	44.5	83.0	48.7	47.6
Disability pensions	44.8	49.4	52.6	48.9	67.4	41.5	57.0	46.8
Survivor pensions	76.1	80.6	58.8	79.8	70.0	95.6	45.5	88.8
Unemployment benefits	59.1	53.0	47.9	68.7	42.5	47.3	42.5	51.8
Permanent SA benefits	74.1	59.3	43.0	78.0	62.3	66.3	83.6	71.6
Temporary SA benefits	80.7	94.9	78.8	93.2	80.3	59.7	76.3	76.3

Source: Polish Household Budget Survey, 1998, and author's computations.

* Computed as a difference between benefits received by a household and benefits received by women.

All items: net, in current prices; in cash and in kind (when applicable).

a Households have been grouped according to the main source of income (compare: GUS).
b Including households living on temporary jobs.

Table A2.18
Social benefits received by women, by income decile in Poland, 1998

Social benefits received by women

					Income decile[a] number						
	1	2	3	4	5	6	7	8	9	10	Total
					PLN, per capita, per month						
Benefits received by women (total)	33.54	42.24	48.65	55.13	71.56	86.55	102.97	124.03	140.68	142.46	84.79
Retirement pensions	7.30	10.27	13.31	18.52	29.22	41.45	57.44	74.86	90.52	90.09	43.30
Disability pensions	8.83	9.86	16.09	17.28	22.51	25.18	24.80	24.33	22.01	17.21	18.81
Survivor pensions	3.16	4.93	5.56	6.75	7.58	11.04	13.87	18.99	23.33	27.87	12.31
Unemployment benefits	1.62	2.71	2.72	2.07	2.61	1.69	1.16	0.89	0.74	0.53	1.68
Permanent SA benefits	1.16	1.69	1.28	0.74	1.25	0.69	0.46	0.32	0.32	0.11	0.80
Temporary SA benefits	2.93	2.41	1.16	0.86	0.76	0.36	0.16	0.28	0.05	0.03	0.90

Table A2.18 (continued)
Social benefits received by women, by income decile[a] number in Poland, 1998

| Social benefits received by women | Income decile[a] number | | | | | | | | | | |
	1	2	3	4	5	6	7	8	9	10	Total
	Percent (benefits received by household = 100)										
Benefits received by women (total)	50.3	51.8	51.2	51.5	51.7	53.1	53.2	51.1	50.0	49.4	51.1
Retirement pensions	57.6	53.6	50.1	50.6	48.3	50.3	50.8	48.8	45.1	43.9	47.6
Disablity pensions	42.7	40.3	45.8	44.9	48.5	49.5	48.6	43.7	50.0	48.4	46.8
Survivor pensions	82.9	88.1	82.0	80.8	78.9	86.3	87.9	89.3	93.3	93.9	88.8
Unemployment benefits	33.8	49.0	52.7	48.7	65.6	55.1	56.4	62.4	64.0	60.7	51.8
Permanent SA benefits	66.3	82.3	80.1	74.7	68.7	66.5	53.9	55.6	77.8	100.0	71.6
Temporary SA benefits	76.1	83.7	71.7	81.6	82.0	87.9	67.7	85.9	35.2	9.0	76.3

Source: Polish Household Budget Survey, 1998, and author's computations.

*   Computed as a difference between benefits received by a household and benefits received by women.

All items: net, in current prices; in cash and in kind (when applicable).

[a]   Households have been grouped according to the main source of income (compare: GUS).

Social benefits received by women

Table A2.19
Social benefits received by women by family type in Poland, 1998

Benefits received by women (total)	Single person	Parents + 1 child	Parents + 2 children	Parents + 3+ children	Single parent with children	Other hhlds with children	Other hhlds without children	Total
					PLN, per capita, per month			
Total social benefits	394.25	26.31	15.02	16.65	90.03	60.70	137.69	84.79
Retirement pensions	233.32	5.86	1.12	0.61	5.54	24.19	82.23	43.30
Disablity pensions	45.28	11.51	4.60	2.81	13.09	15.43	35.20	18.81
Survivor pensions	109.45	0.28	0.15	0.35	26.74	9.66	12.09	12.31
Unemployment benefits	1.15	1.73	1.85	1.45	1.64	1.77	1.69	1.68
Permanent SA benefits	1.30	0.34	0.36	0.77	6.53	0.88	0.69	0.80
Temporary SA benefits	0.54	0.56	0.58	1.46	6.40	1.00	0.57	0.90

Family type

Table A2.19 (*continued*)
Social benefits received by women by family type in Poland, 1998

Social benefits received by women

	Single person	Parents + 1 child	Parents + 2 children	Parents + 3+ children	Single parent with children	Other hhlds with children	Other hhlds without children	Total
				Percent (benefits received by household = 100)				
Benefits received by women (total)	79.3	36.0	40.6	39.5	81.1	55.8	43.7	51.1
Retirement pensions	78.1	23.9	24.1	20.6	74.0	55.9	39.7	47.6
Disability pensions	64.6	35.8	34.7	28.7	80.2	49.7	46.5	46.8
Survivor pensions	98.8	88.9	88.1	87.1	96.9	76.3	80.2	88.8
Unemployment benefits	53.7	55.7	61.8	50.8	100.0	48.9	45.7	51.8
Permanent SA benefits	84.1	63.5	59.6	70.6	91.1	71.2	64.7	71.6
Temporary SA benefits	46.2	76.0	69.3	79.9	95.4	78.3	71.3	76.3

Source: Polish Household Budget Survey, 1998, and author's computations.

* Computed as a difference between benefits received by a household and benefits received by women.

All items: net, in current prices; in cash and in kind (when applicable).

Table A2.20
Share of selected social benefits in household income in Poland, 1988–1999

All households	1988	1989	1990	1991	1992	1993	1994	1995	1996	1997	1998	1999
	Percent (household income = 100)											
Income	100.00	100.00	100.00	100.00	100.00	100.00	100.00	100.00	100.00	100.00	100.00	100.00
Total social benefits	23.08	22.33	26.15	33.57	32.73	31.71	31.68	32.48	31.11	30.66	31.70	31.02
Family and nursing allowances	4.16	5.40	4.15	4.42	4.15	3.42	2.70	1.97	1.78	2.11	1.15	1.24
Family allowance	na	na	na	na	na	na	na	na	1.26	1.05	0.97	1.04
Nursing allowance	na	na	na	na	na	na	na	na	0.52	0.22	0.18	0.20
Child raising benefit	0.16	0.08	0.20	0.33	0.31	0.37	0.28	0.26	0.26	0.24	0.20	0.20
Maternity benefit	0.14	0.14	0.16	0.15	0.12	?	?	?	0.08	0.10	0.09	0.10
SA benefit for pregnant women	na	na	na	na	na	na	na	na	0.01	0.01	0.02	0.02
Benefits from Alimony Fund	na	na	na	na	na	na	na	na	na	na	0.14	0.17

Notice: Major changes of HBS methodology since 1993. Data of the two sub-periods displayed in the above table are not fully comparable.

All items considered: net; since 1993 – disposable incomes. Incomes for all households: until 1992 – author's computations (weighted averages).

[a] Including households living on temporary jobs (social benefit as a main source of the household income does not include pensions).
[b] Until 1992 excluding households of the self-employed (households living on social benefit were put into a separate group).

Source: 1988–1989: Published data. *Budżety gospodarstw domowych w [rok]*, GUS, Warszawa [rok wyd.] and author's computation.
1990–1995: Published data. *Statystyczny opis jakości życia 1990–1995*, GUS, Warszawa 1997, Table 50.
1996–1999: Unpublished data. Author's computations based on individual records from HBS conducted by GUS.

Table A2.21
Mean time of professional work by gender (in hours and minutes per day)*

Type of activity	Total	Men	Women
Total			
• 1984	7.12	7.57	6.21
• 1996	6.55	7.40	6.00
Main activity of non-agricultural employees			
• 1984	7.44	8.00	7.25
• 1996	7.49	8.17	7.11
Main activity in agriculture			
• 1984	5.12	6.22	4.15
• 1996	5.29	6.30	4.24

* For persons aged 18 and over.

Source: *Time Use Survey 1996*, Central Statistical Office, Warsaw, 1999, p.137.

Table A2.22
Frequency of work by gender[*]

Type of activity	Total	Men	Women
Total			
· 1984	54.3	64.7	46.0
· 1996	43.5	53.1	35.6
Main activity of non-agricultural employees			
· 1984	35.2	44.3	27.9
· 1996	14.2	18.0	11.0
Main activity in agriculture			
· 1984	15.5	15.7	15.3
· 1996	13.4	15.4	11.7

[*] As a percentage of persons aged 18 and over.

Source: Time Use Survey 1996, Central Statistical Office, Warsaw, 1999, p.139.

Table A2.23
Time use by gender in 1996

Type of activity	Women	Men
Professional work		
Mean time (in hours)*	6.00	7.28
Frequency of work (percentage of employed persons)	28.8	44.5
Education		
Mean time (in hours)*	5.06	5.09
Frequency of work (percentage of persons who in education)	20.0	17.9
Household work		
Mean time (in hours)*	4.50	2.36
Frequency of work (percentage of employed persons)	93.5	80.1
Meal preparation		
Mean time (in hours)*	2.20	0.52
Frequency of work (percentage of persons who prepare meals)	86.5	44.1
Cleaning		
Mean time (in hours)*	1.04	0.58
Frequency of work (percentage of persons who clean)	77.9	48.4
Shopping and services		
The mean time (in hours)*	0.48	0.55
Frequency of work (percentage of persons who shop and use services)	44.0	23.6
Care for adults		
Mean time (in hours)*	0.57	1.0
Frequency of work (percentage of persons caring for adults)	3.4	0.9
Child care		
Mean time (in hours)*	1.47	1.19
Frequency of work (percentage of persons caring for children)	32.9	20.2

*   Time is given in hours and minutes.

Source: *Time Use Survey 1996*, Central Statistical Office, Warsaw, 1999, p.108.

Table A2.24
Institutional child care

	1990	1999
Nurseries and kindergartens		
Number of nurseries and nursery wards	1,412	469
Places in nurseries (in thousands)*	95.8	32
Children in nurseries during the year (in thousands)*	137.5	56.9
Places in nurseries per 1,000 children up to age 3 in urban areas*	104	50
Children in nurseries per 1,000 children up to age 3*	42	23
Number of kindergatrens	12,308	8,733
Number of pre-school sections at primary schools	13,565	10,152
Places in kindergartens (in thousands)	896.7	726.2
Children in kindergartens (in thousands)	856.6	719.6
Children in pre-school sections at primary schools (in thousands)	375.3	199.5
Children attending pre-school education establishments per 1,000 of children aged		
3–6 years	471	499
3–5 years	295	328
6 years	952	967
Children attending kindergartens per 1,000 of children aged	.	
3–6 years	328	391
6 years	467	600
Children attending kindergartens per 100 places	96	99
Children attending kindergartens per kindergarten	70	82

Source: *Statistical Yearbook 2000*, Central Statistical Office, Warsaw, 2000.

Table A2.25

State and *gmina's* budgets spending on nurseries and kindergartens in relation to GDP, 1990–1998

Item	1990	1991	1992	1993	1994	1995	1996	1997	1998
GDP (in millions PLN)	59,624	86,076	122,324	165,782	223,917	306,318	385,448	469,372	549,467
Spending on:									
Nurseries	60.1	81.5	85.8	90.8	105.4	128.5	150.9	169.7	—
Kindergartens	278.4	486.7	587.9	761.2	947.9	1,251.1	1,551.1	1,851.2	—
As a percentage of GDP									
Spending on:									
Nurseries	0.10	0.09	0.07	0.05	0.04	0.04	0.03	0.03	—
Kindergartens	0.46	0.56	0.48	0.45	0.42	0.40	0.40	0.39	—

— Data not available.

Source: Author's own calculations based on Statistical Yearbooks 1997, 1998.

Table A2.26
Changes in the number of children in nurseries and kindergartens in 1989–1999

Children in facilities per 1,000 in a given age group	1989	1990	1991	1992	1993	1994	1995	1996	1997	1998	1999
Children in nurseries (aged 0–2)	44	42	31	26	23	22	22	24	25	23	23
Children in kindergartens (aged 3–6)	340	328	298	332	334	348	356	363	370	384	391

Source: Statistical Yearbooks 1990, 1996, 2000.

Year	Number of births (in thousands)	Total fertility rate			Extra marital births (per 100 births)			Mean age at	
		Total	Urban	Rural	Total	Urban	Rural	First birth	Any birth
1990	547,7	2,078	1,817	2,506	6.2	7.8	4.4	23.3	26.2
1995	433,1	2,039	1,401	1,958	9.5	12.0	6.5	23.5	26.9
1996	428,2	1,580	1,371	1,924	10.2	12.8	7.8	23.6	26.9
1997	412,7	1,508	1,305	1,843	11.0	13.7	7.8	24.1	27.1
1998	395,6	1,431	1,251	1,730	11.6	14.3	8.3	24.2	27.2
1999	382	1,366	1,201	1,640	11.7	14.4	8.4	—	—

Table A2.27
Selected fertility indicators, Poland 1990–1999

Source: *Statistical Yearbook of Demography,* Central Statistical Office, different issues; *Recent Demographic Development in Europe, 1999,* Council of Europe, Strasbourg, 1999; *Recent Demographic Development in Europe, 2000,* Council of Europe, Strasbourg, 2000.

Table A2.28
Nuptiality parameters of women, 1990–1999

Years	Total first marriage rate of women	Mean age of women at first marriage
1990	0.91	22.6
1995	0.65	22.8
1996	0.64	23.4
1997	0.64	23.4
1998	0.61	23.3
1999	0.63	—

Source: *Recent Demographic Development in Europe, 2000,* Council of Europe, Strasbourg, 2000.

Table A2.29
Unemployed without unemployment benefits
as percentage of the number of unemployed by sex, 1998–2000

	1998	1999	2000
Unemployed women without the unemployment benefit as percentage of the number of unemployed women	82	82	83
Unemployed men without the unemployment benefit as percentage of the number of unemployed men	70	71	73

Table TA.1
Household income and selected social benefits by household type, Poland, 1988–1999

Household type/Benefit	1988	1989	1990	1991	1992	1993	1994	1995	1996	1997	1998	1999
	PLN per capita per month (in current prices)											
Worker/employee												
Income	2.98	11.60	56.30	97.90	142.83	176.61	234.69	301.26	395.90	486.03	545.91	591.99
Family and nursing allowances	0.17	0.81	2.91	5.41	7.10	7.26	7.30	6.56	7.14	12.39	6.89	7.72
Family allowance	na	na	na	na	na	na	na	na	6.19	6.20	6.01	6.70
Nursing allowance	na	na	na	na	na	na	na	na	0.95	0.80	0.88	1.02
Child raising benefit	0.00	0.01	0.13	0.40	0.43	0.71	0.68	0.80	1.07	1.25	1.11	1.31
Maternity benefit	0.01	0.02	0.12	0.20	0.24	?	?	?	0.45	0.60	0.75	0.88
SA benefit for pregnant women	na	na	na	na	na	na	na	na	0.02	0.05	0.06	0.04
Benefits from Alimony Fund	na	na	na	na	na	na	na	na	na	na	0.79	0.82
Farmer												
Income	3.48	13.44	57.73	82.39	117.33	157.72	205.18	282.35	340.03	438.61	406.47	411.14
Family and nursing allowances	0.01	0.07	0.44	1.27	2.88	3.39	4.01	4.42	5.42	7.21	4.88	5.81
Family allowance	na	na	na	na	na	na	na	na	3.19	3.60	4.41	5.16
Nursing allowance	na	na	na	na	na	na	na	na	2.23	0.63	0.47	0.66
Child raising benefit	0.00	0.00	0.04	0.15	0.23	0.37	0.42	0.42	0.63	0.74	0.57	0.72
Maternity benefit	0.00	0.00	0.01	0.04	0.08	?	?	?	0.00	0.00	0.04	0.08
SA benefit for pregnant women	na	na	na	na	na	na	na	na	0.05	0.03	0.10	0.09
Benefits from Alimony Fund	na	na	na	na	na	na	na	na	na	na	0.05	0.13

Table TA.1 *(continued)*
Household income and selected social benefits by household type, Poland, 1988–1999

Household type/Benefit	1988	1989	1990	1991	1992	1993	1994	1995	1996	1997	1998	1999
					PLN per capita per month (in current prices)							
Farmer/worker												
Income	3.20	12.45	59.63	93.02	129.36	145.37	194.56	260.80	322.19	397.42	419.02	438.01
Family and nursing allowances	0.10	0.61	2.41	4.60	6.23	6.27	6.40	6.38	7.68	13.50	8.51	10.13
Family allowance	na	na	na	na	na	na	na	na	6.02	6.75	7.66	8.93
Nursing allowance	na	na	na	na	na	na	na	na	1.66	0.88	0.85	1.20
Child raising benefit	0.00	0.01	0.09	0.34	0.53	0.66	0.63	0.83	1.06	0.93	1.12	1.14
Maternity benefit	0.01	0.02	0.12	0.18	0.22	?	?	?	0.47	0.85	0.51	0.59
SA benefit for pregnant women	na	na	na	na	na	na	na	na	0.00	0.03	0.02	0.04
Benfits from Alimony Fund	na	na	na	na	na	na	na	na	na	na	0.28	0.25
Pensioner												
Income	2.52	8.45	49.34	94.59	126.58	185.71	245.00	319.68	402.36	494.22	552.58	595.99
Family and nursing allowances	0.05	0.22	1.18	2.38	3.58	3.81	4.48	5.02	6.63	3.97	3.15	3.44
Family allowance	na	na	na	na	na	na	na	na	2.13	1.99	2.03	2.32
Nursing allowance	na	na	na	na	na	na	na	na	4.50	1.72	1.12	1.11
Child raising benefit	0.01	0.02	0.10	0.17	0.41	0.32	0.24	0.37	0.47	0.44	0.46	0.44
Maternity benefit	0.00	0.02	0.02	0.03	0.06	?	?	?	0.03	0.13	0.13	0.08
SA benefit for pregnant women	na	na	na	na	na	na	na	na	0.02	0.01	0.06	0.08
Benefits from Alimony Fund	na	na	na	na	na	na	na	na	na	na	0.57	0.78

Table TA.1 (continued)
Household income and selected social benefits by household type, Poland, 1988–1999

Household type/Benefit	1988	1989	1990	1991	1992	1993	1994	1995	1996	1997	1998	1999
					PLN per capita per month (in current prices)							
Self-employed												
Income	—	—	—	—	—	218.85	297.69	386.13	487.68	618.00	654.74	715.88
Family and nursing allowances	—	—	—	—	—	6.09	6.94	4.30	3.95	6.47	4.22	4.89
Family allowance	—	—	—	—	—	na	na	na	3.28	3.24	3.61	3.97
Nursing allowance	—	—	—	—	—	na	na	na	0.67	0.60	0.65	0.92
Child raising benefit	—	—	—	—	—	0.51	0.64	0.99	0.84	0.99	1.18	1.24
Maternity benefit	—	—	—	—	—	?	?	?	0.28	0.59	0.48	0.66
SA benefit for pregnant women	—	—	—	—	—	na	na	na	0.01	0.00	0.00	0.00
Benefits from Alimony Fund	—	—	—	—	—	na	na	na	na	na	0.12	0.18
Living on social benefit[a]												
Income	—	—	—	—	—	95.33	125.87	155.89	200.71	232.09	298.60	300.48
Family and nursing allowances	—	—	—	—	—	7.69	8.48	9.91	10.91	22.36	13.66	17.97
Family allowance	—	—	—	—	—	na	na	na	9.66	11.18	11.07	14.26
Nursing allowance	—	—	—	—	—	na	na	na	1.25	2.00	2.58	3.71
Child raising benefit	—	—	—	—	—	2.87	3.29	3.74	4.23	6.05	5.73	4.66
Maternity benefit	—	—	—	—	—	?	?	?	0.31	0.36	0.00	0.13
SA benefit for pregnant women	—	—	—	—	—	na	na	na	0.17	0.72	1.35	1.23
Benefits from Alimony Fund	—	—	—	—	—	na	na	na	na	na	7.16	9.56

Table TA.1 *(continued)*
Household income and selected social benefits by household type, Poland, 1988–1999

Household type/ Benefit	1988	1989	1990	1991	1992	1993	1994	1995	1996	1997	1998	1999
					PLN per capita per month (in current prices)							
All households												
Income	2.96	11.23	55.27	95.34	134.03	173.62	230.93	300.56	383.48	473.38	522.52	560.07
Family and nursing allowances	0.12	0.61	2.29	4.21	5.57	5.94	6.24	5.93	6.83	9.99	6.00	6.95
Family allowance	na	na	na	na	na	na	na	na	4.84	4.99	5.07	5.82
Nursing allowance	na	na	na	na	na	na	na	na	1.99	1.05	0.94	1.13
Child raising benefit	0.00	0.01	0.11	0.31	0.42	0.64	0.64	0.78	0.99	1.13	1.04	1.14
Maternity benefit	0.00	0.02	0.09	0.14	0.17	?	?	?	0.29	0.46	0.47	0.54
SA benefit for pregnant women	na	na	na	na	na	na	na	na	0.03	0.06	0.09	0.10
Benefits from Alimony Fund	na	na	na	na	na	na	na	na	na	na	0.74	0.95

Notice:

Major changes of HBS methodology since 1993. Data of the two sub-periods displayed in the above table are not fully comparable.
All incomes considered: net; since 1993—disposable incomes. Incomes for all households: until 1992—author's computations (weighted averages).

[a] Including households living on temporary jobs (social benefit as a main source of the household income does not include pensions).

[b] Until 1992 excluding households of the self-employed (households living on social benefit were not put into a separate group).

Source: 1988–1989: Published data. *Budżety gospodarstw domowych w [rok]*, GUS, Warszawa [rok wyd.] and author's computation.
1990–1995: Published data. *Statystyczny opis jakości życia 1990–1995*, GUS, Warszawa 1997, Tabl.50.
1996–1999: Unpublished data. Author's computations based on individual records from HBS conducted by GUS.

Table TA.2

Share of selected social benefits in household income by household type, Poland, 1988–1999

Household type/Benefit	1988	1989	1990	1991	1992	1993	1994	1995	1996	1997	1998	1999
					Percent (household income = 100)							
Worker/employee												
Income	100.00	100.00	100.00	100.00	100.00	100.00	100.00	100.00	100.00	100.00	100.00	100.00
Family and nursing allowances	5.61	6.97	5.17	5.53	4.97	4.11	3.11	2.18	1.80	2.55	1.26	1.30
Family allowance	na	na	na	na	na	na	na	na	1.56	1.27	1.10	1.13
Nursing allowance	na	na	na	na	na	na	na	na	0.24	0.16	0.16	0.17
Child raising benefit	0.14	0.07	0.23	0.41	0.30	0.40	0.29	0.27	0.27	0.26	0.20	0.22
Maternity benefit	0.19	0.14	0.22	0.21	0.17	?	?	?	0.11	0.13	0.14	0.16
SA benefit for pregnant women	na	na	na	na	na	na	na	na	0.01	0.01	0.01	0.01
Alimonies from Alimony Fund	na	na	na	na	na	na	na	na	na	na	0.14	0.14
Farmer												
Income	100.00	100.00	100.00	100.00	100.00	100.00	100.00	100.00	100.00	100.00	100.00	100.00
Family and nursing allowances	0.25	0.48	0.77	1.54	2.46	2.15	1.95	1.57	1.59	1.64	1.20	1.41
Family allowance	na	na	na	na	na	na	na	na	0.94	0.82	1.08	1.25
Nursing allowance	na	na	na	na	na	na	na	na	0.65	0.14	0.12	0.16
Child raising benefit	0.04	0.02	0.06	0.19	0.20	0.23	0.20	0.15	0.19	0.17	0.14	0.18
Maternity benefit	0.00	0.01	0.02	0.04	0.07	?	?	?	0.00	0.00	0.01	0.01
SA benefit for pregnant women	na	na	na	na	na	na	na	na	0.02	0.01	0.02	0.02
Alimonies from Alimony Fund	na	na	na	na	na	na	na	na	na	na	0.01	0.03

Table TA.2 (continued)
Share of selected social benefits in household income by household type, Poland, 1988–1999

Household type/Benefit	1988	1989	1990	1991	1992	1993	1994	1995	1996	1997	1998	1999
					Percent (household income = 100)							
Farmer/worker												
Income	100.00	100.00	100.00	100.00	100.00	100.00	100.00	100.00	100.00	100.00	100.00	100.00
Family and nursing allowances	3.21	4.89	4.04	4.94	4.81	4.31	3.29	2.45	2.38	3.40	2.03	2.31
Family allowance	na	na	na	na	na	na	na	na	1.87	1.70	1.83	2.04
Nursing allowance	na	na	na	na	na	na	na	na	0.51	0.22	0.20	0.27
Child raising benefit	0.10	0.04	0.14	0.37	0.41	0.45	0.32	0.32	0.33	0.23	0.27	0.26
Maternity benefit	0.18	0.13	0.21	0.19	0.17	?	?	?	0.15	0.18	0.10	0.10
SA benefit for pregnant women	na	na	na	na	na	na	na	na	0.00	0.01	0.00	0.01
Alimonies from Alimony Fund	na	na	na	na	na	na	na	na	na	na	0.07	0.06
Pensioner												
Income	100.00	100.00	100.00	100.00	100.00	100.00	100.00	100.00	100.00	100.00	100.00	100.00
Family and nursing allowances	1.79	2.55	2.39	2.52	2.83	2.05	1.83	1.57	1.65	0.80	0.57	0.58
Family allowance	na	na	na	na	na	na	na	na	0.53	0.40	0.37	0.39
Nursing allowance	na	na	na	na	na	na	na	na	1.12	0.35	0.20	0.19
Child raising benefit	0.33	0.18	0.21	0.18	0.33	0.17	0.10	0.12	0.12	0.09	0.08	0.07
Maternity benefit	0.04	0.25	0.03	0.03	0.04	?	?	?	0.01	0.03	0.02	0.01
SA benefit for pregnant women	na	na	na	na	na	na	na	na	0.01	0.00	0.01	0.01
Benefits from Alimony Fund	na	na	na	na	na	na	na	na	na	na	0.10	0.13

Table TA.2 (*continued*)

Share of selected social benefits in household income by household type, Poland, 1988–1999

Household type/Benefit	1988	1989	1990	1991	1992	1993	1994	1995	1996	1997	1998	1999
						Percent (household income = 100)						
Self-employed												
Income	—	—	—	—	—	100.00	100.00	100.00	100.00	100.00	100.00	100.00
Family and nursing allowances	—	—	—	—	—	2.78	2.33	1.11	0.81	1.05	0.64	0.68
Family allowance	—	—	—	—	—	na	na	na	0.67	0.52	0.55	0.55
Nursing allowance	—	—	—	—	—	na	na	na	0.14	0.10	0.10	0.13
Child raising benefit	—	—	—	—	—	0.23	0.21	0.26	0.17	0.16	0.18	0.17
Maternity benefit	—	—	—	—	—	?	?	?	0.06	0.13	0.09	0.12
SA benefit for pregnant women	—	—	—	—	—	na	na	na	0.00	0.00	0.00	0.00
Benefits from Alimony Fund	—	—	—	—	—	na	na	na	na	na	0.02	0.02
Living on social benefit[a]												
Income	—	—	—	—	—	100.00	100.00	100.00	100.00	100.00	100.00	100.00
Family and nursing allowances	—	—	—	—	—	8.07	6.74	6.36	5.44	9.63	4.57	5.98
Family allowance	—	—	—	—	—	na	na	na	4.81	4.82	3.71	4.75
Nursing allowance	—	—	—	—	—	na	na	na	0.62	0.86	0.86	1.24
Child raising benefit	—	—	—	—	—	3.01	2.61	2.40	2.11	2.61	1.92	1.55
Maternity benefit	—	—	—	—	—	?	?	?	0.15	0.08	0.00	0.02
SA benefit for pregnant women	—	—	—	—	—	na	na	na	0.09	0.31	0.45	0.41
Benefits from Alimony Fund	—	—	—	—	—	na	na	na	na	na	2.40	3.18

Table TA.2 *(continued)*
Share of selected social benefits in household income by household type, Poland, 1988–1999

Household type/Benefit	1988	1989	1990	1991	1992	1993	1994	1995	1996	1997	1998	1999
	Percent (household income = 100)											
All households												
Income	100.00	100.00	100.00	100.00	100.00	100.00	100.00	100.00	100.00	100.00	100.00	100.00
Family and nursing allowances	4.16	5.40	4.15	4.42	4.15	3.42	2.70	1.97	1.78	2.11	1.15	1.24
Family allowance	na	na	na	na	na	na	na	na	1.26	1.05	0.97	1.04
Nursing allowance	na	na	na	na	na	na	na	na	0.52	0.22	0.18	0.20
Child raising benefit	0.16	0.08	0.20	0.33	0.31	0.37	0.28	0.26	0.26	0.24	0.20	0.20
Maternity benefit	0.14	0.14	0.16	0.15	0.12	?	?	?	0.08	0.10	0.09	0.10
SA benefit for pregnant women	na	na	na	na	na	na	na	na	0.01	0.01	0.02	0.02
Benefits from Alimony Fund	na	na	na	na	na	na	na	na	na	na	0.14	0.17

Note:

Major changes of HBS methodology since 1993. Data of the two sub-periods displayed in the above table are not fully comparable.
All incomes considered: net; since 1993—disposable incomes. Incomes for all households: until 1992—author's computations (weighted averages).

a Including households living on temporary jobs (social benefit as a main source of the household income does not include pensions).

b Until 1992 excluding households of the self-employed (households living on social benefit were not put into a separate group).

Source: 1988–1989: Published data. *Budżety gospodarstw domowych w [rok]*, GUS, Warszawa [rok wyd.] and author's computation.
1990–1995: Published data. *Statystyczny opis jakości życia 1990–1995*, GUS, Warszawa 1997, Table 50.
1996–1999: Unpublished data. Author's computations based on individual records from HBS conducted by GUS.

Chapter 5
Women's Views
on Social Security Reform:
Qualitative Survey

Silke Steinhilber

The central question investigated in this study is how social security reforms undertaken since the transition in the Czech Republic, Hungary, and Poland have influenced gender relations and women's employment and life choices. Did these reforms contribute to greater gender equality, detract from it, or have a more or less neutral impact? Public opinion in the three countries is diverse and sometimes contradictory on this question. There is, however, a widely shared perception that social security, especially maternity, child care, and family benefits, exerts a significant influence on gender relations in the world of work and at home. Moreover, this influence has subtle dimensions that are not always apparent in national statistics.

As can be observed in the three national studies, gaps in existing data prevent the drawing of firm conclusions about a number of gender-related issues. While data on changes in national social security caseloads and program expenditures are usually available, these do not reveal the actual impact of reforms on the work and life choices of women and men. Even where changes in behavior are observable, it is difficult to establish firm causality in the complex and rapidly changing environments in Central Europe. A further difficulty is a lack of survey data across the three countries on what gender equality actually means to women and on their assessment of whether social security reforms have affected its realization. Without these perceptions, there is a danger that the authors and/or readers may impose their own values on the situation and thus misinterpret the meaning or impact of the reforms.

To help address these information gaps in the national studies, we have sought a variety of first-hand opinions on the gender impact of social security reforms in the three countries. A qualitative questionnaire was administered to collect the views and perceptions of women's organizations, government officials, and the social partners, and these responses were supplemented by a series of in-depth personal interviews.

Before presenting the findings, the limitations of the approach should be noted. The survey was small and selectively drawn, consisting of 37 questionnaire responses and 13 in-depth interviews. As such, it cannot serve as the basis for conclusions about women at large or even about the full membership of the organizations surveyed. What it does provide is some selective first-hand insights into how women in organizations with a concern about gender conceive of equality and how they assess the impact of social security reforms on the actual behavior of people they know and observe. We present these perceptions as interesting anecdotal information, suggestive of broader patterns but in need of verification by further research. We hope our findings will serve to encourage such investigation.

The survey and interviews covered four areas, as will the following text: first, women's concept of fairness and gender equality in social security, second, the actual impact of reforms on women's work, family and retirement choices, third, women's voices in the reform process, and lastly, prospects for further promoting gender equality under current social policy regimes.

1. Fairness and Gender Equality in Social Security

Thirteen years after the transformation began in Central Europe, there is still wide disagreement about the appropriate role of the state in providing social security. While virtually everyone agrees that the previous social security systems provided too much redistribution and state involvement, there is much disagreement about the optimal balance between individual and collective responsibility today. This disagreement was strongly reflected in the survey.

Some respondents, in particular from the business community, emphasized that the withdrawal of the state from social provisioning and the promotion of individual responsibility have not gone far enough. Others noted the negative consequences which the state withdrawal and the privatization of some social security schemes have caused among large groups of the population.

On balance, most respondents held that under current conditions the state should still play a strong role, and social security should serve to redistribute income to even out existing and growing inequalities. Most respondents emphasized that there is an even greater need for social solidarity now, given the harsh economic environment. Under conditions of high unemployment and low wages, solidarity is required not only to support those in need but also to keep society from falling apart, as trade union respondents in all countries were quick to assert.

Gender equality was widely accepted by the respondents as an appropriate goal for social security law and practice. There was less agreement, however, about its practical meaning in this context. The survey reflected three distinct perspectives. For a large number of respondents, it means formal equal treatment of women and men by all social security schemes. Consequently, they called for abolishing any kind of differences between women and men, commonly with the exception of maternity protection, understood in the narrow sense of a limited leave period. For others, gender equality can, or for some it must, include differential treatment of women and men. Since women face disadvantages in other fields, especially in the labour market, social security should help to ameliorate inequalities resulting from these disadvantages. Thus the promotion of gender equality would include some kind of preferential treatment for women, or affirmative action schemes, for at least as long as women's disadvantages persist. A smaller group held that social security should be structured to support women who pursue goals traditionally associated with women's social roles. They assert that women should seek to fulfill themselves first in their homes, and then in work. These respondents were less concerned with inequality in labour markets or social security than with ensuring support for women whose life choices reflect this order of priorities. Some were even reluctant to subscribe to the goal of gender equality on the grounds that such an emphasis on equal – individual – rights and social security entitlements creates a divide between women and men.

Instead, they preferred to use the notion of 'partnership' and argued that the family should be treated as a whole by social security policy.

Many respondents felt that there is limited public awareness of gender inequality and discrimination. As a consequence, public support for special measures for women is not easy to achieve. Instead, as some respondents pointed out, under conditions of a tight labour market many consider it more important to maintain or create jobs for men so that they can provide for their families. It appears that despite the continuous, strong attachment of women to the workforce in all three countries, a significant group of the population continues to regard women's income as supplementary; and their views have been reinforced by difficult economic conditions.

One particularly knotty problem for advocates of gender equality is the retirement age, which is lower for women than men in many CEE countries. In this environment, achieving equality in the formal sense generally implies a loss of benefits for women. Among the respondents, most Hungarians and Czechs were in favor of a preferential retirement age for women (as previously shown, Hungary has enacted a law which will equalize the retirement age, while the Czech Republic has chosen to maintain an age differential). A majority of Polish respondents opted for equal retirement ages, but the opposing group was almost equally strong. As shown in the national studies, the equalization of pension ages was more controversial in Poland than in the other two countries (and the difference in pension age has so far been maintained there), so the Polish responses may be colored by that controversy. When asked to interpret the debate about retirement ages, Polish respondents explained that a large majority of women perceived the equalization as a loss of privileges rather than an issue of equality. Quite understandably, women close to retirement were most involved, while younger women found it harder to relate to the topic and assess the impact of the Polish pension reform. It was also reported that younger and more highly educated women, particularly from urban environments, tended to oppose the earlier retirement age for women. Respondents from all three countries cited the argument that women are more exhausted than men from having worked the double shift of paid employment and unpaid housework. Some also argued that, given insufficient or unaffordable child care, the caring role of grandmothers is becoming an essential support for younger women who wish to work.

Finally, respondents expressed strong concern for the welfare of children, especially those in large families. In all three countries, such families have been among the first to feel the effects of massive changes and the children are at significant risk for falling into poverty.[1] When asked about the role of family benefit schemes, respondents were divided, both between the three countries and within. Support for means testing based on household income was somewhat stronger among respondents from Hungary and Poland. In the Czech Republic, roughly equal numbers thought that family benefits should be paid out as universal benefits or dependent on household income.

2. The Impact of Reforms on Women's Work, Family and Retirement Choices

Survey respondents reported that they see quite some continuity between the layout of social security schemes today and those before the transformation. They emphasized this continuity particularly in the case of maternity and family benefits, and less so in the case of child care provisions. However, respondents also felt that existing benefits have become less effective as support to a family's income. Also, benefits have become more difficult to use, according to survey respondents, because of a harsher working environment and a higher level of insecurity in the job market, which makes many workers reluctant to assert their rights or take advantage of provisions such as extended leave. Respondents were most dissatisfied with pension reforms in the three countries but, at the same time, found these reforms more difficult to assess.

In terms of social support for families, most respondents felt that it has generally become more difficult for parents, especially mothers, to combine work and family responsibilities over the past decade. This is particularly true outside big cities due to a combination of loss of employment, lack of means of transportation and loss of affordable child care. Czech respondents unanimously felt that the situation of women has become more difficult after the reforms. In Poland a majority of respondents thought that women today

---

[1]   This concern is consistent with household survey data in all three countries, which shows that family size is an important predictor of poverty.

face more discrimination at the workplace than before because of their family responsibilities. Insufficient and overly expensive child care creates further difficulties for parents, as Hungarian respondents in particular emphasized.

Respondents in all three countries agree that it is more costly today for couples to raise children. This increased cost is commonly interpreted as one reason for the steeply declining birthrate in all three countries. Respondents have different interpretations of the specific factors which influence prospective parents' decision-making. While low wages and family incomes play an important role everywhere, in Hungary respondents saw a strong impact from the elimination of subsidies for food and baby products. In the Czech Republic and in Poland in turn, respondents first mentioned the lack of affordable housing. They all emphasized as well the changing values and preferences of young people.

The low level of benefits during child rearing periods creates barriers for parents to take advantage of existing parental leave. And restrictions tied to the receipt of parental benefits inhibit the smooth transition between parenting and employment. For example, respondents criticized that it is not allowed that parents work, even limited hours, while on parental leave, or participate in training courses, or use existing child care facilities. It is not uncommon therefore that parents on leave, for example in the Czech Republic, break this regulation.

A few Polish respondents pointed out that it has become so 'normal' for employees not to use the three-year parental leave provisions that there is not even a public discussion about the very low level of benefits. Consequently, parents look for private, commercial solutions or rely on family support. Large numbers of ads for private child care in Polish newspapers illustrate this privatization of child care. Czech respondents mentioned the growing number of women who take early retirement, often leading to reduced pension benefits for the rest of their lives, in order to take care of their grandchildren.

Not only do low wages and low replacement rates make it difficult to take advantage of existing protection. It also appears that benefits that are intended to protect workers sometimes operate to their disadvantage in periods of tight labour markets and insufficient law enforcement. Respondents reported that many women are afraid to take advantage of existing benefits out of fear of losing their jobs. This problem was raised particularly by Polish respondents, but also by women in Hungary and the Czech Republic. The perceived weak enforcement of existing legal provisions and protection mechanisms contributes to a widespread feeling of insecurity. In this context, it is puzzling that while the statutory maternity leave in Poland has remained 100 percent, it is here that most respondents felt strongly that maternity benefits are less generous than they used to be. Employers' changed expectations and the tight labour market have created an environment in which *de jure* entitlements are not perceived to be useful in practice. It is a common practice, as respondents related, that the employment relationship is formally terminated when a woman goes on maternity leave, but with an informal promise of reemployment after the leave. The promise, however, was not kept in a number of cases of which the respondents were aware, leaving no legal remedies to the laid-off woman.

Respondents disagreed about whether the costs of maternity and child care leave are real for employers or merely perceived. In Poland, some argued that such protection makes women more costly employees, and 'overprotection is negative for the general business environment, and international competitiveness.' Others stressed that, under a system of pooled risk, maternity benefits for individual employees are not directly paid for by the employer so that there are no real costs involved. Instead, they blame employers' prejudices and stereotypes of younger women, which they felt cannot be easily influenced by social security legislation.

There was wide agreement that existing benefits for parents do not provide sufficient incentives for men to take parental leave. Respondents everywhere offered one explanation: Given that men typically have higher incomes than women, the family income is more negatively affected if the father goes on leave. So what would happen if child care were better compensated? Hungarian respondents were quite optimistic that under different income conditions, more men would take parental leave. Czech respondents tended to share this optimism but Poles, less so. They emphasized that in addition to income, cultural questions play an important role. Traditional stereotypes about mothers' and fathers' roles continue to determine parents' decisions about the sharing of care work and their behavior in response to family benefits, even when both parents are equally entitled. Also, respondents everywhere mentioned that employers have not yet become accustomed to the idea that their male employees also have family responsibilities, and so many fathers face employers' resistance. Some respondents also said that men may perceive a challenge to their own male identities when considering parental leave.

Respondents nevertheless appreciated the fact that parental leave is now available everywhere for both men and women under equal conditions. For families with a highly paid woman, the possibility for fathers to take parental leave has created an attractive new alternative. The extent of its use, however, will depend on changes in the labour market, as well as on a softening of strict gender stereotypes.

Respondents reported that the gender division of tasks in the home has not changed greatly over the last decade and that women continue to bear a larger burden of unpaid home work. Resistance against a change in traditional gender roles is reportedly strong. As respondents explain, in recent debates about caring in Poland, arguments are sometimes couched in the terminology of 'children's rights' or 'children's needs,' both by women and men, to justify why it is the mother who should take over the role of full-time care giver. Some respondents observe men taking over more family responsibilities than before, in particular among the younger generation. Others stress that today more men are taking over at least some family responsibilities. But several respondents noted astutely that this trend does not mean that, compared to the population, this is a large group of men.

It appears that the transition from parental leave back to employment is often difficult. Initiatives to support returning parents, mostly women, are not common or well known, as respondents explain. In Hungary and the Czech Republic, such initiatives were popular among respondents.

Dissatisfaction with pension laws was widespread among respondents. A large majority did not believe that women's needs are well-reflected in the old-age security systems currently in place. At the same time, respondents found the impact of pension reform difficult to assess (it is of course possible that general dissatisfaction with the pension systems has been growing throughout the entire population, both women and men, since the latter could not be detected by this survey). Among the respondents, Poles showed most dissatisfaction with the pension reform, noting that a continuing early retirement age in private savings schemes, and the elimination of redistribution toward low income workers will make women's situation in old age much more difficult in coming years. Hungarian respondents also fear the negative consequences for women under the new pension system, but they appeared less certain about these negative effects. Czech respondents in turn expressed uncertainty when asked if the reform of their pension system has brought disadvantages for women.

3.   Women's Voices in the Reform Process

Most respondents expressed dissatisfaction with the processes by which social security reforms had been enacted in their countries. There were three common concerns: a lack of openness and transparency in reform deliberations, insufficient analysis of the gender impact of reforms, and limited involvement of women's organizations in the political decision-making process. The Polish responses were most critical with respect to the lack of openness and transparency. Hungarians expressed a similar concern, while Czech respondents were somewhat more satisfied with the public decision-making process. But consultation with women's organizations was not seen as satisfactory anywhere.

In explaining weak political participation by women, respondents from all three countries perceived that they were systematically disadvantaged by several conditions: lack of representation in high-level decision-making bodies; difficulties in obtaining detailed and timely information on the reforms without having such positions of access; and weak cooperation among their own organizations. Weak cooperation between women's organizations was explained in part from divergent organizational perspectives on gender issues and priorities, resulting in different, even contradictory, goals. Cooperation occurred to some extent in Hungary, but respondents from Poland and the Czech Republic described it as less successful.

In explaining deficient attention to the gender impacts of reforms, respondents pointed out that social security has less immediate and direct gender impacts than the problems of gender discrimination that women experience in labour markets every day. Thus, for women with limited time to devote to public policy debates, these issues were probably overshadowed by more immediate concerns. The lack of attention was seen as part of the larger problem of low transparency in policy making. It was also pointed out that, as predominantly low-income workers, women stood to lose more from reforms which reduced redistribution in social security; and advocates of these reforms were probably more eager to publicize their benefits than their disadvantages.

4. Prospects for Further Promoting Gender Equality under Current Social Policy Regimes

A large majority of respondents argued that promotion of gender equality should receive more attention in national social policy. They perceived an urgent need for greater emphasis on women's economic and social rights, as well as for more support for women who are balancing employment and family responsibilities. They argued that over the course of the last decade, public awareness of discrimination and gender inequality in the labour market has increased; however, this has not happened to the same extent for social security issues.

Respondents stated that recent advances in legislation on equal opportunities have largely been consequences of the EU accession process. They felt that resistance to such changes would have been far greater without this pressure.

Respondents described recent discussions in all three countries of special non-discrimination/equal opportunity laws. Draft laws have been developed, but nowhere has such a law been approved yet. Lamenting this situation, many respondents expressed concern that government commitments to gender equality are only formal and linked to EU accession, reflecting no deeper value change. As illustrations, some respondents noted that sex-specific job announcements are not outlawed in any of the three countries, that women victims of discrimination do not know where to turn to for assistance, and that women whom they know encounter discrimination when attempting to return from parental leave to employment.

Respondents also expressed concern about unresolved social security reform issues that have predictable gender impacts. In Poland, it is not yet clear if gender neutral annuities are to be used in the second, private, pension pillar, or if private pension funds will instead be allowed to differentiate benefit levels between women and men based on their average life expectancies. In

Hungary, there are discussions about the possible introduction of a notional defined contribution scheme in the public pension pillar. Citing experiences in Poland, Hungarian respondents fear that this will have a negative impact on the pension benefits of all but the highest paid women. Similarly, the support of working parents through tax preferences rather than direct benefits, as in Hungary, was seen as disadvantageous to single-parent and low-income families.

Many women suffer from the gap between legislation and actual practice in the world of work, and see themselves as far more limited in their employment and life choices than the law indicates. Citing maternity protection, respondents pointed out that many women do not use these benefits out of fear of losing their jobs or being disadvantaged when they return to work.

A few respondents focused on parental leave and child care benefits as central for promoting gender equality. To make parental leave available for men everywhere is seen as a positive step. But respondents were also concerned that the incentives provided by existing schemes are not sufficient to induce large numbers of men to use the benefits. Many argued for a more proactive policy towards men aimed at encouraging more equal sharing of family responsibilities.

At the same time, most respondents expressed a recognition that social security can go only so far in overcoming persistent gender stereotypes and inequalities in the labour market and society, which they viewed as the central constraint on women's life and work choices.

Nearly unanimously, respondents saw a need for capacity building among women on gender and social security, as well as on social security generally, as a prerequisite for greater success in bringing gender issues to the forefront of public attention in social security reform debates. Representatives of trade unions and some non-governmental organizations observed that many of their members have difficulties following the financial and macroeconomic arguments used in discussions of pension reform. Moreover, it is hard, not only for women, to assess the long-term consequences of social security reforms. Tellingly, several individual respondents stated that they had been reluctant to respond to the survey because they do not consider themselves to be social security experts. In this context, several respondents pointed out that the survey, interviews, and national research functioned as a kind of awareness-raising and mobilizing tool.

www.ingramcontent.com/pod-product-compliance
Lightning Source LLC
Chambersburg PA
CBHW061001280326
41935CB00009B/793